DATE DUE

THE
NUCLEAR
FAMILY
IN CRISIS

THE NUCLEAR FAMILY IN CRISIS:
THE SEARCH FOR AN ALTERNATIVE

EDITED AND WITH AN INTRODUCTION BY

Michael Gordon

THE UNIVERSITY OF CONNECTICUT

HARPER & ROW, PUBLISHERS
New York/Evanston
San Francisco/London

To Andra and Jennifer

CONTENTS

PREFACE *ix*

INTRODUCTION *1*

I HISTORICAL PERSPECTIVES ON COMMUNAL FAMILIES 23

1 Plato on Women and the Family *25*
2 GILLIAN LINDT GOLLIN, Family Surrogates in Colonial America: The Moravian Experiment *44*
3 WILLIAM M. KEPHART, Experimental Family Organization: An Historico-Cultural Report on the Oneida Community *59*

II THE FAMILY IN THE KIBBUTZ 79

4 MELFORD E. SPIRO, Is the Family Universal?—The Israeli Case *81*
5 LESLIE and KAREN RABKIN, Children of the Kibbutz *93*
6 YONINA TALMON, Aging in Israel, A Planned Society *101*

III THE FAMILY IN SOCIALIST AND WELFARE NATIONS 117

7 URIE BRONFENBRENNER, The Changing Soviet Family *119*
8 JAN MYRDAL, Li Kuei-ying, Woman Pioneer, Aged 32 *143*
9 ELINA HAAVIO-MANNILA, The Position of Finnish Women: Regional and Cross-National Comparisons *154*

IV THE FAMILY AND THE CURRENT COMMUNAL MOVEMENT 171

10 ROSABETH MOSS KANTER, Communes *173*
11 GAETON FONZI, The New Arrangement *180*
12 DAVID E. SMITH and JAMES L. STERNFIELD, Natural Child Birth and Cooperative Child Rearing in Psychedelic Communes *196*
13 LARRY L. and JOAN M. CONSTANTINE, The Group Marriage *204*

INDEX 223

PREFACE

The idea for this book grew out of a graduate seminar I taught in the spring of 1970. The course began as a fairly traditional macrosociological treatment of the family in industrial societies. However, it soon became apparent that the assumed "fit" on a systems level between the nuclear family and the demands of an industrial society overlooks the problems faced by individuals living in such familial settings. This led us to consider the communal family as an alternative form, which provides at least partial answers to some of these problems. The following fall I reorganized my undergraduate course along similar lines. I found, somewhat to my surprise, that many of my students showed great interest in communal families, and no longer unquestioningly assumed they would ultimately form nuclear families.

My experiences in these courses served as a guide in the writing, selection of articles, and organization of this book. I have devoted a considerable amount of space in the introduction to a discussion of the place of the nuclear family in industrial societies. I have done this not only because the nuclear family is the form to which alternatives have been sought (though this in itself would be sufficient reason), but more importantly because such a discussion is necessary if the reader is to comprehend the role of family and kinship in society and how it has changed and is changing. An attempt has also been made to explore the sources of tension within nuclear families that are contributing to the growing appeal of communal families.

The readings have been chosen to provide insight into communal family life in historical, cross-cultural, and contemporary perspectives. The articles in each part illustrate various dimensions of communal family life, many of which touch on the points raised in the introduction. Taken as a whole they should offer a comprehensive picture of this family form.

To the students in the seminar mentioned above I owe a special debt. The introductory essay contains many ideas that grew out of our discussions. A number of people read drafts of my contributions to the book, among them "Colt" Denfeld, Floyd Dotson, Jerold Heiss, and Penelope Shankweiler. They should in no way be seen as condoning many of the statements contained in the book; nevertheless, their advice and effort was greatly appreciated. Two people at Harper & Row deserve recognition: Luther Wilson, the sociology editor; and Joan Zwaska, who guided this book through production. A special note of thanks is due my wife, Roberta Gordon, who not only helped copy edit this book, but also compiled the index.

M.G.

INTRODUCTION

This book is a collection of articles dealing with alternative family forms, for the most part in a communal setting. From them we shall see that the desire to modify and change existing institutions has a long history, and that there is considerable continuity between the wave of communalism of today and those of the eighteenth and nineteenth centuries. We shall also learn that this phenomenon is confined as little by geographic borders as it is by time and has taken root in culturally diverse settings. Throughout the book, however, our focus will not be on communalism per se, but rather on communes as milieus in which experimentation with modification of family forms has occurred, though in one section we shall deal with the family in socialist and welfare nations.

The first part of this introductory essay will review the controversy that has surrounded the place of the nuclear family in industrial society, not only because the nuclear family is the form from which communal alternatives have generally been sought, but also because an understanding of it is necessary for a more general appreciation of the role of the family institution in society. The second part will look at some of the sources, actual and potential, of tension, dissatisfaction, and stress confronting individuals living in nuclear families and then explore how the communal family is in certain ways better able to meet these problems. Because the articles that have been reprinted discuss almost all facets of the communal family it is not necessary to deal with it in any depth here; the introductions to each section, it is hoped, will provide a basis for enabling the reader to see continuity throughout the book.

Some definition of frequently encountered terms is required. The term *nuclear family* refers to a unit consisting of husband, wife, and dependent offspring. The nuclear family is generally contrasted with the *extended family*, typically a residential unit composed of husband, wife, dependent offspring, and married sons and their spouses and offspring. Deplorably, these terms are often used sloppily, so that we will find a nuclear family with an adult member in residence in addition to the mother and father (e.g., an unmarried sibling of the latter or a widowed parent) being referred to as an extended family.

The extended family as defined above is seldom actually encountered in any society, preindustrial or industrial. In fact, Gideon Sjoberg has argued that such families have historically been found only among the wealthy élites in feudal cities; they alone could support such a unit in the preindustrial period.[1] What we do see in many peasant societies is a modified extended family; here only one son returns upon marriage to live with the family. This is the family form described in such classic studies of peasant communities as Arensberg and Kimball's *Family and Community in Ireland* and Miner's *St. Denis*.[2]

Until recently, it was assumed that the Industrial Revolution (i.e., the factory system of production, its concomitant technology, and the associated form of urbanism) had resulted in the extended family's being superseded by the nuclear family. As is the case with many such generalizations, it contains an element of truth despite its being basically in error. Increasingly sound historical evidence is becoming available to support the position that the nuclear family was the prevailing residential unit long before the Industrial Revolution. Investigations of town records and parish registers in England by Peter Laslett and E. A. Wigley, members of the Cambridge Group, and of similar documents in this country by John Demos and Philip Greven, have shown that sixteenth- and seventeenth-century families were nuclear in character, and in this respect virtually identical with contemporary families.[3] Nonetheless, a qualification is required: Because the primary economic activity of such families was agriculture, most of the wealth they possessed was in the form of land. Ideally, the family's holdings would be large enough to divide among the sons, but inevitably most families found themselves in a position where there was only enough land to support a single family. This meant that just one son could inherit the family holdings and with his wife take up residence in the paternal home. A frequent if not universal condition of the son's taking over the farm was that his parents would remain in the home and be provided for until their

[1] Gideon Sjoberg, *The Preindustrial City* (New York: Free Press, 1960), p. 159.

[2] Conrad M. Arensberg and Solon T. Kimball, *Family and Community in Ireland* (Gloucester, Mass.: Peter Smith, 1961); Horace Miner, *St. Denis* (Chicago: Phoenix Books, 1963). Both the Arensberg and Kimball and the Miner studies were carried out in the 1930s. Evidence of the persistence of this pattern is found, among other places, in Dorrian Apple Sweetser, "Urbanization and the Patrilineal Transmission of Farms in Finland," *Acta Sociologica*, 7 (1964): 215–224.

[3] Peter Laslett, *The World We Have Lost* (New York: Scribner's, 1965); E. A. Wigley, *Industrial Growth and Population Change* (Cambridge: Cambridge University Press, 1961); John Demos, *A Little Commonwealth* (New York: Oxford University Press, 1970); Philip J. Greven, Jr., *Four Generations* (Ithaca, N.Y.: Cornell University Press), 1970.

death. Still, what should be kept in mind is that it was only for a brief period—between the father's retirement and his death—that these families could be spoken of as extended, and even then in a modified way. Moreover, in the United States, because an enormous amount of land was available during the preindustrial period, even inheriting sons did not have to wait for a father's retirement to start a family. What the Industrial Revolution did, then, by shifting a large part of the population out of agriculture, was to undermine this temporary and modified extended familism.

If the size of the residential unit was not affected by industrialization, what of the larger kinship network? This is a two-pronged question because kinship networks must be viewed on more than one level: (1) Who are involved? and (2) What is the nature of the relationship among them? Many have argued that urban-industrial kinship is but a shrunken remnant of the glorious past when cousins, uncles, and aunts were all a functionally important and conspicuous part of life.[4] If, however, we compare kinship priorities in seventeenth-century New England with those of today, we see more similarity than difference. Demos reports the following on Plymouth Colony:

> Direct bloodlines were accorded a special sort of precedence in the family feelings of the colonists: a man was involved, first of all, with his wife and children, and then with his grandchildren. Somewhat less intense was the relation to his own brothers and sisters, and to their children. Parent-child; grandparent-grandchild; brother (or sister)-brother (or sister); uncle (or aunt)-nephew (or niece): this was the general order of priority. . . . First cousins may have been recognized as such—but the fact implied no special feelings or responsibilities.[5]

A study in the early 1960s of kinship in a medium-size American industrial city found that

> When attention turns from parents and siblings, the kin of orientation, to cousins and other secondary relatives, one is hard-pressed to find great significance in such relationships among young adult [married] Greensborites. . . . On the whole the young adults consider these relationships—to aunts, uncles, cousins, and so on—to be functionally irrelevant.[6]

These two pictures separated by two hundred years can hardly be seen as indicative of great social changes.

[4] Pitirim A. Sorokin et al., eds., A Systematic Source Book in Rural Sociology (Minneapolis: University of Minnesota Press, 1931), vol. 2, chap. 10.

[5] Demos., op. cit., p. 124.

[6] Bert N. Adams, Kinship in an Urban Setting (Chicago: Markham, 1968), p. 165.

It is considerably more difficult to describe patterns of kinship interaction in the preindustrial setting than it is to describe kinship priorities. The documents demographic historians use to ascertain the latter do not give us information on the reciprocal obligations and services performed by kin and the occasions for them. The available materials deal with such things as the transference of property, estates, and apprenticeships. In all of these matters we learn that kinship was a key consideration, but this tells us little about the more mundane aspects of kinship interaction. Nonetheless, the subject can be approached obliquely. The nostalgic image many hold of preindustrial life is one in which geographic mobility is almost negligible, and thus families are seen as building up large bodies of kin in the surrounding area. Here again, demographic data suggest this may not have been the case:

> Far from being permanently rooted in the soil of the same villages from time beyond the memories of men, countless rural English families in the late sixteenth and early seventeenth centuries were uprooted, mobile and nuclear, dependent upon the soil yet independent of particular places. So extensive was the mobility of the rural population, in Elizabethan and Stuart England that, as an English historian has estimated, by 1641 "only 16 percent of our agricultural population had a hundred years in the same village behind them."[7]

Similarly, while in the early years of colonial settlement in New England there was, at least for the first three generations, a certain amount of geographic stability, the pressures of diminishing land and opportunity encouraged and ultimately resulted in considerable mobility.[8] All this does not mean that current patterns of mobility are not greater than preindustrial patterns, but rather that the extent of preindustrial stability has been exaggerated.

However, the amount of mobility in industrial societies has also probably been exaggerated. For example, a recent study disclosed that 74 percent of the married persons with living mothers in a working-class section of London and 66 percent in the middle-class London suburb had seen their mother either in the previous week or in the foregoing 24 hours.[9] These findings are by no means atypical. This would suggest that if geographic

[7] Greven, *op. cit.*, p. 265.

[8] *Ibid.* Greven mentions similar patterns among the early residents of Andover, Massachusetts. Fourth-generation sons began to move into Connecticut and New Hampshire. See Chapter 7.

[9] Peter Willmott and Michael Young, *Family and Class in a London Suburb* (London: Routledge & Kegan Paul, 1960), p. 33. See also Ethel Shanas *et al.*, *Old People in Three Industrial Societies* (London, Routledge & Kegan Paul, 1968), p. 174.

mobility has increased with industrialization, it has not resulted in the fragmentation of close kin. Moreover, we should keep in mind that technological advances enable persons who are separated from their families by considerable distances to maintain contacts through telephone, letters, and visits.

If it is correct to assume that the amount of distance separating kin is currently not fantastically greater than was the case in preindustrial settings, what, if anything, can be inferred about the services kin perform for each other? Studies of peasant societies indicate that kin are called upon in situations where the nuclear family is unable to meet the demands made upon it. For example, Miner, in his research on a rural French-Canadian village in the 1930s, reports that young farmers with small children had to depend upon brothers or other male relatives in order to cope with certain agricultural tasks until the male children were old enough to help out.[10] This and similar studies also find that kin are used to deal with other emergency situations, for example, sickness and death, and strong sentiment is associated with these obligations. Arensberg and Kimball note, "In fact, failure to fulfill the patterns of conduct demanded by extended family obligations leads often to punitive action on the part of the aggrieved party."[11]

The nature of life in industrial society is such that many of the circumstances that would have previously necessitated the aid of kin have attenuated or been removed. The separation of the economic and domestic spheres means that a person's occupational role is formally defined and there will be few occasions in connection with his work that will require the aid of kin. Obviously, this is less true for those involved in small family businesses or farms than it is for those employed by large corporations, but we must remember that the former make up a small and shrinking part of the population. Furthermore, many activities such as home building and repair in which extended kin were sometimes involved are now, for the most part, the domain of specialists whose services are formally contracted for, though here again kin may play a role. There still remain, however, situations for which kin are deemed the most appropriate sources of aid.

The 1950s and 1960s saw several studies of urban kinship interaction. Among the earliest was Marvin Sussman's research, first in New Haven and later in Cleveland,[12] where he determined that intergenerational ties between married adults and their parents were prevalent and manifested themselves in a number of ways—most conspicuously in help during ill-

[10] Miner, *op. cit.*, p. 81. Miner reports that an unrelated male is turned to only as a last resort.

[11] Arensberg and Kimball, *op. cit.*, p. 77.

[12] Marvin B. Sussman, "The Help Pattern in the Middle-Class Family," *American Sociological Review*, 18 (February 1953): 22–28; Marvin B. Sussman, "The Isolated Nuclear Family: Fact or Fiction?" *Social Problems*, 6 (Spring 1959): 333–340.

ness, babysitting, and financial aid. While there were class differences in amount and frequency, such assistance took place in all strata. Similar patterns were discovered in other cities as well.[13]

Findings such as these make us question the notion that kinship patterns as they currently exist represent a vestige of the idealized ways and relationships that prevailed in the past. To be sure, some changes have occurred, but not of the type or magnitude that was previously believed. Visiting is still the most common social activity, even though the kin *may* live farther from each other than they would have during the preindustrial era. And kin are still the first people turned to for help, financial and otherwise. All in all, then, kinship patterns have shown great durability.

While the composition of the residential unit and kinship interaction may not have been dramatically affected by industrialization, the same is not true of the functional role of the family. The family changed from a unit of production to a unit of consumption. This transformation is well documented in Smelser's *Social Change in the Industrial Revolution*, a study which focuses on English families involved in cotton cloth production in the period from 1770 to 1840.[14] Throughout most of the eighteenth century, cotton cloth was produced under the "putting-out," or "cottage," system, in which farming families spun and wove cotton on a contract basis during the time remaining from their agricultural work. This represented a form of manufacturing transitional between that used for home consumption and the coming factory system. What is important is that it involved the family as a unit in the productive process, with economic authority residing in the father, as it did in agricultural activity. There was, of course, a division of labor—the father wove, the mother spun, and the children engaged in subsidiary tasks—but this in no way undermined the authority patterns associated with traditional agrarian pursuits.

With the introduction of factory methods of production, the father began to work outside the home, thus destroying the family-based economy. The implications and ramifications of this disengagement of work and home were very great indeed.

We may view what happened in terms of a general shrinkage of familial functions in various institutional spheres. Prior to the emergence of the factory system, boys learned the arts of husbandry and weaving from their fathers in what amounted to an apprentice system.[15] For the population

---

[13] See also Scott Greer, "Urbanism Reconsidered: A Comparative Study of Local Areas in a Metropolis," *American Sociological Review*, 21 (February 1956): 19–25; Morris Axelrod, "Urban Structure and Social Participation," *American Sociological Review*, 21 (February 1956): 13–18.

[14] Neil J. Smelser, *Social Change in the Industrial Revolution* (Chicago: University of Chicago Press, 1959).

[15] The apprenticing of children in Colonial America is a topic of mild historical controversy. Edmund S. Morgan, in *The Puritan Family* (Boston: Boston Public Library, 1944), claims that it was common for Puritan parents to apprentice their

involved in industrial production, this was no longer possible for two reasons. First, the father was now not at home during the work day. Second, and perhaps more important, the tasks demanded of most factory employees were so simple as not to warrant any but the most rudimentary training. Obviously, this was not as much the case for girls. Training in homemaking skills remained a family matter or a mother-daughter affair. But, as Smelser indicates, the emergence of compulsory education, for both boys and girls, in the first half of the nineteenth century, in part a response to industrialization, added the final blow to the separation of the educational sphere from the home. Now, for a good portion of the day and for a significant number of years, children would leave home to be trained in formal schools.

THE FAMILY IN INDUSTRIAL
AND POSTINDUSTRIAL SOCIETY

The more current situation of the family in industrial or postindustrial society is also a topic of interest and disagreement among sociologists. Talcott Parsons has viewed the family as still responding to the societal differentiation brought about by the Industrial Revolution. Focusing on the middle-class American family, he sees it moving toward, if it has not already arrived at, a situation in which it is limited to two "basic" and "irreducible" social-psychological functions: ". . . First, the primary socialization of children so that they can truly become members of the society into which they have been born; second, the stabilization of adult personalities of the population of the society."[16] For Parsons, it is the psychological experiences the child has within the relatively isolated nuclear family that lay the foundation for his later participation in the occupational milieu. Moreover, he sees it as the agency best prepared to manage this task of creating a personality type suited to the demands of a highly rational industrial society.

The "stabilization of adult personalities," as Parsons would have us understand the terms, refers to the nuclear family as the center of emotional support and affective expression in a society where all other spheres are given over to detachment and calculation. The nuclear family has become the place to which individuals return, so to speak, to refuel their emotional lives in order to be able to plunge back refreshed into the hard and demanding workaday world.

Not all sociologists have been as sanguine as Parsons in their appraisal of

children to other families for fear that if they were kept at home they would be spoiled. The data Demos, *op. cit.*, presents suggest that this practice may not have been as common as Morgan, who offers little in the way of empirical data, would have us believe.

[16] Talcott Parsons and Robert F. Bales, *Family, Socialization and Interaction Process* (New York: Free Press, 1955), p. 16.

the harmony between the nuclear family and industrial society. In a recent book, *Families Against the City*, Richard Sennett takes issue with Parsons' position and argues that the nuclear family has cut itself off from participation in the larger society.[17] He contrasts Parsons' views with those of the French historian Philippe Ariès, whose position, in his influential *Centuries of Childhood*, is that the nuclear family represents a retreat from society and that since the thirteenth century the family has moved from a large corporate form strongly enmeshed in society at all levels, to the more or less nuclear form we know today.[18] Sennett maintains that implicit in Ariès' work is the notion that

> as a result of the growth of privacy in the family, and the rationale of better training of the young in a more isolated, controlled setting, Ariès argues the intensive family of the industrial era cast the members of the home who did not work into a retreat from the world at large. . . . This historical confluence denied young people a chance to create a fund of experience with, and judgment about, other people. Presumably this ineptitude would reflect itself when young went out in the world, to work or marry. [19]

While Sennett's interpretation of Ariès is open to question, he does, nevertheless, offer some data to support his own thesis. Drawing upon census and city directory figures for the period between 1870 and 1890 for what he calls the Union Park section of Chicago, he compares the mobility of fathers and sons in extended families and nuclear families and finds that the fathers and sons in extended families were more economically mobile than those fathers and sons in nuclear families.[20] Sennett uses the term "extended family" for residential units with one or more adults in addition to the parents, a form which, in fact, is a variant of the nuclear family. He explains this differential mobility as a result of the experiences of children in "extended families" that were denied to children in nuclear families. For example:

> The practice of not "talking business," of leaving behind the office and what one did there when work was done for the day, would be an unnatural mode for the adult family members, whereas it would be natural when only one member

[17] Richard Sennett, *Families Against the City* (Cambridge, Mass.: Harvard University Press, 1970).

[18] Philippe Ariès, *Centuries of Childhood* (New York: Vintage Books, 1962). Ariès' thesis that the family in the West has been moving toward a nuclear form since the thirteenth century is frequently cited to discount the often posited relationship between industrialization and the nuclear family.

[19] Sennett, *op. cit.*, p. 65.

[20] Sennett uses the term "Union Park" to describe an area in West Chicago of forty square blocks bounded by Union Park on the west and Halstead Street on the east. The data on mobility are found in Chapter 9.

> of the family worked, as in most nuclear families. In this way, the minority families [i.e., the extended families] built a bridge between home and city life outside it.
>
> .   .   .
>
> One's work was not something that could be kept from the family, in the sense that one would be evaluated as a family member apart from it: there were others within the family circle who were also striving outside and who provided a point of reference, or in some cases may have supplemented or helped one's own efforts. In either event, the split between home and work was harder to maintain; the two worlds became interwoven and, for these families in Union Park, the outcome was favorable for the work experience of the family leader.[21]

He goes on to say that the children benefited by hearing discussions of the work world from adults who were successfully competing in it. Thus, the greater success of sons from extended families was due to socialization experiences within the family unit. For Sennett, then, the nuclear family is not suited to the preparation of persons for participation in industrial society. We shall return to Sennett's writings on the current urban family later in this essay and in a different context.

Sennett notwithstanding, Parsons is not alone in his assertion that the nuclear family is suited to meet the demands of an industrial society. Most students of the family have assumed the same thing. Even William Goode, the staunchest critic of those who see simple one-to-one relationships between industrialization and the nuclear family, generally views the conjugal form as one which articulates well with industrialization. However he has raised a point not found in the writings of other proponents of the "fit" hypothesis, viz., Is the conjugal family the form *best* suited for an industrial society?

> In analyzing the fit of the conjugal family system with the demands of an urban, bureaucratic technology, we left open the question as to whether an *alternative* family system might meet these demands still better. If that earlier theoretical analysis was correct, then there *is* an alternative, some variant of a communal "family" pattern. Plato's variant was of course even more radical than the present-day ideal Chinese version, but in both, as in the more extreme forms of the kibbutz, the aim is to reduce the claims of kin to, at most, a weak tie between parents and children. Then, each individual may be used as best fits the needs of industrialization, not those of his family (or his own).[22]

---

[21] Sennett, *op. cit.*, pp. 209–210.

[22] William J. Goode, *World Revolution and Family Patterns* (New York: Free Press, 1963), p. 24.

Goode obviously recognizes that a communal family form might better serve the needs of an industrial society than a conjugal one, but given his concern with the system, he does not, in any depth, consider the needs of individuals within such societies. In the next portion of this essay an attempt will be made to consider certain problems facing individuals living in nuclear families and concomitantly show how communal families provide at least partial answers to these problems.

Women
and the Family

Industrialization created the possibility of the emancipation of women, but has hardly brought about its reality. With such consumer goods as bread and cloth being produced outside the home, women were at least potentially freed from some of their domestic responsibilities and in a position to seek outside employment. Virtually from the beginning of the industrial era some have done so, but generally out of economic necessity and as an adjunct to and an extension of their roles of wives and mothers. Among the reasons more women have not gone into the marketplace, according to Goode, is that they are seen as being the only persons suited to care for their own children and they are given little or no relief from this task. Additionally, as Goode goes on to show, their housekeeping has not been made easier.

> Every study of the time allocation of mothers shows that housewives work extremely long hours. For those who have assumed otherwise, let me remind them that the washing machine brings back into the home a job that an earlier generation delegated to lower-class labor or the laundry; that the vacuum cleaner merely raises standards without substantially speeding up work; that the electric sewing machine is exactly analogous to the washing machine. On the other hand, the organized activities of children have become so complex, and the number of objects in the house so numerous, that even the middle-class housewife must spend much of her time in essentially administrative activities when she is not laboring with her hands.[23]

All of this means that many women are prevented from working outside the home. Among the lower strata, economic necessity keeps a goodly number employed, but for those whose husbands' incomes provide means sufficient to maintain appropriate life styles, few work and fewer still think of their job as a career—that is, "as a necessary and intrinsic part of their destiny."[24]

[23] *Ibid.*, pp. 15–16.
[24] *Ibid.*, p. 16.

The fruits of this situation are apparent in many ways. For one thing, while women today make up 37 percent of the work force in the United States, they are concentrated in service occupations—for example, one-third are secretaries, saleswomen, general private household workers, teachers in elementary schools, bookkeepers, waitresses, or professional nurses. Furthermore, ". . . they earn less than men in all kinds of jobs, and their unemployment rate is higher. . . . The gap between the earnings of women and of men has been steadily widening since 1956."[25] These discrepancies are only partly explainable in terms of the demands made on women's time by domestic responsibility. Nor do discriminatory admission and employment policies provide the whole answer. Perhaps the most nefarious element in this scheme is the more general educational and socialization process, what Sandra and Daryl Bem have called "training the woman to know her place."[26]

Data that indicate women hold themselves and their work in lower esteem than they do men and their work are becoming increasingly available. Goldberg finds that in an experimental situation women rate the same story higher when it is ascribed to a male rather than to a female author—that is, to John T. McKay vs. Joan T. McKay.[27] Terman and Tyler conclude that despite better academic performance, girls' self-opinion declines through adolescence while their opinion of boys and boys' abilities improves.[28] Likewise, Lipinski, using Thematic Aperception Test-type pictures (a projective technique), showed that girls attributed more imagery interpretable in terms of achievement to pictures with males than to those with females.[29]

Where are the roots of this differential evaluation? One does not have to look far. While Norwegian mothers in one study overwhelmingly (95 percent) felt that boys and girls should be reared similarly, they were in much less (77 percent) agreement with regard to both helping with housework.[30] Half of the mothers also thought that boys should receive a better education than should girls. Often the process is more subtle. A study of

[25] Marijean Suelzle, "Women in Labor," *Trans*-action, 8 (November–December 1970): 50.

[26] Sandra L. Bem and Daryl J. Bem, "Case Study of a Nonconscious Ideology: Training the Woman to Know Her Place," in Daryl J. Bem, ed., *Beliefs, Attitudes, and Human Affairs* (Belmont, Calif.: Brooks/Cole, 1970) pp. 89–99.

[27] Philip Goldberg, "Are Women Prejudiced Against Women?" *Trans*-action, 5 (April 1968): 28–30.

[28] Lewis Terman and Leona Tyler, "Psychological Sex Differences," in Leonard Carmichael, ed., *Manual of Child Psychology* (2d ed.; New York: John Wiley, 1954), pp. 1064–1114.

[29] Beatrice Lipinski, *"Sex-Role Conflict and Achievement in College Women."* Unpublished Doctoral dissertation, University of Cincinnati, 1965.

[30] Sverre Brun-Gulbrandsen, "Sex Role and the Socialization Process," in Edmund Dahlström, ed., *The Changing Roles of Men and Women* (London: Gerald Duckworth, 1967), p. 63.

mothers and infants revealed that by the time the babies were six months old the women were already touching and speaking more to their girls while at play than to their boys. By thirteen months of age these same children were showing sex differences in coping with frustration and separation that plausibly, though not definitely, can be connected with the earlier differential treatment.[31]

There is some reason to believe that women who escape conventional role definitions and opt for careers are those whose socialization experience has in some ways been different from that of those women who choose the more usual wife-mother role. In attempting to separate college girls who were committed to a career from those who were not, Almquist and Angrist found that the former were no less attractive than the latter and their social lives were no less full (two frequently encountered explanations), but rather that the career-bound coeds had mothers who were involved in careers, thus lending credence to the argument that role models are an important determinant of work orientation.[32] But it goes further than the mere presence of a role model. While Almquist and Angrist were not interested in the differential socialization of their subjects, might we not infer that the mothers of the career-oriented women students not only provided them with a role model but also in their socialization instilled certain values and created personality traits which led to their ultimate career decision?

Perhaps the most dramatic finding of all is that which emerged in Poloma's recent study of married professional women, all of whom were physicians, lawyers, or professors.

> In analyzing the responses of 53 dual professional couples, it became apparent that *the assumption of a professional role by the wife does not mean a drastic change in family roles.* In only one case did we find the dual profession insuring an egalitarian family. . . . In all other cases, the wife was *responsible* for the traditional feminine tasks. . . . Our data yielded no indication that either men or women desire to see an equal *sharing* of both masculine and feminine roles. The wives (so long as their husbands were able to provide adequately) preferred not to *have to* work in the same ways their husbands did, leaving the provider role and its corresponding rights and duties as his domain. In return they

[31] S. Goldberg and M. Lewis, "Play Behavior in the Year-Old Infant: Early Sex Differences," *Child Development,* 40 (March 1969): 21–31.

[32] Elizabeth M. Almquist and Shirley S. Angrist, "Career Salience and Atypicality of Occupational Choice Among College Women," *Journal of Marriage and the Family,* 32 (May 1970): 242–249; Elizabeth M. Almquist and Shirley S. Angrist, "Role Model Influences in College Women's Career Aspirations," *Merrill-Palmer Quarterly,* 17 (July 1971): 263–279.

accepted their prime responsibilities to be in the area of homemaking and child care.[33]

These women even went so far as not to earn more than their husbands did, where such a possibility existed, for fear of disrupting the conventional definition of the husband as the main provider. What is significant about this research is that it shows how deeply ingrained is the conventional division of labor within the home and how even women who have been able to overcome the by no means slight obstacles for them in the professions cleave to their conventional domestic roles rather than push for a truly equal division of labor. What Friedan speaks of as the "Feminine Mystique" seems to have taken its toll here.[34]

There is some reason to believe that an important source of the inferior psychological and vocational status of women is to be found in the family. Given the nuclear family as we know it, it is difficult to improve the situation. This is starkly brought out in studies of women in socialist and welfare nations—some of these are included in this collection—which indicate that while more women may work and have better jobs than do American women (e.g., 75 percent of Soviet physicians are women, 7 percent of U.S. physicians), their domestic responsibilities are not lightened to any degree (apart from facilities for the care of children, which we shall discuss below), and thus they are doubly burdened: They work full time and take care of their homes as well.

To be sure, some attempt to resolve this problem is being made in those countries. One of the major advances is what we have come to call the day care center, a facility for preschool children during the working day. Nonetheless, only about 14 percent of Sweden's and 23 percent of the USSR's preschoolers are in such centers.[35] The figures for this country represent only a token effort; moreover, the children have to be picked up at the end of the day and cared for so that cooking, cleaning, and associated chores still go on.

Sweden is committed at the highest levels of government to sexual equality; at the same time, it espouses the nuclear family.[36] The hope is that children can be educated to accept the absence of sex role differences in child and home care. It is in this way, the government believes, that a generation can be raised which will permit the liberation of men as well as the liberation of women. "Liberation of men" means a situation in which men, if they feel suited for it and comfortable with it, will be able to stay home and assume responsibility for what has previously been defined as the

---

[33] Margaret M. Poloma, "The Myth of the Egalitarian Family: Familial Roles and the Profesionally Employed Wife." Paper presented at the Sixty-fifth Annual Meeting of the American Sociological Association, Washington, D.C., September 1970, p. 21.

[34] Betty Friedan, *The Feminine Mystique* (New York: Dell, 1963).

[35] "Day Care: The Boom Begins," *Newsweek* (December 7, 1970), 95.

[36] Dahlström, *op. cit., passim.*

woman's province. More importantly, the government hopes to create a setting in which both sexes can realize their talents uncontaminated by conventional sexual role distinctions. The success of such a program, when grounded in the nuclear family, remains to be seen.

More radical theoreticians maintain that change is not possible within the context of the nuclear family. They argue that only in a communal environment, where child rearing and other domestic responsibilities are taken out of the hands of women and given to the community, can women truly be emancipated and offensive sex roles abolished. This theme appears as far back as Plato's *Republic* and more recently, as we shall see, in the writings and communities of nineteenth- and twentieth-century utopians. These experiments came a long way toward liberating women—they removed most of the more onerous aspects of the female role: cleaning, cooking, and child rearing; and more importantly they permitted a more complete participation of women in the work force, unquestionably a major accomplishment. But what none of these communities did, and this holds for the kibbutzim of the present day as well as for a nineteenth-century community like Oneida, was provide true egalitarianism in the sense of women having a proportionate share of the work which the community defined as the most important and prestigious. Thus Melford Spiro in his study of one Israeli kibbutz discusses at length what he speaks of as "the problem of the women": The great majority (88 percent) of the women worked in the less esteemed "service" branch rather than in the "agricultural" branch.[37] In a kibbutz society, which emphasizes occupations that show economic (i.e., directly productive) return, this difference inevitably leads to invidious comparisons and a feeling of dissatisfaction on the part of women that their sex is being used to keep them down. Thus women find themselves engaged in the most narrow form of housework—for example, washing clothes or cooking all day—hardly an improvement over the diverse domestic tasks of women outside the communal setting.

The persistence of sex role distinctions in kibbutzim indicates how deep lying such sentiments are. Still, the kibbutz has come a very long way in the direction of the emancipation of women, and the fact that they are agricultural communities *may* impose certain constraints in terms of the physical demands of labor. Perhaps when information becomes available on the new urban kibbutzim we shall see more equality. Still, whatever shortcomings current experiments reveal, the communal setting may be the only one in which women can be truly emancipated.

The Elderly
and the Family

It was mentioned earlier that one of the consequences of the patterns of residence associated with industrialization was the undermining of

[37] Melford E. Spiro, *Kibbutz* (New York: Schocken Books, 1970), pp. 221–236.

what might be called preindustrial social security patterns, or more specifically, the "contractual" obligation of the inheriting son to care for his aging parents in return for being given the family farm. This is not to say that the only reason parents were looked after in their later years was that they had established a son in a livelihood, but rather that the agricultural inheritance arrangement was an institutionalized means that provided for people as vigor and health declined. As we shall see, there no longer exist generally accepted patterns of behavior between children and their elderly parents. Furthermore, the nuclear family in industrial society is faced with a number of problems in this connection that did not exist for the preindustrial family or even for families in the earlier phases of the industrial era.

Approaching this matter from the broadest perspective, it becomes evident that the status of the elderly in society has been altered, especially in the work world. While there is some reason to believe that the ascendancy accorded to old age in the preindustrial world has been exaggerated,[38] nevertheless, as vocational tasks increasingly demand skills that are passed on by formal agencies of socialization, the role played by the mature in the transmission of knowledge has declined. Moreover, with the accession of performance criteria over seniority criteria in bureaucratized settings, the value assigned to years has also diminished. The problem is compounded by the advent of forced retirement, in some cases at a reduced age. This means that many still-active people must leave an area that gives great meaning to their lives. And, as we shall show, retirement often results in serious financial problems because of the drastically reduced income. In concert, all of these factors act to push the elderly to the perimeters of society, and to create for some a sense of futility and uselessness.[39]

Another important factor is that there are many more older people now than there previously were. For example, in 1900, persons sixty-five years of age and older made up 4.1 percent of the U.S. population; in 1970, they made up 9.9 percent.[40] Because of these increased numbers various nations have been forced to think in terms of special programs for them, and more and more young and middle-aged adults are confronted with difficult personal decisions. As Burgess indicates, the choices are troublesome:

> (a) Should adult children offer an aging parent or parents a home? (b) What should be the *moral* and legal responsibility

[38] Ariès, *op. cit.*, points out that prior to the eighteenth century "the old man was regarded as ridiculous" (p. 31). Old age, then, was not always held in high esteem.

[39] One can easily exaggerate the postretirement difficulties of the elderly; many make successful adjustments, but the problems discussed in the text are those common to nearly all.

[40] Edward G. Stockwell, "Some Notes on the Changing Age Composition of the Population of the United States," *Rural Sociology*, 29 (March 1964): 69; and *Statistical Abstracts of the United States* (Washington, D.C.: U.S. Bureau of the Census, 1971), p. 23.

of children for the financial support of indigent parents? and (c) What if any should be the reciprocal roles of aging parents and their adult married sons and daughters? At present, then, there is confusion and conflict because the relationship of the older and younger generation has not been redefined in terms of the present situation.[41]

A factor contributing to these dilemmas is the differential life expectancy of men and women. In 1920, it was 53.6 years for men and 54.6 for women; by 1968, it was 66.6 and 74.0, respectively.[42] This reflects itself in household composition to the extent that "at seventy-five and over, more than 40 percent of all men are still living with a spouse in their own household in contrast to less than 15 percent of the women."[43] This obviously means that now there are many more widows, who, because of this status, are in a particularly poor position to deal with certain of the afflictions associated with aging, one of the most important of which is loneliness: ". . . Isolation in old age is an immense social problem, affecting upwards of three-quarters of a million individuals in Britain alone. Many live in conditions of discomfort or misery and are particularly vulnerable in illness or infirmity. Society is only slowly awakening to their needs."[44] Some feel that such isolation has been overstated. They point to such findings as that reported in a major study of aging in three industrial societies (Denmark, Great Britain, and the United States): Over three-fifths of the older parents had seen at least one child on the day of the interview and another 20 percent had seen a child in the week preceding the interview.[45] How do we reconcile frequency of visitation and loneliness? Part of the answer is to be found in household composition. The Shanas et al. research came up with the following distribution of household type for those over sixty-five years: living alone, never married, 4–8 percent; married couple, 35–45 percent; married couple and married or single children, 7–14 percent; widowed (or divorced or separated) parent and married or unmarried children, 9–20 percent; widowed (sometimes divorced or separated) living alone, 22–28 percent.[46] From these figures we learn that more than a quarter of this over-sixty-five population is living alone, and the proportion is even greater for those over seventy-five years. These people are extremely dependent upon kin, specifically their offspring, for relief from their solitude. Even though they may see their children with some regularity—and

[41] Quoted in Harold E. Smith, "Family Interaction Patterns of the Aged: A Review," in Arnold Rose and Warren Peterson, eds., Older People and Their Social World (Philadelphia: F. A. Davis, 1965), p. 149.

[42] Statistical Abstracts of the United States, op. cit., p. 53.

[43] Gordon F. Streib, "Old Age and the Family: Facts and Forecasts," American Behavioral Scientist, 14 (September–October 1970): 29.

[44] Peter Townsend, The Family Life of Old People (Baltimore: Penguin, 1963), p. 236.

[45] Shanas et al., op. cit., p. 174.

[46] Ibid., p. 218.

a by no means insignificant number of such persons live too far from their children to make this possible very often—the visits may be brief (stopping by to say hello on the way home from work) and the periods between visits socially arid. Even those widowed parents living with a child or children may be in an empty house during the day, but their situation is better than that of those who live alone.

Irrespective of residential and visiting patterns, children are still the first to whom the elderly turn for financial aid. The importance of this becomes evident when some facts about the relationship between old age and economic hardship are examined. A Senate task force recently indicated that three out of ten old persons, in contrast to one out of nine young persons, were definable as living in poverty in 1967; about half of the single elderly had incomes under $1500, and incomes of $1000 or less were reported by a quarter of these people.[47] The Senate group concluded that there is little reason for optimism; without governmental action their financial situation would not improve. In view of the pervasive money shortage among them, it is surprising that only 4 percent of the aged in this country receive *regular* payments from their children. One should realize, though, that those who need the aid the most have children who themselves are in economic straits.[48] This does not mean that children do not offer any financial assistance to parents. As Rosow says, "People look only to their closest family members, primarily children, for financial aid, and there are no functional substitutes for them among other personal associates."[49] During times of economic need, children do respond; friends and neighbors are virtually never called upon in this capacity.

For care during illness, a recurrent and serious problem, the elderly often turn to friends and neighbors after resort to children. The well-being of the aged is dependent on their grown children to such an extent that even in industrial societies children are a form of social security.

All that has been said up to this point is intended to convey the problematic character of old age in industrial society and the nuclear family patterns that exist to cope with it. The picture is not complete, because in recent years various partial solutions have emerged that seem to offer the possibility of reconciling the nuclear family and the aged. For the elderly who have not been rendered infirm by illness, there has been public and private construction of facilities specifically for them. These range from specially designed apartment houses (containing resident medical staffs and located near shopping areas) to self-contained communities comprising homes or apartments purchased, generally at considerable expense, by retired persons. In recent years retirement communities have literally

[47] *Economics of Aging: Toward a Full Share in Abundance* (Washington, D.C.: U.S. Senate Special Committee on Aging, March 1969).

[48] Streib, *op. cit.,* p. 31.

[49] Irving Rosow, "Old People, Their Friends and Neighbors," *American Behavioral Scientist,* 14 (September–October 1970): 60.

boomed in this country, if for no other reason than that they are seen by speculators as potentially good investments, but only a small affluent group is able to take advantage of them.[50]

These provisions for housing are important; several studies have shown that the elderly lead much fuller social lives when they are near each other. They interact more frequently and with a greater number of people. This is, of course, facilitated by their shared experiences and interests. It has also been shown that when the aged have contemporaries as neighbors they fare better during illness: "In areas with high concentration of the aged, neighbors basically provide the care for these most dependent people [those without local children] even in longer more serious illness. Under these conditions, of those who live alone but have comparatively few old neighbors, one-third go completely without any care in contrast to fourteen percent of those with many old neighbors."[51] However successful this approach of concentrating the elderly may be, to some it represents an offensive form of segregation, a pushing out of one group. At this point, though, there is little reason to believe that more than a small fraction of the aged population will be involved in it in the foreseeable future.

The family in the commune offers a more complete and in many ways a more humane solution to the problem of the aged. But the current communal movement in this country has yet to show much concern with this issue, which is not surprising in view of its youthful composition (for the most part people under thirty). If the communes are able to survive, old age will ultimately become an issue, as it did in the more long-lived nineteenth-century communes and has in the current kibbutzim. Because the literature on the kibbutz is much fuller than that on the nineteenth-century communal movement, we can again turn to it, as we did in our discussion of the place of women, to learn about the elderly in that setting.

The situation of the elderly on the kibbutz is more complicated than one might initially think. The movement from work to retirement is transitional; workers slowly relinquish their economic activity or are transferred to less demanding tasks. Upon complete retirement, no one confronts the financial crises common among less than affluent retirees in a noncommunal setting. Individual physical needs are as adequately met as they had been. To be sure, contacts within the community are reduced as a consequence of withdrawal from the work sphere but family relations assume greater salience. Because of their new leisure, grandparents can take on responsibilities for the grandchildren that were previously impossible; they can care for the youngsters during the daily visiting periods if the parents are too tired, or they can be in charge of them when the parents are away from

---

[50] See, for example, R. P. Walkley *et al., Retirement Housing in California* (Berkeley, Calif.: Diablo Press, 1960).

[51] Rosow, *op. cit.,* p. 64.

the kibbutz. Such attentions are often reciprocated by adult children, who visit aged parents when they are ill, bring them food when they find it difficult to go to the dining hall, and meet their other needs as well. Talmon quite correctly points out that this give-and-take occurs in a setting where the demands made are really not great and require little in the way of sacrifice or the reorganization of one's life.[52]

All this notwithstanding, life is not completely rosy for the elderly on the kibbutz. These are communities that prize productive labor above all else, and people are valued in accordance with their contributions. Therefore, it is not to be wondered at that retired persons often find it difficult to adjust to their new dependence, even though the community does not question their right to it. When Talmon compared aging members of the kibbutzim with members' parents who were living on kibbutzim but who themselves were not members in the fullest sense of the word, she found the latter to be more satisfied than the former. This puzzling difference she explained by the fact that the members' parents had not been imbued with the work ethic of the retired members.[53] Moreover, the situation they faced on the kibbutzim was better than what they faced outside.

The dissatisfaction of retired kibbutz members has been thought by some critics to be indicative of the failure of the kibbutz to deal with the problem of the elderly.[54] It is perhaps more correct to say that as was the case with women, the kibbutz has come a long way toward resolving many of the difficulties associated with old age, but it still has some way to go. As the Talmon article shows, these problems have been recognized, and attempts are being made to deal with them.

SOCIAL ISOLATION
AND THE FAMILY

In the preceding section of this essay, we have discussed two sources of strain between the nuclear family and life in industrial society, and how communal families reduce this strain. Now we turn to a third source, one that in many ways is just coming to the fore: familial isolation. On a structural level, the roots of the isolation have been present for some time, but in terms of subjective awareness and distress they are only now emerging.

In view of our earlier attempt to discount certain notions about the family in industrial society, it may appear paradoxical that we are now raising the specter of familial isolation. What we have maintained up to this point is that the small nuclear family has been the predominate residential form since long before the Industrial Revolution and that we have

---

[52] Yonina Talmon, "Aging in Israel, A Planned Society," *American Journal of Sociology*, 67 (November 1961): 288–289. (Reprinted in this collection.)

[53] *Ibid.*, p. 291.

[54] Streib, *op. cit.*, pp. 36–37.

been subjected to the myth of the extended rural family. Furthermore, while we have recognized that certain services currently performed by extrafamilial agencies were once performed by kin, the number of kin with whom families interact and, more importantly, live, has not changed significantly. From what, then, does the "new" isolation arise?

In *The Community Press in an Urban Setting*, Morris Janowitz introduced the concept of the "community of limited liability," referring to the narrow nature of the individual's commitments to his community and his willingness to withdraw when his needs are not met by the community.[55] This theme has been developed further by Scott Greer in his valuable discussions of the character of urban life.[56] Neither of these two men, however, looks specifically at the family and familism in these settings.

If the individual's liability to the community is limited, to what is his liability extensive? We shall argue that it is to the family. Parsons, as we have seen, maintains that the nuclear family is the center of the affective life of persons in industrial societies, but it is the center of social life as well. More significantly, it has been argued, most cogently by Richard Sennett, that the modern family has increasingly cut itself off from the larger society.

In "The Brutality of Modern Families," Sennett has drawn important contrasts *not* between contemporary and preindustrial families but rather between current suburban families and working-class immigrant families at the turn of the century.[57] He does not fall prey to a romantization of the latter's life; he recognizes their poverty and hardship, but nonetheless feels there was a pervasive civility then that is absent now. Drawing upon Louis Wirth's famous essay "Urbanism as a Way of Life," he points out that the character of city life was such as to break down the insularity of the ethnic enclaves that formed in the immigrant sections.[58] The round of daily activity brought both adults and children in contact with a variety of people and experiences:

> This life . . . required an urbanity of outlook, and multiple, often conflicting points of social contact, for these desperately poor people to survive. They *had* to make this diversity in their lives, for no one or two or three institutions in which they lived could provide for all their needs. . . . It is the mark of a sophisticated life style that localities become crossed in

---

[55] Morris Janowitz, *The Community Press in an Urban Setting* (New York: Free Press, 1952).

[56] Scott Greer, *The Emerging City* (New York: Free Press, 1962).

[57] Richard Sennett, "The Brutality of Modern Families," *Trans*-action, 7 (September 1970): 29–37. Sennett develops the ideas in this article more fully in *The Uses of Disorder* (New York: Knopf, 1970).

[58] Louis Wirth, "Urbanism as a Way of Life," *American Journal of Sociology*, 44 (July 1938): 1–24.

conflicting forms, and this sophistication was the essence of these poor people's lives.[59]

Loss of this diversity is the price, Sennett feels, that people have paid for their prosperity. In the last fifty years, the children and grandchildren of these immigrants have, upon reaching the middle class, turned in upon themselves and fashioned a family life of great intensity, at the expense of extrafamilial diversity. The suburbs have added to this development by reducing the possibility of any sort of external variety. They have furthered the homogenization and the insulation of family life, and have made the threat of the outside world even greater.

While all of this was happening, Sennett feels that there arose a commitment both to the deindividualization of family roles and a taboo on overt conflict. Thus, "a good family of this sort is a family whose members talk to each other as equals, where the children presume to the lessons of experience and the parents try to forget them."[60] Dignity, according to Sennett, resides not in separateness or individuality, but in equality. This equality breeds a tolerance only for those who share the same attitude and life style. The family becomes a "microcosm" of the world for its members. As one of his informants put it, nothing "really important" in human relationships occurs outside the home. All of this, he argues, has resulted in a situation where familial conflict is seen as an indication of failure: ". . . The guilt-over-conflict syndrome is significant because it is too deeply held a presupposition about family life: people look, for example, at conflicts between generations as an evil, revealing some sort of rottenness in the familial social fabric, rather than as an inevitable and natural process of historical change."[61] Taken together, the emergence of these values and the insularity of the nuclear family have created an atmosphere which Sennett has labeled a "brutal" one.

While some may feel Sennett's presentation of the middle-class family to be extreme and exaggerated, he is not alone. Similar voices have been raised, not only by other sociologists such as Philip Slater, but by psychiatrists as well, perhaps most notably by David Cooper, a founder with R. D. Laing of the Philadelphia Association, in *The Death of the Family*.[62] Like Sennett, he is in agreement with Philip Ariès' position that since the mideighteenth century the family has increasingly encroached upon the life space of the individual: "The family form of social existence that characterizes all our institutions essentially destroys autonomous initiative by its defining nonrecognition of what I have called the proper dialectic

[59] Sennett, "The Brutality of Modern Families," *op. cit.*, p. 31.
[60] *Ibid.*, p. 33.
[61] *Ibid.*, p. 34.
[62] David Cooper, *The Death of the Family* (New York: Pantheon, 1970). See also Philip E. Slater, *The Pursuit of Loneliness* (Boston: Beacon Press, 1970); R. D. Laing, *The Politics of the Family* (Toronto: Canadian Broadcasting Publications, 1969).

of solitude and being with other people."[63] Life as we know it in nuclear families, according to Cooper, prevents us from realizing ourselves and our potential to be by ourselves. Of greater weight, it restricts our lives emotionally by offering "the illusion of the quantifiability of love"—that is, that we have only so much love to offer and this love is exhausted in a monogamous relationship. He feels that if we are to create settings that permit involvement and personal growth we have to adopt some sort of communal alternative.

> A commune is a microsocial structure that achieves a viable dialect between solitude and being-with-others; it implies either a common residence for the members, or at least a common work and experience area, around which residential situations may be spread out peripherally; it means that love relationship become diffused between members of the commune network far more than is the case with the family system, and this means, of course, that sexual relationships are not restricted to some socially approved two-person, man-woman arrangement; above all, because this strikes most centrally at repression, it means that children should have totally free access to adults beyond their biological parental couple.[64]

To be sure, the views of Sennett and Cooper are not identical. Nevertheless, it is of great significance that a sociologist and a psychiatrist, as well as others in their disciplines, coming out of very different traditions and starting with very diverse theoretical perspectives, have come up with such surprisingly similar views. These men, by tapping what may be seen as incipient currents in Western society, give great insight into some of the key forces that are pushing some of us to seek a communal alternative.

For most, communal life represents an attempt to involve the individual in the larger community, to destroy the notion that the world outside the family is hostile and cold and that only in the bosom of the family can love and safety be found. For some, as we shall see, this has meant turning away from the nuclear family and seeking group or multilateral marriages. For others, it has meant cleaving to the nuclear family but in a communal context where group participation is a necessary and desired part of life. Whatever shape family life takes, and there are many intermediary forms between complete monogamy and complete group marriage, the central idea is always the same: Break down the barrier between people and permit freedom and growth.

At this point, we cannot say with any certainty whether family life in the commune will resolve the problems we have explored in this essay. The papers that follow suggest that at least partial answers have been found in this setting. Who knows but that these new experiments may be the wave of the future.

[63] Cooper, *op. cit.*, p. 140.
[64] *Ibid.*, pp. 44–45.

I
HISTORICAL PERSPECTIVES ON COMMUNAL FAMILIES

We begin this section dealing with historical perspectives on the communal family with excerpts from Plato's *The Republic,* a description of a utopia, in order to convey how early in human thought the idea of moving away from conventional family patterns arose—not to mention the fact that many of his major themes will be echoed in the discussions of actual communities in this volume. Plato is concerned with reducing the potentiality of conflict between the individual's allegiance to the state and allegiance to the family; hence his desire to abolish the latter. He also sees doing away with the family as a means to allow eugenic reproduction, although his treatment of the subterfuge of drawing lots indicates his awareness of the tension that will result when the state or the commune attempts to regulate sexual intercourse. Kephart's paper on Oneida in this section focuses on the same problem in an actual community.

We also learn that Plato was a proponent of woman's liberation: ". . . If we are to set women to the same tasks as men, we must teach them the same thing. They must have the same two branches of training for mind and body and also be taught the art of war, and they must receive the same treatment." His discussion of the topic is extraordinarily up-to-date. If his language and examples were altered slightly, there would be no difficulty in believing the work to be from a contemporary pen.

Gollin's article on the Moravians is an excellent examination of family life in a highly religious utopian community. Of particular interest is her analysis of community failure. The choir system was introduced to reduce familial influence and provide an alternative structure, but it fell short as an agency for the socialization of succeeding generations. This neatly illustrates the importance of the family unit in the socialization and ultimate recruitment of new members to a community. If the prevailing techniques produce children who are not suited to membership, as was the case with the Moravians, decline is inevitable. We shall see that such relatively successful communities as the *kibbutzim* have created procedures of socialization that cohere with the group's aims and needs.

Gollin's piece also is of importance because of the type of communal family described in it. The reader must realize that Gollin is dealing with a very special kind of monogamy: one in which the community exercised a great amount of control over mate selection, and one in which, at least in the early years of marriage, the couple did not live together. Here the balance between communal and family allegiances was managed by substantially diminishing not only the role of the family in various institutional spheres, but the relationship among man and wife and children as well.

Kephart, in the article that follows, presents a comprehensive description of what is perhaps the most important, and revolutionary, experiment in family reorganization to have taken place in any American utopian community. Few present-day communes have adopted such radical departures from the nuclear family, and of those none so systematically and successfully as Oneida. Because, as Kephart tells us, the diaries dealing with this aspect of the venture have been destroyed, we will never know definitely how much conflict accompanied the domestic rearrangement. Evidence suggests that the problems were not as great as one might imagine, though this may in large part be explainable in terms of the members' strong religious commitments and the charismatic role played by Noyes.

Oneida would be significant if only for its experiment in complex marriage, but it also adopted a program of selective breeding, referred to as "stirpiculture." Like Plato, Noyes wanted the community to produce children who were physically and mentally sound. Unlike Plato, he did not have to worry about resentment of those who were denied parenthood because an unusual and effective form of birth control permitted even those not selected for procreative purposes to engage in intercourse.

1

PLATO ON WOMEN
AND THE FAMILY

THE EQUALITY OF WOMEN

Before proceeding to the central paradox, the rule of the
philosopher-king, Socrates explains how the Guardians are to
"have wives and children in common." The common life of
the Guardians, it now appears, involves that men and women
shall receive the same education and share equally in all
public duties: women with the right natural gifts are not to
be debarred by difference of sex from fulfilling the highest
functions. So when the best Guardians are selected for training as Rulers, the choice may fall upon a woman. At Athens,
where women lived in seclusion and took no part in politics,
this proposal would appear revolutionary. It is the theme of
one of Aristophanes' later comedies, *Women in Parliament*
(*Ecclesiazusae*), which shows that the question of women's
right's was in the air as early as 393 B.C.

This topic is introduced as if it were a digression. Socrates
is interrupted as he starts upon a description of the degenerate
types of constitution and human character.

Nevertheless, I continued, we are now within sight of the clearest possible
proof of our conclusions, and we ought not to slacken our efforts.

No, anything rather than that.

If you will take your stand with me, then, on this point of vantage to
which we have climbed, you shall see all the forms that evil takes, or at
least all that it seems worth while to look at.

Lead the way and tell me what you see.

What I see is that, whereas there is only one form of excellence, imper-
fection exists in innumerable shapes, of which there are four that specially
deserve notice.

What do you mean?

It looks as if there were as many types of character as there are distinct
varieties of political constitution.

How many?

Five of each.

Will you define them?

Yes, I said. One form of constitution will be the form we have been

REPRINTED with permission of the publisher from *The Republic of Plato*, translated
and with introduction and notes by F. M. Cornford, New York and London: Oxford University Press, First American Edition, 1945, pp. 144–168.

describing, though it may be called by two names: monarchy, when there is one man who stands out above the rest of the Rulers; aristocracy, when there are more than one.[1]

True.

That, then, I regard as a single form; for, so long as they observe our principles of upbringing and education, whether the Rulers be one or more, they will not subvert the important institutions in our commonwealth.

Naturally not.

Such, then, is the type of state or constitution that I call good and right, and the corresponding type of man. By this standard, the other forms in which a state or an individual character may be organized are depraved and wrong. There are four of these vicious forms.

What are they?

Here I was going on to describe these forms in the order in which, as I thought, they develop one from another, when Polemarchus, who was sitting a little way from Adeimantus, reached out his hand and took hold of his garment by the shoulder. Leaning forward and drawing Adeimantus towards him, he whispered something in his ear, of which I only caught the words: What shall we do? Shall we leave it alone?

Certainly not, said Adeimantus, raising his voice.

What is this, I asked, that you are not going to leave alone?

You, he replied.

Why, in particular? I inquired.

Because we think you are shirking the discussion of a very important part of the subject and trying to cheat us out of an explanation. Everyone, you said, must of course see that the maxim "friends have all things in common" applies to women and children. You thought we should pass over such a casual remark!

But wasn't that right, Adeimantus? said I.

Yes, he said, but "right" in this case, as in others, needs to be defined. There may be many ways of having things in common, and you must tell us which you mean. We have been waiting a long time for you to say something about the conditions in which children are to be born and brought up and your whole plan of having wives and children held in common. This seems to us a matter in which right or wrong management will make all the difference to society; and now, instead of going into it thoroughly, you are passing on to some other form of constitution. So we came to the resolution which you overheard, not to let you off discussing it as fully as all the other institutions.

I will vote for your resolution too, said Glaucon.

In fact, Socrates, Thrasymachus added, you may take it as carried unanimously.

---

[1] The question whether wisdom rules in the person of one man or of several is unimportant. In the sequel the ideal constitution is called kingship or aristocracy (the rule of the best) indifferently.

You don't know what you are doing, I said, in holding me up like this. You want to start, all over again, on an enormous subject, just as I was rejoicing at the idea that we had done with this form of constitution. I was only too glad that my casual remark should be allowed to pass. And now, when you demand an explanation, you little know what a swarm of questions you are stirring up. I let it alone, because I foresaw no end of trouble.

Well, said Thrasymachus, what do you think we came here for—to play pitch-and-toss or to listen to a discussion?

A discussion, no doubt, I replied; but within limits.

No man of sense, said Glaucon, would think the whole of life too long to spend on questions of this importance. But never mind about us; don't be faint-hearted yourself. Tell us what you think about this question: how our Guardians are to have wives and children in common, and how they will bring up the young in the interval between their birth and education, which is thought to be the most difficult time of all. Do try to explain how all this is to be arranged.

I wish it were as easy as you seem to think, I replied. These arrangements are even more open to doubt than any we have so far discussed. It may be questioned whether the plan is feasible, and even if entirely feasible, whether it would be for the best. So I have some hesitation in touching on what may seem to be an idle dream.

You need not hesitate, he replied. This is not an unsympathetic audience; we are neither incredulous nor hostile.

Thank you, I said; I suppose that remark is meant to be encouraging.

Certainly it is.

Well, I said, it has just the opposite effect. You would do well to encourage me, if I had any faith in my own understanding of these matters. If one knows the truth, there is no risk to be feared in speaking about the things one has most at heart among intelligent friends; but if one is still in the position of a doubting inquirer, as I am now, talking becomes a slippery venture. Not that I am afraid of being laughed at—that would be childish —but I am afraid I may miss my footing just where a false step is most to be dreaded and drag my friends down with me in my fall. I devoutly hope, Glaucon, that no nemesis will overtake me for what I am going to say; for I really believe that to kill a man unintentionally is a lighter offense than to mislead him concerning the goodness and justice of social institutions. Better to run that risk among enemies than among friends; so your encouragement is out of place.

Glaucon laughed at this. No, Socrates, he said, if your theory has any untoward effect on us, our blood shall not be on your head; we absolve you of any intention to mislead us. So have no fear.

Well, said I, when a homicide is absolved of all intention, the law holds him clear of guilt; and the same principle may apply to my case.

Yes, so far as that goes, you may speak freely.

We must go back, then, to a subject which ought, perhaps, to have been treated earlier in its proper place; though, after all, it may be suitable that the women should have their turn on the stage when the men have quite finished their performance, especially since you are so insistent. In my judgment, then, the question under what conditions people born and educated as we have described should possess wives and children, and how they should treat them, can be rightly settled only by keeping to the course on which we started them at the outset. We undertook to put these men in the position of watchdogs guarding a flock. Suppose we follow up the analogy and imagine them bred and reared in the same sort of way. We can then see if that plan will suit our purpose.

How will that be?

In this way. Which do we think right for watchdogs: should the females guard the flock and hunt with the males and take a share in all they do, or should they be kept within doors as fit for no more than bearing and feeding their puppies, while all the hard work of looking after the flock is left to the males?

They are expected to take their full share, except that we treat them as not quite so strong.

Can you employ any creature for the same work as another, if you do not give them both the same upbringing and education?

No.

Then, if we are to set women to the same tasks as men, we must teach them the same things. They must have the same two branches of training for mind and body and also be taught the art of war, and they must receive the same treatment.

That seems to follow.

Possibly, if these proposals were carried out, they might be ridiculed as involving a good many breaches of custom.

They might indeed.

The most ridiculous—don't you think?—being the notion of women exercising naked along with the men in the wrestling-schools; some of them elderly women too, like the old men who still have a passion for exercise when they are wrinkled and not very agreeable to look at.

Yes, that would be thought laughable, according to our present notions.

Now we have started on this subject, we must not be frightened of the many witticisms that might be aimed at such a revolution, not only in the matter of bodily exercise but in the training of women's minds, and not least when it comes to their bearing arms and riding horseback. Having begun upon these rules, we must not draw back from the harsher provisions. The wits may be asked to stop being witty and try to be serious; and we may remind them that it is not so long since the Greeks, like most foreign nations of the present day, thought it ridiculous and shameful for men to be seen naked. When gymnastic exercises were first introduced in Crete and later at Sparta, the humorists had their chance to make fun of them; but when experience had shown that nakedness is better uncovered than muffled up, the laughter died down and a practice which the reason approved ceased to look ridiculous to the eye. This shows how idle it is to think anything ludicrous but what is base. One who tries to raise a laugh at any spectacle save that of baseness and folly will also, in his serious moments, set before himself some other standard than goodness of what deserves to be held in honor.

Most assuredly.

The first thing to be settled, then, is whether these proposals are feasible; and it must be open to anyone, whether a humorist or serious-minded, to raise the question whether, in the case of mankind, the feminine nature is capable of taking part with the other sex in all occupations, or in none at all, or in some only; and in particular under which of these heads this business of military service falls. Well begun is half done, and would not this be the best way to begin?

Yes.

Shall we take the other side in this debate and argue against ourselves? We do not want the adversary's position to be taken by storm for lack of defenders.

I have no objection.

Let us state his case for him. "Socrates and Glaucon," he will say, "there is no need for others to dispute your position; you yourselves, at the very outset of founding your commonwealth, agreed that everyone should do the one work for which nature fits him." Yes, of course; I suppose we did. "And isn't there a very great difference in nature between man and woman?" Yes, surely. "Does not that natural difference imply a corresponding difference in the work to be given to each? Yes. "But if so, surely you must be mistaken now and contradicting yourselves when you say that men and women, having such widely divergent natures, should do the same things?" What is your answer to that, my ingenious friend?

It is not easy to find one at the moment. I can only appeal to you to state the case on our own side, whatever it may be.

This, Glaucon, is one of many alarming objections which I foresaw some time ago. That is why I shrank from touching upon these laws concerning the possession of wives and the rearing of children.

It looks like anything but an easy problem.

True, I said; but whether a man tumbles into a swimming pool or into midocean, he has to swim all the same. So must we, and try if we can reach the shore, hoping for some Arion's dolphin or other miraculous deliverance to bring us safe to land.[2]

I suppose so.

Come then, let us see if we can find the way out. We did agree that

[2] The musician Arion, to escape the treachery of Corinthian sailors, leapt into the sea and was carried ashore at Taenarum by a dolphin, Herod.

different natures should have different occupations, and that the natures of man and woman are different; and yet we are now saying that these different natures are to have the same occupations. Is that the charge against us?

Exactly.

It is extraordinary, Glaucon, what an effect the practice of debating has upon people.

Why do you say that?

Because they often seem to fall unconsciously into mere disputes which they mistake for reasonable argument, through being unable to draw the distinctions proper to their subject; and so, instead of a philosophical exchange of ideas, they go off in chase of contradictions which are purely verbal.

I know that happens to many people; but does it apply to us at this moment?

Absolutely. At least I am afraid we are slipping unconsciously into a dispute about words. We have been strenuously insisting on the letter of our principle that different natures should not have the same occupations, as if we were scoring a point in a debate; but we have altogether neglected to consider what sort of sameness or difference we meant and in what respect these natures and occupations were to be defined as different or the same. Consequently, we might very well be asking one another whether there is not an opposition in nature between bald and long-haired men, and, when that was admitted, forbid one set to be shoemakers, if the other were following that trade.

That would be absurd.

Yes, but only because we never meant any and every sort of sameness or difference in nature, but the sort that was relevant to the occupations in question. We meant, for instance, that a man and a woman have the same nature if both have a talent for medicine; whereas two men have different natures if one is a born physician, the other a born carpenter.

Yes, of course.

If, then, we find that either the male sex or the female is specially qualified for any particular form of occupation, then that occupation, we shall say, ought to be assigned to one sex or the other. But if the only difference appears to be that the male begets and the female brings forth, we shall conclude that no difference between man and woman has yet been produced that is relevant to our purpose. We shall continue to think it proper for our Guardians and their wives to share in the same pursuits.

And quite rightly.

The next thing will be to ask our opponent to name any profession or occupation in civic life for the purposes of which woman's nature is different from man's.

That is a fair question.

He might reply, as you did just now, that it is not easy to find a satisfactory answer on the spur of the moment, but that there would be no difficulty after a little reflection.

Perhaps.

Suppose, then, we invite him to follow us and see if we can convince him that there is no occupation concerned with the management of social affairs that is peculiar to women. We will confront him with a question: When you speak of a man having a natural talent for something, do you mean that he finds it easy to learn, and after a little instruction can find out much more for himself; whereas a man who is not so gifted learns with difficulty and no amount of instruction and practice will make him even remember what he has been taught? Is the talented man one whose bodily powers are readily at the service of his mind, instead of being a hindrance? Are not these the marks by which you distinguish the presence of a natural gift for any pursuit?

Yes, precisely.

Now do you know of any human occupation in which the male sex is not superior to the female in all these respects? Need I waste time over exceptions like weaving and watching over saucepans and batches of cakes, though women are supposed to be good at such things and get laughed at when a man does them better?

It is true, he replied, in almost everything one sex is easily beaten by the other. No doubt many women are better at many things than many men; but taking the sexes as a whole, it is as you say.

To conclude, then, there is no occupation concerned with the management of social affairs which belongs either to woman or to man, as such. Natural gifts are to be found here and there in both creatures alike; and every occupation is open to both, so far as their natures are concerned, though woman is for all purposes the weaker.

Certainly.

Is that a reason for making over all occupations to men only?

Of course not.

No, because one woman may have a natural gift for medicine or for music, another may not.

Surely.

Is it not also true that a woman may, or may not, be warlike or athletic? I think so.

And again, one may love knowledge, another hate it; one may be high-spirited, another spiritless?

True again.

It follows that one woman will be fitted by nature to be a Guardian, another will not; because these were the qualities for which we selected our men Guardians. So for the purpose of keeping watch over the commonwealth, woman has the same nature as man, save in so far as she is weaker.

So it appears.

It follows that women of this type must be selected to share the life and duties of Guardians with men of the same type, since they are competent and of a like nature, and the same natures must be allowed the same pursuits.

Yes.

We come round, then, to our former position, that there is nothing contrary to nature in giving our Guardians' wives the same training for mind and body. The practice we proposed to establish was not impossible or visionary, since it was in accordance with nature. Rather, the contrary practice which now prevails turns out to be unnatural.

So it appears.

Well, we set out to inquire whether the plan we proposed was feasible and also the best. That it is feasible is now agreed; we must next settle whether it is the best.

Obviously.

Now, for the purpose of producing a woman fit to be a Guardian, we shall not have one education for men and another for women, precisely because the nature to be taken in hand is the same.

True.

What is your opinion on the question of one man being better than another? Do you think there is no such difference?

Certainly I do not.

And in this commonwealth of ours which will prove the better men— the Guardians who have received the education we described, or the shoe-makers who have been trained to make shoes?[3]

It is absurd to ask such a question.

Very well. So these Guardians will be the best of all the citizens?

By far.

And these women the best of all the women?

Yes.

Can anything be better for a commonwealth than to produce in it men and women of the best possible type?

No.

And that result will be brought about by such a system of mental and bodily training as we have described?

Surely.

We may conclude that the institution we proposed was not only practicable, but also the best for the commonwealth.

Yes.

The wives of our Guardians, then, must strip for exercise, since they will be clothed with virtue, and they must take their share in war and in the other social duties of guardianship. They are to have no other occupation; and in these duties the lighter part must fall to the women, because of the

---

[3] Elementary education will be open to all citizens, but presumably carried further (to the age of 17 or 18) in the case of those who show special promise.

weakness of their sex. The man who laughs at naked women, exercising their bodies for the best of reasons, is like one that "gathers fruit unripe,"[4] for he does not know what it is that he is laughing at or what he is doing. There will never be a finer saying than the one which declares that whatever does good should be held in honor, and the only shame is in doing harm.

That is perfectly true.

ABOLITION OF THE FAMILY FOR THE GUARDIANS

The principle, "Friends have all things in common," is now applied by abolishing private homes and families for the Guardians (only), so that they may form a single family. The chief aims are: (1) to breed and rear children of the highest type by the eugenic methods used in breeding domestic animals; (2) to free the Guardians from the temptation to prefer family interests to those of the whole community; (3) to ensure the greatest possible unity in the state.[5] There must be no private property in women and children. It is in this negative sense that wives and children are to be held in common; anything like promiscuity would defeat the eugenic purpose even more than it is now defeated where individuals are allowed free choice of partners. Hence sexual intercourse is to be more strictly controlled and limited by the Rulers than it has ever been in civilized society—a fact which has escaped some hasty readers of inaccurate translations. This throws on the Rulers an invidious task. They will be protected from the imputation of favoritism or personal spite by making it appear that the choice of partners is made by drawing lots, which they will in fact secretly manipulate.

Plato does not seem to have thought out very clearly the details of his marriage regulations. Some obscure points will be dealt with in notes.

So far, then, in regulating the position of women, we may claim to have come safely through with one hazardous proposal, that male and female Guardians shall have all occupations in common. The consistency of the argument is an assurance that the plan is a good one and also feasible. We are like swimmers who have breasted the first wave without being swallowed up.

---

[4] An adapted quotation from Pindar.

[5] Herodotus records that a northern people, the Agathyrsi, held their women in common, in order that they might all be brothers and kinsmen and have no envy or hatred towards one another. In the Laws, Plato maintains that communism, extended to the whole state, would be ideal. But as a practical proposal he abandons it even for the Rulers.

Not such a small wave either.

You will not call it large when you see the next.

Let me have a look at the next one, then.

Here it is: a law which follows from that principle and all that has gone before, namely that, of these Guardians, no one man and one woman are to set up house together privately: wives are to be held in common by all; so too are the children, and no parent is to know his own child, nor any child his parent.

It will be much harder to convince people that that is either a feasible plan or a good one.

As to its being a good plan, I imagine no one would deny the immense advantage of wives and children being held in common, provided it can be done. I should expect dispute to arise chiefly over the question whether it is possible.

There may well be a good deal of dispute over both points.

You mean, I must meet attacks on two fronts. I was hoping to escape one by running away: if you agreed it was a good plan, then I should only have had to inquire whether it was feasible.

No, we have seen through that maneuver. You will have to defend both positions.

Well, I must pay the penalty for my cowardice. But grant me one favor. Let me indulge my fancy, like one who entertains himself with idle day-dreams on a solitary walk. Before he has any notion how his desires can be realized, he will set aside that question, to save himself the trouble of reckoning what may or may not be possible. He will assume that his wish has come true, and amuse himself with settling all the details of what he means to do then. So a lazy mind encourages itself to be lazier than ever; and I am giving way to the same weakness myself. I want to put off till later that question, how the thing can be done. For the moment, with your leave, I shall assume it to be possible, and ask how the Rulers will work out the details in practice; and I shall argue that the plan, once carried into effect, would be the best thing in the world for our commonwealth and for its Guardians. That is what I shall now try to make out with your help, if you will allow me to postpone the other question.

Very good; I have no objection.

Well, if our Rulers are worthy of the name, and their Auxiliaries likewise, these latter will be ready to do what they are told, and the Rulers, in giving their commands, will themselves obey our laws and will be faithful to their spirit in any details we leave to their discretion.

No doubt.

It is for you, then, as their lawgiver, who have already selected the men, to select for association with them women who are so far as possible of the same natural capacity. Now since none of them will have any private home of his own, but they will share the same dwelling and eat at common tables, the two sexes will be together; and meeting without restriction for exercise and all through their upbringing, they will surely be drawn towards union with one another by a necessity of their nature—necessity is not too strong a word, I think?

Not too strong for the constraint of love, which for the mass of mankind is more persuasive and compelling than even the necessity of mathematical proof.

Exactly. But in the next place, Glaucon, anything like unregulated unions would be a profanation in a state whose citizens lead the good life. The Rulers will not allow such a thing.

No, it would not be right.

Clearly, then, we must have marriages, as sacred as we can make them; and this sanctity will attach to those which yield the best results.[6]

Certainly.

How are we to get the best results? You must tell me, Glaucon, because I see you keep sporting dogs and a great many game birds at your house; and there is something about their mating and breeding that you must have noticed.

What is that?

In the first place, though they may all be of good stock, are there not some that turn out to be better than the rest?

There are.

And do you breed from all indiscriminately? Are you not careful to breed from the best so far as you can?

Yes.

And from those in their prime, rather than the very young or the very old?

Yes.

Otherwise, the stock of your birds or dogs would deteriorate very much, wouldn't it?

It would.

And the same is true of horses or of any animal?

It would be very strange if it were not.

Dear me, said I; we shall need consummate skill in our Rulers, if it is also true of the human race.

Well, it is true. But why must they be so skilful?

Because they will have to administer a large dose of that medicine we spoke of earlier. An ordinary doctor is thought good enough for a patient who will submit to be dieted and can do without medicine; but he must be much more of a man if drugs are required.

True, but how does that apply?

It applies to our Rulers: it seems they will have to give their subjects a considerable dose of imposition and deception for their good. We said, if

6 In the *Laws* "Plato's view of marriage is very far from being merely physical. It has its moral and even its religious side" (Barker, *Greek Political Theory*, 329).

you remember, that such expedients would be useful as a sort of medicine.

Yes, a very sound principle.

Well, it looks as if this sound principle will play no small part in this matter of marriage and child-bearing.

How so?

It follows from what we have just said that, if we are to keep our flock at the highest pitch of excellence, there should be as many unions of the best of both sexes, and as few of the inferior, as possible, and that only the offspring of the better unions should be kept.[7] And again, no one but the Rulers must know how all this is being effected; otherwise our herd of Guardians may become rebellious.

Quite true.

We must, then, institute certain festivals at which we shall bring together the brides and the bridegrooms. There will be sacrifices, and our poets will write songs befitting the occasion. The number of marriages we shall leave to the Rulers' discretion. They will aim at keeping the number of the citizens as constant as possible, having regard to losses caused by war, epidemics, and so on; and they must do their best to see that our state does not become either great or small.[8]

Very good.

I think they will have to invent some ingenious system of drawing lots, so that, at each pairing off, the inferior candidate may blame his luck rather than the Rulers.

Yes, certainly.

Moreover, young men who acquit themselves well in war and other duties, should be given, among other rewards and privileges, more liberal opportunities to sleep with a wife,[9] for the further purpose that, with good

---

[7] That is, "kept as Guardians." The inferior children of Guardians were to be "thrust out among the craftsmen and farmers." A breeder of race-horses would keep the best foals, but not kill the rest.

[8] Plato seems to forget that these rules apply only to Guardians. If the much larger third class is to breed without restriction, a substantial rise in their numbers might entail suspension of all childbirth among Guardians, with a dysgenic effect. Plato, however, feared a decline, rather than a rise, in the birth-rate. (The state described in the Laws is always to have 5,040 citizens, each holding one inalienable lot of land.)

The "number of marriages" may include both the number of candidates admitted at each festival and the frequency of the festivals. But it is perhaps likely that the festivals are to be annual, so that women who had borne children since the last festival would be remarriageable. If so, at each festival a fresh group will be called up, consisting of all who have reached the age of 25 for men or 20 for women since the previous festival. Some or all of these will be paired with one another or with members of older groups. The couples will cohabit during the festival, which might last (say) for a month. The marriages will then be dissolved and the partners remain celibate until the next festival at earliest. [T]he resulting batch of children will all be born between 7 and 10 months after the festival.

[9] Not to have several wives at once, but to be admitted at more frequent intervals to the periodic marriage festivals, not necessarily with a different wife each time.

excuse, as many as possible of the children may be begotten of such fathers.

Yes.

As soon as children are born, they will be taken in charge by officers appointed for the purpose, who may be men or women or both, since offices are to be shared by both sexes. The children of the better parents they will carry to the crèche to be reared in the care of nurses living apart in a certain quarter of the city. Those of the inferior parents and any children of the rest that are born defective will be hidden away, in some appropriate manner that must be kept secret.[10]

They must be, if the breed of our Guardians is to be kept pure.

These officers will also superintend the nursing of the children. They will bring the mothers to the crèche when their breasts are full, while taking every precaution that no mother shall know her own child; and if the mothers have not enough milk, they will provide wet-nurses. They will limit the time during which the mothers will suckle their children, and hand over all the hard work and sitting up at night to nurses and attendants.

That will make child-bearing an easy business for the Guardians' wives.

So it should be. To go on with our scheme: we said that children should be born from parents in the prime of life. Do you agree that this lasts about twenty years for a woman, and thirty for a man? A woman should bear children for the commonwealth from her twentieth to her fortieth year; a man should begin to beget them when he has passed "the racer's prime in swiftness,"[11] and continue till he is fifty-five.

Those are certainly the years in which both the bodily and the mental powers of man and woman are at their best.

If a man either above or below this age meddles with the begetting of children for the commonwealth, we shall hold it an offence against divine and human law. He will be begetting for his country a child conceived in darkness and dire incontinence, whose birth, if it escape detection, will not have been sanctioned by the sacrifices and prayers offered at each marriage festival, when priests and priestesses join with the whole community in praying that the children to be born may be even better and more useful citizens than their parents.

You are right.

The same law will apply to any man within the prescribed limits who touches a woman also of marriageable age when the Ruler has not paired them. We shall say that he is foisting on the commonwealth a bastard, unsanctioned by law or by religion.

---

[10] Infanticide of defective children was practiced at Sparta; but the vague expression used does not imply that all children of inferior Guardians are to be destroyed. Those not defective would be relegated to the third class. Promotion of children from that class [would be] provided for.

[11] A poetical quotation, which may, in its original context, have referred to a racehorse, brought to the stud when he had ceased to run.

Perfectly right.

As soon, however, as the men and the women have passed the age prescribed for producing children, we shall leave them free to form a connection with whom they will, except that a man shall not take his daughter or daughter's daughter or mother or mother's mother, nor a woman her son or father or her son's son or father's father; and all this only after we have exhorted them to see that no child, if any be conceived, shall be brought to light, or, if they cannot prevent its birth, to dispose of it on the understanding that no such child can be reared.[12]

That too is reasonable. But how are they to distinguish fathers and daughters and those other relations you mentioned?

They will not, said I. But, reckoning from the day when he becomes a bridegroom, a man will call all children born in the tenth or the seventh month sons and daughters, and they will call him father. Their children again he will call grandchildren, and they will call his group grandfathers and grandmothers; and all who are born within the period during which their mothers and fathers were having children will be called brothers and sisters. This will provide for those restrictions on unions that we mentioned; but the law will allow brothers and sisters to live together, if the lot so falls out and the Delphic oracle also approves.[13]

---

[12] The unofficial unions might be permanent. The only unions barred as incestuous are between parents and children, or grandparents and grandchildren (all such are included, since, if a woman cannot marry her father's father, a man cannot marry his son's daughter). It seems to follow that Plato did not regard the much more probable connections of brothers and sisters as incestuous; and if so, he would see no reason against legal marriage of real brothers and sisters, who would not know they were so related. Such unions were regular in Egypt; and some modern authorities deny that they are dysgenic. Greek law allowed marriage between brother and half-sister by a different mother.

[13] This last speech deals with two distinct questions: (1) avoidance of incestuous unions as above defined; (2) legal marriage of brothers and sisters.

(1) Since the elderly people forming unofficial unions are not to know who are their parents or children, they must avoid all persons who could possibly be so related to them. This is easy, if cohabitation in legal marriage is confined to the duration of a marriage festival and the children of any parent must therefore belong to a batch born in the seventh or tenth month after any festival at which that parent has been married. (Most ancient authorities denied that a child could be born in the eighth month.) If a register was kept, a man could be told all the dates in question without being told who were his real children.

(2) After explaining how incestuous unions can be avoided by a man treating certain whole groups as his parents or children or grandparents or grandchildren, Plato adds that all persons "born within the period during which their mothers and fathers (not *his* father and mother) were having children" will be called "brothers" and "sisters." If unions of real brothers and sisters are not incestuous, this clause has nothing to do with avoidance of incest. It only adds to the definition of nominal parents and children and grandparents and grandchildren, a definition of those who will call one another "brothers" and "sisters," whether they are really so related or

Very good.

This, then, Glaucon, is the manner in which the Guardians of your commonwealth are to hold their wives and children in common. Must we not next find arguments to establish that it is consistent with our other institutions and also by far the best plan?

Yes, surely.

We had better begin by asking what is the greatest good at which the lawgiver should aim in laying down the constitution of a state, and what is the worst evil. We can then consider whether our proposals are in keeping with that good and irreconcilable with the evil.

By all means.

Does not the worst evil for a state arise from anything that tends to rend it asunder and destroy its unity, while nothing does it more good than whatever tends to bind it together and make it one?

That is true.

And are not citizens bound together by sharing in the same pleasures and pains, all feeling glad or grieved on the same occasions of gain or loss; whereas the bond is broken when such feelings are no longer universal, but any event of public or personal concern fills some with joy and others with distress?

Certainly.

And this disunion comes about when the words "mine" and "not mine," "another's" and "not another's" are not applied to the same things throughout the community. The best ordered state will be the one in which the largest number of persons use these terms in the same sense, and which accordingly most nearly resembles a single person. When one of us hurts his finger, the whole extent of those bodily connections which are gathered up in the soul and unified by its ruling element is made aware and it all shares as a whole in the pain of the suffering part; hence we say that the

---

not. Probably, it is meant that these will be all the Guardians born in the same generation (in a vague sense). Since there is no question of incest, these persons will never need to inquire about dates of marriage and birth, if they wish to form a union.

The last sentence refers to both topics of the previous one: (1) avoidance of incestuous unions, (2) legal marriage of real brothers and sisters. It has been held that Plato regarded such marriages as incestuous and that the Oracle was to guard against them. But either the Rulers knew how all Guardians were related or they did not. If (as seems likely) they did know, they could avoid arranging such marriages without invoking an oracle to negative their own proposals. If they did not (though it would be folly to keep no registers if *any* incest was to be avoided), then how could the Oracle know? Granted that Plato did not hold marriage of brothers and sisters to be incestuous, the Rulers could sometimes knowingly arrange such marriages. The Oracle might be asked once for all to approve the whole scheme of marriage laws, or it might be formally invoked at each festival. If it raised no objection, the Rulers would be protected from any charge of violating religious law.

man has a pain in his finger. The same thing is true of the pain or pleasure felt when any other part of the person suffers or is relieved.

Yes; I agree that the best organized community comes nearest to that condition.

And so it will recognize as a part of itself the individual citizen to whom good or evil happens, and will share as a whole in his joy or sorrow.

It must, if the constitution is sound.

It is time now to go back to our own commonwealth and see whether these conclusions apply to it more than to any other type of state. In all alike there are rulers and common people, all of whom will call one another fellow citizens.

Yes.

But in other states the people have another name as well for their rulers, haven't they?

Yes; in most they call them masters; in democracies, simply the government.

And in ours?

The people will look upon their rulers as preservers and protectors.

And how will our rulers regard the people?

As those who maintain them and pay them wages.

And elsewhere?

As slaves.

And what do rulers elsewhere call one another?

Colleagues.

And ours?

Fellow Guardians.

And in other states may not a ruler regard one colleague as a friend in whom he has an interest, and another as a stranger with whom he has nothing in common?

Yes, that often happens.

But that could not be so with your Guardians? None of them could ever treat a fellow Guardian as a stranger.

Certainly not. He must regard everyone whom he meets as brother or sister, father or mother, son or daughter, grandchild or grandparent.

Very good; but here is a further point. Will you not require them, not merely to use these family terms, but to behave as a real family? Must they not show towards all whom they call "father" the customary reverence, care, and obedience due to a parent, if they look for any favor from gods or men, since to act otherwise is contrary to divine and human law? Should not all the citizens constantly reiterate in the hearing of the children from their earliest years such traditional maxims of conduct towards those whom they are taught to call father and their other kindred?

They should. It would be absurd that terms of kinship should be on their lips without any action to correspond.

In our community, then, above all others, when things go well or ill with any individual everyone will use that word "mine" in the same sense and say that all is going well or ill with him and his.

Quite true.

And, as we said, this way of speaking and thinking goes with fellow-feeling; so that our citizens, sharing as they do in a common interest which each will call his own, will have all their feelings of pleasure or pain in common.

Assuredly.

A result that will be due to our institutions, and in particular to our Guardians' holding their wives and children in common.

Very much so.

But you will remember how, when we compared a well-ordered community to the body which shares in the pleasures and pains of any member, we saw in this unity the greatest good that a state can enjoy. So the conclusion is that our commonwealth owes to this sharing of wives and children by its protectors its enjoyment of the greatest of all goods.

Yes, that follows.

Moreover, this agrees with our principle that they were not to have houses or lands or any property of their own, but to receive sustenance from the other citizens, as wages for their guardianship, and to consume it in common. Only so will they keep to their true character; and our present proposals will do still more to make them genuine Guardians. They will not rend the community asunder by each applying that word "mine" to different things and dragging off whatever he can get for himself into a private home, where he will have his separate family, forming a center of exclusive joys and sorrows. Rather they will all, so far as may be, feel together and aim at the same ends, because they are convinced that all their interests are identical.

Quite so.

Again, if a man's person is his only private possession, lawsuits and prosecutions will all but vanish, and they will be free of those quarrels that arise from ownership of property and from having family ties. Nor would they be justified even in bringing actions for assault and outrage; for we shall pronounce it right and honorable for a man to defend himself against an assailant of his own age, and in that way they will be compelled to keep themselves fit.

That would be a sound law.

And it would also have the advantage that, if a man's anger can be satisfied in this way, a fit of passion is less likely to grow into a serious quarrel.

True.

But an older man will be given authority over all younger persons and power to correct them; whereas the younger will, naturally, not dare to strike the elder or do him any violence, except by command of a Ruler. He will not show him any sort of disrespect. Two guardian spirits, fear and reverence, will be enough to restrain him—reverence forbidding him to lay hands on a parent, and fear of all those others who as sons or brothers or fathers would come to the rescue.

Yes, that will be the result.

So our laws will secure that these men will live in complete peace with one another; and if they never quarrel among themselves, there is no fear of the rest of the community being divided either against them or against itself.[14]

No.

There are other evils they will escape, so mean and petty that I hardly like to mention them: the poor man's flattery of the rich, and all the embarrassments and vexations of rearing a family and earning just enough to maintain a household; now borrowing and now refusing to repay, and by any and every means scraping together money to be handed over to wife and servants to spend. These sordid troubles are familiar and not worth describing.

Only too familiar.

Rid of all these cares, they will live a more enviable life than the Olympic victor, who is counted happy on the strength of far fewer blessings than our Guardians will enjoy. Their victory is the nobler, since by their success the whole commonwealth is preserved; and their reward of maintenance at the public cost is more complete, since their prize is to have every need of life supplied for themselves and for their children; their country honors them while they live, and when they die they receive a worthy burial.

Yes, they will be nobly rewarded.

Do you remember, then, how someone who shall be nameless reproached us for not making our Guardians happy: they were to possess nothing, though all the wealth of their fellow citizens was within their grasp? We replied, I believe, that we would consider that objection later, if it came in our way: for the moment we were bent on making our Guardians real guardians, and molding our commonwealth with a view to the greatest happiness, not of one section of it, but of the whole.

Yes, I remember.

Well, it appears now that these protectors of our state will have a life better and more honorable than that of any Olympic victor; and we can hardly rank it on a level with the life of a shoemaker or other artisan or of a farmer.

I should think not.

However, it is right to repeat what I said at the time: if ever a Guardian tries to make himself happy in such a way that he will be a guardian no longer; if, not content with the moderation and security of this way of

---

[14] [Plato notes earlier in *The Republic* that]: "Revolution always starts from the outbreak of internal dissension in the ruling class."

living which we think the best, he becomes possessed with some silly and childish notion of happiness, impelling him to make his power a means to appropriate all the citizens' wealth, then he will learn the wisdom of Hesiod's saying that the half is more than the whole.

My advice would certainly be that he should keep to his own way of living.

You do agree, then, that women are to take their full share with men in education, in the care of children, and in the guardianship of the other citizens; whether they stay at home or go out to war, they will be like watch-dogs which take their part either in guarding the fold or in hunting and share in every task so far as their strength allows. Such conduct will not be unwomanly, but all for the best and in accordance with the natural partnership of the sexes.

Yes, I agree.

2

FAMILY SURROGATES
IN COLONIAL AMERICA:
THE MORAVIAN EXPERIMENT*

Gillian Lindt Gollin

Traditionally, the family has guaranteed the supply of new members to society and has also been entrusted with the initial responsibility for the socialization and social control of the young. The preservation of existing social values and structures is thus powerfully determined by the extent to which the family is successful in performing these functions.

What little evidence we have suggests that the family in Colonial America was no exception to this pattern. But the evidence is scanty, and generalizations purporting to measure the degree of success of the Colonial family, where they exist at all, are often contradictory. Thus Morgan concludes that the primacy of family-centered concerns in Puritan settlements in turn undermined their political structure.[1] Bailyn, on the other hand, cites the development of formal institutions of learning during the Colonial period as evidence of the declining importance of the family.[2] He emphasizes the uniqueness of the type of family structure which emerged in response to early American conditions—a recurrent theme in virtually all of the histories of the family in the Colonial period.[3]

The recent work of such European scholars as Ariès has, however, raised questions as to the validity even of this generalization. Ariès's study of the transformation of the European family system from the Middle Ages to the present suggests that many of the developments, such as the shift from

FROM Gillian Lindt Gollin, "Family Surrogates in Colonial America: The Moravian Experiment," *Journal of Marriage and the Family*, 31, No. 4 (November 1969): 650–658. Reprinted by permission of the National Council on Family Relations and the author.

* The materials on the Moravian family reported in this paper are treated more fully in my larger study of the Brethren, *Moravians in Two Worlds: A Study of Changing Communities* (New York: Columbia University Press, 1967). An earlier draft of this paper was presented at the meetings of the American Sociological Association in Boston, August 1968. The author is indebted to the Board of Elders of the Northern Province of the Church of the United Brethren in America for permission to examine and quote from materials in the Provincial Archives of the Moravian Church, North, in Bethlehem, Pennsylvania. The research assistance of Mark L. Littman and editorial criticism of Albert E. Gollin are gratefully acknowledged.

1 Edmund S. Morgan, *The Puritan Family* (New York: Harper Torchbooks, 1966), pp. 161–186.

2 Bernard Bailyn, *Education in the Forming of American Society* (New York: Vintage Books, 1960), pp. 22–44.

3 *Ibid.*, pp. 21–29.

extended to conjugal family systems, and the increasing geographic mobility of the individual family members, once regarded as "unique" within the American experience of the Colonial period, have their parallels in the seventeenth and eighteenth-century history of the European family.[4] Unfortunately the classical works on the history of the American family, notably the works of Howard, Calhoun, and Goodsell, shed little light on these issues since they are primarily descriptive and devoid of systematic, comparative frameworks.[5] For example, Howard and Calhoun give the impression that there was very little variation in family structure—geographical or social—and what little there was, was deemed insignificant.[6] Studies by Morgan and Ironside in the 1940s, however, began to suggest that some very significant differences existed, not only between North and South but even within the northern colonies.[7]

One variation, which appears to have been largely ignored in the historical literature on the American family, concerns a social group's values and attitudes towards the institution of the family itself. These values may be positive, negative, or ambivalent. Virtually all of the histories of the American family portray the colonies' value systems of the period as essentially supportive of the institution of the family and emphasize its positive role in the colonization of the New World.

The negative case, although numerically far less significant, existed nevertheless in some colonies. There were groups that perceived the family's influence as actually or potentially threatening to the welfare or interests of the larger society and, in consequence, strove to limit the influence of the family. These groups may be further subdivided into those for whom these negative values were self-imposed and those who were subjected to the values of others. The history of a number of sectarian communities may be cited as illustrations of the former; the history of the treatment of the Negro under slavery provides the best known example of the latter.[8]

[4] Philippe Ariès, *Centuries of Childhood: A Social History of Family Life* (New York: Knopf, 1962), pp. 362–407.

[5] Arthur W. Calhoun, *A Social History of the American Family*, Vol. 1 (Cleveland: Arthur Clark, 1917); Willystine Goodsell, *A History of the Family as a Social and Educational Institution* (New York: Macmillan, 1915); George Elliot Howard, *A History of Matrimonial Institutions Chiefly in England and the United States* (Chicago: University of Chicago Press, 1904).

[6] Calhoun notes that, in spite of some regional variation between North and South, it is still possible to "affirm" their "general similarity" during the Colonial period. *Op. cit.*, p. 10.

[7] Morgan, *op. cit.*, pp. 18, 55–59; Charles E. Ironside, *The Family in Colonial New York* (New York: Columbia University Press, 1942).

[8] The broad outlines of the history of the Negro family have been ably drawn by E. Franklin Frazier in his *The Negro Family in the United States* (Chicago: University of Chicago Press, 1944), chaps. 1–4. However, many of the details essential to our understanding of this institution can only be gleaned from a much more extensive search of primary source materials.

Although a large number of sects settled in the American colonies during the seventeenth and eighteenth centuries, few lasted long enough to permit adequate study of their family system.[9] Of those who survived for some time and who attempted to limit the influence of the traditional family to a significant degree, only two—the Ephrata Brethren and the Moravians—fall properly into the Colonial period.[10] The Ephrata Brethren, under the leadership of Conrad Beissel, founded a religious settlement in Pennsylvania in 1732. It survived for a period of approximately 80 years. The members of this cloister-like community, convinced that any family ties were incompatible with allegiance to the collective goals of their society, adopted an essentially monastic way of life. Although the ultimate collapse of this settlement cannot be attributed to a single cause, it is clear that the Brethren's failure to institutionalize appropriate alternatives to the family for the recruitment of succeeding generations was the single most important element in the breakdown of their community.[11]

The history of the communities of the Moravian Brethren, descendants of the fifteenth-century Protestant church of the Unitas Fratrum, provides a further illustration of a social group whose family system differed radically from that of the "typical" families of Colonial New England or Virginia. Their history also documents the difficulties confronting a community that insists upon the exclusive allegiance of its members to the goals of the community. For participation in the family inevitably detracts to some extent from participation in communal affairs by generating particularistic loyalties which compete with the individual's devotion to communal aims.[12] Most utopian or "intentional" communities, political or religious, have therefore tried either to abolish the institution of the family altogether—as did the Ephrata Brethren—or to delimit severely the influence of the family by relegating the responsibility for child-rearing to an institution less likely to threaten the exclusive allegiance of their members —as did the Moravians and more recently the Israeli kibbutzim.[13]

[9] Arthur Eugene Bestor, Backwoods Utopias (Philadelphia: University of Pennsylvania Press, 1959), pp. 235–237.

[10] The Shakers, although they originally came to this country in 1774, did not really develop their own communities and social institutions until the nineteenth century. The various secular communitarian experiments of the Rappites and the Owenites also belong to a later period.

[11] Oswald Seidensticker, Ephrata: Eine Amerikanische Klostergeschichte (Cincinnati: Mecklenburg und Rosenthal, 1883); Felix Reichman, and Eugene Edgar Doll, Ephrata as Seen by Contemporaries (Allentown, Pa.: Pennsylvania-German Folklore Society, 1954); Chronicon Ephratense, by Brothers Lamech and Agrippa, Ephrata: 1786.

[12] For an interesting discussion of alternate ways of dealing with this problem, see Lewis A. Coser, "Political Functions of Eunuchism," American Sociologolical Review, 29 (December 1964): 880–885.

[13] The Israeli kibbutzim provide an interesting contemporary parallel to the position taken by the Moravians in the eighteenth century. See Yonina Talmon-Garber, "Social Change and Family Structure," International Social Science Journal, 14 (1962):

The Moravian solution to this dilemma was to develop a family surrogate in the form of choirs, which explicitly subordinated a Moravian's familial obligations to his religious duties. This choir system was characteristic of all Moravian settlements throughout the world, in some of which it has survived to this day. Our analysis will focus primarily on the experience of one of their communities, that of Bethlehem, founded in Pennsylvania in 1741, the largest Moravian enclave in North America, whose population during the Colonial period rose to over 1,000 persons.[14]

BETHLEHEM: A MORAVIAN
SETTLEMENT IN COLONIAL AMERICA

The key to understanding this community is to be found in its religious institutions. Throughout this period the day-to-day activities of the Moravians were guided primarily by religious norms and sanctions. Missionary opportunities among the population of the New World, particularly the Indians, provided the raison d'être of the settlement. *Praxis pietatis* rather than doctrinal uniqueness became the cornerstone of their religion.[15] The penetration of religious values into the economy of Bethlehem was crucial for the type of economic system which emerged. The Moravians believed that all worldly goods belonged not to man but to God, Christ being regarded as the sole owner of man's possessions, and the community and choirs mere administrators of God's wealth. Although in theory the Moravians upheld the sanctity of private property, Bethlehem came for a time to interpret the concept of a Christian communitarianism literally. It developed an economy based on communal sharing in production as well as consumption: the community took care of all the material needs of a member in return for both his labor and the fruits of his labor. The occupational structure of Bethlehem was dominated by skilled craftsmen; textiles, clothing, and leather goods constituted their most important products.[16]

During the Colonial period the political institutions of the Moravians showed no clear line of demarcation between sacred and secular power. There was little structural differentiation of authority in communal affairs. In order to ascertain God's verdict on a given issue, the Moravians resorted to the use of the lot. Theocratic authority thus dominated communal affairs.[17] It is within this sociocultural context that the development of the choir system needs to be explored.

468–487; "Mate Selection in Collective Settlements," *American Sociological Review*, 29 (1964): 491–497.

[14] Hellmuth Erbe, *Bethlehem, Pa.: Eine kommunistische Herrnbuter Kolonie des 18. Jahrhunderts*, Herrnhut (Winter 1929): 183–184.

[15] Gillian Lindt Gollin, *Moravians in Two Worlds: A Study of Changing Communities* (New York: Columbia University Press, 1967), pp. 9–22.

[16] *Ibid.*, pp. 138–147.

[17] *Ibid.*, pp. 38–63.

THE ORIGINS AND PRINCIPLES
OF THE CHOIR SYSTEM

This choir system, entailing a rigid stratification of the community according to age, sex, and marital status, emerged as a response to Zinzendorf's early attempts to enrich the spiritual life of the community by providing increased opportunities for prayer, song, study, and testimony.[18] The considerable emphasis placed on the segregation of the sexes in Moravian communities must be understood in the light of their leader's views on this matter; he was well aware of the danger that the emotionalism associated with a religious awakening could be directed toward sensual preoccupations rather than religious objects.

In Bethlehem the principle of choir segregation was incorporated into Spangenberg's original plan for the community, and the building plans were from the outset predicated on the assumption that choirs and not individual families were the social units determining the size of a given household. Infants, children, the single, the married, and the widowed came to live in quarters in which the sexes were kept apart. The extremes to which this principle of the segregation of the sexes was carried are graphically illustrated by an ordinance of the 1740s detailing separate walks for the Single Brethren, Single Sisters, and Married People's choir.[19]

The communal living arrangements of the choirs, though originally motivated by religious considerations, offered an ingenious solution to a variety of economic problems confronting frontier settlements. They reduced very considerably the number of separate dwelling units which would otherwise have had to be built and permitted economies of scale in the feeding, clothing, and employment of the population. Since home industries were developed within the choirs rather than the family, the community was spared the expense of constructing workshops for those with no family ties in Bethlehem. Everyone thus ate, slept, prayed, and worked within his or her choir.[20] The economic responsibilities of the choirs had indeed become far more extensive than those vested in the traditional family of the period, with its heavy reliance on apprenticeship and schooling outside the home.

THE DEVELOPMENT OF
SOCIALIZATION FUNCTIONS

Once the choirs had become established as independent socioeconomic units with their own living, sleeping, and eating quarters, it was inevitable that their role in the socialization of their charges should be similarly

---

[18] Protokolle der Synode in Gotha, June 16, 1740, Provincial Archives of the Moravian Church, North, Bethlehem, Pennsylvania.

[19] Diarium seit de Arrivée de See und Pilgergemeine in Bethlehem, am 21. Juni, 1742, Herrnhut Archives; quoted in Erbe, op. cit., p. 28.

[20] Ibid., pp. 41–42.

broadened. The nature and consequences of this broader role varied for the different choirs. According to their leader, Zinzendorf, choir socialization began even before the child was born:

> When the marriage has been consecrated to the Lord and the mother lives in continuous interaction with the Savior, one may expect that already in the mother's womb the children form a choir, that is, a grouping of the community consecrated to the Lord's work.[21]

To this end pregnant women were expected to be particularly painstaking in their religious devotions. In their choir meetings they would discuss with their supervisors many of the issues, both religious and social, associated with the birth of a child.

Such indoctrination as to the place of the child in the community greatly facilitated taking infants away from their mothers at a very early age. In Bethlehem the chief supervisor of the children's nursery noted that

> the mothers plead, almost with tears in their eyes, that they (their children) may be placed in the nursery, as soon as they have been weaned.[22]

Generally children were taken away from their parents and put under institutional care at the age of one or one and a half. The christening ceremony marked the transfer of responsibility from parent to community.[23]

Now Count Zinzendorf was convinced that the supervisors of the choirs could be trained more systematically than their natural parents, to instill in their charges a devotion to the goals of the community.[24] In practice, supervisors were not always too successful in living up to such demanding norms. Toward the end of his life, Zinzendorf—influenced largely by the failure of the children's choirs to produce the diversity of personnel necessary for filling new posts in the community—reversed his stand and insisted that

> parents of the bourgeoisie shall raise their own children, in order that they may savor the toils of life from childhood on and learn to work. Otherwise we get nothing but princes, priests, and officers, and no common soldiers.[25]

---

[21] Juengerhaus Diarium, September 19, 1755, Herrnhut Archives manuscripts; quoted in Otto Uttendoerfer, *Zinzendorf und die Jugend* (Berlin: Furche Verlag, 1923), p. 85.

[22] Letter of Maria Spangenberg to Zinzendorf, April 21, 1746, Library of Congress manuscripts on Herrnhut. Her testimony should be interpreted with some caution. As head of the children's choir, she is likely to have been predisposed to a favorable point of view.

[23] Johannes Plitt, Denkwuerdigkeiten aus der Geschichte der Brueder Unitaet, 1841, Vol. 3, unpaginated manuscript. Bethlehem Archives manuscripts.

[24] Verlass der Nazarether Conferenz, 1758, Bethlehem Archives manuscripts.

[25] Juengerhaus Diarium, November 11, 1750, Herrnhut Archives manuscripts; quoted in Uttendoerfer, *op. cit.*, p. 85.

The Moravians had failed to foresee that the type of education provided by the choirs, though eminently suitable for persons contemplating a career in the professions, was unlikely to motivate children to pursue humbler careers.

At the age of five or six, children were segregated by sex—the little girls and little boys aged six to 12 thus forming their own choirs. It was in these choirs that the children received their formal schooling, which for Colonial times (or our own) was extensive, including instruction in six or seven languages, mathematics, history, geography, art, and music.[26] The older boys and older girls comprised the two choirs of those aged 12 to 17. It was here that both boys and girls were apprenticed to a specific trade and taught the necessary skills. Their training was not restricted to the acquisition of trade or professional skills; the choir supervisors were, for instance, also expected to help them solve "the social problems so pressing among youth of that age."[27]

Finally, at the age of 17 the children would be initiated into the Single choirs. These choirs proved to be important for individuals who might otherwise have retained a marginal status within the traditional kinship structure of the period. The newcomer was granted membership in a ready-made primary group in which a variety of religious and social activities went hand in hand with a heavy work load; little time was left to develop a sense of loneliness.

Upon marriage the Brother or Sister would continue his work in the Married People's choir. Provisions were made to give this choir a house of its own and couples, especially in the early years did not generally live together. Arrangements were made to set aside a time and place for each couple to meet in privacy once a week.[28] In the early years there appears to have been relatively little antagonism toward such living arrangements among the married persons. Because of the disproportionate share of young people in the original immigrant population of Bethlehem, separate choirs for widows and widowers did not come into being for several decades. They served to strengthen the reintegration of older people into the life of the community and generally provided for an effective utilization of their skills.

THE ACQUISITION OF FUNCTIONS
OF SOCIAL CONTROL

When socialization is inadequate, control of behavior of the community becomes necessary to maintain the system. In Bethlehem weekly choir

[26] For a comprehensive history of Moravian education in America, see Mabel Haller, *Early Moravian Education in Pennsylvania, Transactions of the Moravian Historical Society,* 15 (Bethlehem Pa.: Times Publishing Co., 1953).

[27] Juengerhaus Diarium, November 12, 1750, Herrnhut Archives manuscripts; quoted in Uttendoerfer, *op. cit.,* p. 101.

[28] Clarence E. Beckel, "Early Marriage Customs of the Moravian Congregation in Bethlehem, Pa.," *Pennsylvania-German Folklore Society,* 3 (1938): 5.

"speakings" (*Sprechen*) required every individual to discuss and review his past actions with a choir supervisor, who in turn would give advice and admonition where necessary. The eighteenth century Moravian living under the choir system in a closed community could not readily avoid such confessionals: He could not eat, sleep, or work without coming face to face with his supervisor. The authority vested in the status of the choir supervisors was considerable. They could deprive individuals of their right to attend religious or social gatherings of the choir, reduce an individual's weekly pay, or force him to retire to solitary quarters.[29] Sexual misdemeanors constituted a recurrent problem for the Moravians, even in the pioneering years of the community.

Twenty years after the creation of the choirs, they had become largely independent socioeconomic units under whose care the Moravian was nurtured and guided literally from cradle to grave. A Synod of the Moravian Church in 1764 insisted that

> the choir regulations, particularly those concerning the separation of the sexes . . . are *principia stantis et cadentis ecclesiae* upon which the persistence or decline of the community depends.[30]

The choir, in short, rather than the family, had taken on the functions of socialization and control. Since the choirs made it eminently clear that children belonged more to the community than to parents, parental authority was for a number of decades almost nonexistent. This gradual emergence of the choir system as a family surrogate was neither intended nor anticipated by the vast majority of eighteenth-century Moravians. Documents of the period were filled with discussions of a host of pressing social problems, but none of these shows any awareness of the possible implications of choir development for the structure of the traditional family.[31]

As the number of choir members increased, the choirs were faced with a dilemma. On the one hand their expansion attested to the success of the undertaking and confirmed the choir's ability to attract new members. On the other hand this increase was jeopardizing the effectiveness of the socialization function by destroying the intimate character of the primary group. For a while the problem was resolved through the creation of

[29] Verlass des Richter kolleg. Herrnhut Archives manuscripts.

[30] Synodal Verlaz, Marienborn, 1764, Bethlehem Archives manuscripts.

[31] A number of Moravian historians have insisted that the choir as family surrogate was at all times regarded as a temporary expedient to be removed as soon as the social and economic conditions of the community improved. However, contemporary records fail to substantiate this assertion, for it was only after the choir institutions had succeeded in making important inroads into the family structure that a few persons voiced concern about the possible outcome of such developments. Even von Damnitz, the earliest and the most outspoken critic of the choir system, never regarded this aspect of choir expansion as a "temporary expedient." It was only after the choir system had failed that such rationalizations came to be made.

further subdivisions within any one choir.[32] Ultimately, however, even these smaller choir units grew too large to socialize new members adequately.

MARITAL NORMS
AND BEHAVIOR

The emergence of the choir system as a family surrogate had some serious repercussions for the maintenance of monogamy in Bethlehem. The Moravians could not successfully reduce the saliency of an individual's family role as a spouse, parent, or child, without attempting to control the very act—marriage—which symbolized the taking on of new statuses within the family. The Brethren's redefinition of the marital bond and their specification of the conditions governing mate selection provide further evidence of their attempt to subordinate family interests to the religious goals of the community. Matrimony was viewed as a religious matter in which the interests of the community and God overshadowed any personal inclinations or desires that individual candidates might have. Marriage was regarded as instrumental for the attainment of religious goals, because it permitted individuals to "minister unto the religious needs of members of the opposite sex."[33] It thus enlarged the field of service within which the Moravian could legitimately follow his religious calling and social pursuits. Husband and wife participated equally in their work; the woman as the "helpmeet" of her husband shared jointly whatever positions her husband occupied.

It was assumed that every single Brother or Sister of marriageable age was automatically a candidate for marriage. If an individual wished nevertheless to remain single, he or she had first to convince the Elders of the religious merits of such a step. The general procedure was for the supervisors of the Single choirs to nominate prospective candidates for admission to the Married choirs. These nominations were then discussed by the Elders Conference of Bethlehem, and character references of the individuals were examined. When these were deemed satisfactory, suggestions were made as to who should be married to whom.[34]

The authority of the community in matters of marital selection was not unlimited. The Elders, including Zinzendorf himself, were authorized only to make suggestions, not to issue orders. But the matter of acceptance or refusal of such suggestions did not rest solely with the candidates concerned. The recommendations of the community had to be ratified by God himself. The Moravians resorted to the use of the lot as a means of eliciting the will of God whenever an important decision had to be made. Its appli-

---

[32] Maria Spangenberg to Zinzendorf, April 17, 1746; quoted in Erbe, *op. cit.*, pp. 42–43.

[33] *Ibid.*, p. 36.

[34] Protokolle de Synode von 1769, p. 124. Bethlehem Archives manuscripts.

cation to marriage was but one of many uses.[35] Recourse to the lot in questions of mate selection thus absolved the community Elders of ultimate responsibility for their suggestions. And the fact that God himself had indicated approval of a particular union was far more likely to silence the personal doubts of such candidates than would have been the case had the community Elders made such a recommendation on their own.

PROBLEMS IN
CONTROLLING MARRIAGES

Once the community had clearly defined the conditions under which the marital state was to be preferred to that of the single person, the leaders were confronted with an obligation to insure that adequate opportunities for marriage did exist. A reasonably balanced sex ratio and an age distribution favorable to marriage thus became a basic requirement for every self-contained Moravian community. Yet Bethlehem was continually plagued by a serious shortage of nubile women. In 1754, at the height of activity of the General Economy, there was only one single Sister for every seven single Brethren.[36] Although some attempt was made to provide spouses from overseas Moravian settlements, no definite migration policy was ever put into practice.[37]

The Moravian leaders' attempts to induce members of the Single choirs to accept the choice of spouse recommended to them met with varying degrees of success, as the following letter from Spangenberg to Zinzendorf indicates:

> Now when I left you, you entrusted me with the following mission: Once a year we were to go over all our Single Brethren and Sisters and ask ourselves whether any of them should be recommended for marriage. Well, that was an assignment which could not have been made more difficult for me had you ordered me to move mountains. I have great difficulty with Brother Gottlieb, who otherwise is such a good soul. With Annie Rosel, who normally is our pride and joy, it goes no more readily. . . . But dear me, what does one do when the marriage offer miscarries, *ergo* when a Brother or Sister just won't, or at least not willingly?[38]

By the 1750s quite a number of Moravians were rebelling against the restrictions on marriage with outsiders. They had left Europe often with

[35] For an elaboration of the procedures involved in the drawing of lots, see Gollin, *op. cit.*, pp. 54–58.

[36] Erbe, *op. cit.*, p. 183.

[37] See J. W. Jordan, "Moravian Immigration to Pennsylvania," *Pennsylvania Magazine of History and Biography*, 3 (1879): 528–537.

[38] Spangenberg in a letter to Zinzendorf, August 1755, Library of Congress manuscript on Herrnhut.

the assurance that they would be married as soon as they had spent a few years in America. Yet the continued shortage of women in Bethlehem prevented them from doing so within the community, and marriage with "natives of Pennsylvania" continued to be prohibited by Zinzendorf.[39]

Although such segregation from the influence of the outside world was essential to Zinzendorf's ideal of a "closed" community, the young people appear to have been less and less willing to permit the church to control their marriage chances and choices. By 1770 the leaders were forced to admit that the number of non-Moravians brought into the settlements through marriage had increased rapidly in recent years.[40] Their influence gave added impetus to forces working for change. From this point on, communal authority over marital affairs declined rapidly.

MARRIAGE TRENDS

Data on marriage rates in eighteenth-century Bethlehem show that marriages were declining both absolutely and relative to the total population.[41] The social implications of this decline become even more serious when one bears in mind that the tradition of prospective immigrants to Bethlehem marrying immediately prior to their departure for America was widely practiced in the early years of the community but was abandoned after midcentury, when almost all the immigrants were single. This would indicate that after 1750 the actual percentage of the total population which was single rose very considerably, while the proportion of married couples declined consistently. The skewed sex ratio of the community unquestionably contributed to the decline in the marriage rate.

Finally, a word needs to be said about remarriages. Since the marital status was considered to be a precondition for the fulfillment of many occupational assignments, the community frequently insisted upon early remarriage where one had lost his or her spouse.[42] The Moravian, like the Puritan, was under strong pressure to remarry, though the reasons underlying preference of the marital status differed.[43] In Bethlehem we find that during the years 1742–1800 approximately one marriage out of

[39] Zinzendorf in a letter to the Supervisor of the Single Sisters choir, September 1752, Bethlehem Archives manuscripts.

[40] Kenneth G. Hamilton, *John Ettwein and the Moravian Church During the Revolutionary Period* (Bethlehem, Pa.: Times Publishing Company, 1940), p. 83.

[41] Data on marriages and marriage rates were computed from the Marriage Records of the Bethlehem Congregation, Memorabilia concerning population generally recorded at the end of each year in Diarium Bethlehem, as well as in the respective choir diaries, Bethlehem Archives manuscripts. For further details on these rates, see Gollin, *op. cit.*, pp. 121–123.

[42] Hamilton, *op. cit.*, pp. 52–79.

[43] Goodsell, *op. cit.*, pp. 420–421.

every seven constituted a second marriage for one or the other or both partners.[44]

The central clue to low marriage rates in Bethlehem is to be found not in the religious norms of the Moravians, which consistently and unambiguously defined the status of marriage as preferable to that of the single, but in the demographic, economic, and social conditions which often prevented an individual from marrying even though he or she was willing to take the step. The social structure of the choirs impeded the prospects of marriage of the Moravian, on the one hand by guaranteeing the economic support of the Single Brethren and Sisters and, on the other, by insisting upon total economic self-sufficiency of the married. Yet the very involvement of the Single Brother in the choir enterprises not only trained him in occupations which were frequently the sole prerogative of his choir but at the same time effectively prevented him from setting up his own business prior to marriage or competing successfully later on.

MODIFICATION AND DECLINE
OF THE CHOIR SYSTEM

Although the choirs of Bethlehem continued, throughout the 1750s and early 1760s, to increase their membership and improve their economic position to a very considerable degree, there were at the same time undertones of discontent.[45] By the sixties this discontent had reached such proportions that the world leaders of the Moravian church, in an attempt to forestall an independent alienation of Moravian congregations in America, took the necessary steps to abrogate the "general economy," the communal economic system under which Bethlehem had flourished for almost 20 years.[46] As a result the choirs were ordered to abandon their communal enterprises, and every choir member from then on received a wage for his work and in return paid the choir for his bed, board, and clothing.[47] The Elders overseas failed however to realize that the choir institutions could not possibly compete with wage scales in the rest of Pennsylvania. Thus what was originally construed as a wage came to represent a mere pittance, and choir members were often forced to look for work outside the community.

[44] Marriage Records of the Bethlehem Congregation, 1742–1792, unpublished typescript, ed. by Clarence E. Beckel, Bethlehem Archives manuscripts.

[45] See especially Peter Boehler's extensive correspondence with Herrnhut, 1751–1754, Bethlehem Archives manuscripts.

[46] Proceedings of the General Synod in London, 1760, Bethlehem Archives manuscripts.

[47] Die Projekte und Vorschlaege zur kuenftigen, Veraenderung der Bethlemischen Oekonomien spezie aber des Ledigen Bruder Haus bettreffend, December 16, 1761, Bethlehem Archives manuscripts.

The decline of the choir system in Bethlehem cannot however be attributed solely to the rigid exclusivism enforced upon them by the German Elders of the Church. Even without interference from abroad, it is doubtful whether the choirs in Bethlehem could have continued for very much longer. The religious enthusiasm of the forties, which had in a very real sense wrought economic miracles in the wilderness of Pennsylvania, had also helped to produce certain unanticipated changes. The very economic success of the choirs had fostered changes in the Moravians' orientation to the world in which they lived.

More specifically, the necessity for pooling all economic and social resources became less obvious as the community's rapid rise to prosperity attracted not only the attention of outsiders but that of the Moravians themselves. As the ethics of the bourgeoisie came to take the place of the early militant spirit of the Brethren, not only did individuals become more interested in making their own profits, but the choirs themselves came to think largely in terms of economic gains rather than spiritual development.[48]

With the growth of prosperity, the economic advantages accruing to choir living arrangements and mass education of the young became less meaningful to the individuals concerned; for many could now afford financially to take care of their own children and to provide them with a home of their own. At the same time one wonders whether the willingness of parents to raise their own children was enhanced only, or even primarily, by the rise in the standard of living. For if one remembers that one of the supposed advantages of this system was that it left the parents free to engage more fully in missionary activities, the resurgence of the family would seem another indicator of a waning religious enthusiasm. It suggests, moreover, that the choirs never succeeded fully in imparting to their charges an acceptance of the choir system as a family surrogate. In the 1760s a start was made on the construction of individual family housing, children's choir institutions were gradually abrogated, and the nursery closed.[49]

With the growing interest in family life, came a corresponding decline in the extent of involvement in the day-to-day activities of the remaining choir institutions. The choirs for the Single Brethren and Sisters, the Widows and Widowers, had by the 1770s degenerated into respectable boarding houses for lodgers who paid rent and whose religious activities had become in many cases the habitual reflexes of past religious enthusiasms.[50] Though the leaders of the Moravians in Europe were able to prevent non-Moravians from settling in Bethlehem for some decades to come, they

---

[48] Hamilton, op. cit., pp. 57–58.

[49] Koeber, Resolutionen und Verfuegungen an das Bethlehemer Oekonomat, April 3, 1761. Bethlehem Archives manuscripts.

[50] The official choir documents, as might be expected, failed to record the disenchantment of the choir members. Evidence of such attitudes was found primarily in letters. The choir diaries became increasingly rigid in style, lacking the spontaneity and disarming frankness so characteristic of the earlier years.

could do little to stem the decline of what was left of the choir system. In 1841 the last of the Bethlehem choirs was disbanded, but the social, economic, and religious influences of the choirs on the community had long since eroded. The family system of the nineteenth-century Moravians re-affirmed the positive values of the conjugal family for society. From this point the Moravian family in Bethlehem becomes indistinguishable from that of the mainstream of town-dwelling families in nineteenth-century America.

CONCLUSION

In detailing the history of the Moravian family system during the eight-eenth century, we have focused on a system which departs radically from the model of the family described as typical of the period in America. The rise and decline of the Moravian family surrogate in a frontier community highlight the strengths and weaknesses, not only of its own system, but also of the traditional Colonial family as portrayed by Calhoun, Morgan, and others. The Moravian choir system, by maximizing the allegiance of its members to the goals of the community, unquestionably facilitated and accelerated the economic and social development of the settlement. More-over, the much greater size of the choir as compared to the typical con-jugal family unit permitted significant economies of scale in meeting the basic human needs for shelter, food, and clothing. At the same time it is clear that such exclusive loyalty to the communal goals was relatively short-lived. Socialization of succeeding generations was far from adequate to insure the maintenance of the society. The community of the Ephrata Brethren died for sheer lack of new members; the Moravians in Bethlehem suffered a slower rate of decline—they produced offspring but failed in the end to convert their children to the socioreligious goals of the founders of the settlement.

This study of the Moravian experience in Bethlehem suggests that under frontier-type conditions the conjugal family is not the only, or even the most effective, structure. Comparisons and evaluations of various types of families and family surrogates need, however, to be approached with caution, since each system must be evaluated with reference to its own immediate social, economic, and political environment.

A second conclusion is methodological in nature: analyses of changing family systems must employ a sufficiently large time span to permit ade-quate detection of trends. Ariès's work, in this respect, is made far easier by the fact that he is delineating trends over several centuries, whereas both Bailyn and Morgan confine their analysis to only one. The tendency of social historians to accept the periodizations made by their more politically oriented colleagues may seriously distort their own analyses of social change. Our own study of the Moravian family system, though oriented primarily to the Colonial period, was not limited to an arbitrary set of dates.

Finally, although this report focused only on the Moravian experience in America, a parallel study of Herrnhut, their major settlement in Germany, enables us to shed some light on the question of the "uniqueness" of the American experience. Our data on Herrnhut do not corroborate the assumption made by most American historians that the American family continued to develop in the seventeenth and eighteenth centuries whereas the European system remained largely unchanged. The Moravian family surrogate in the German community, which was founded only ten years before the American one, did change and become modified in important respects during this same period. In some cases the modifications paralleled the American ones; in others they did not. But throughout the eighteenth century the changes in the family structure of Herrnhut were less radical than those of Bethlehem, both as to the abrogation of the traditional family system and the subsequent decline of the choir as family surrogate. The greater economic and social freedom of pioneer life in the American colonies, cited by Bailyn as a crucial factor in the development of the American family structure, certainly played a part here, even though this lack of restraint was at times more imaginary than real. The Moravians' attempt to develop industries in Bethlehem, for instance, was hampered and ultimately thwarted by British regulations far more severe than those encountered by the Moravians in Herrnhut.[51] Yet the fact that the Moravian community of Bethlehem differed in some important respects from its sister settlement in Germany should not predispose one to conclude that the American experience was "unique." For in that case the German community and every other Moravian settlement that developed variations of its own deserve the same adjective. A more fruitful approach would seem to lie in the study of both similarities and differences in their respective developments, and the analysis of reasons underlying them.

In a recent survey of historical studies of the Colonial family, Rothman asserts:

> If broad generalizations of questionable validity characterize the state of our knowledge it is because the details of the story have not been sorted. [52]

It is hoped that this study of the Moravian family system in Pennsylvania has helped to clarify one small segment of that story.

---

[51] Gollin, *op. cit.*, pp. 177–178.

[52] David J. Rothman, "A Note on the Study of the Colonial Family," *William and Mary Quarterly*, 23 (1966): 633.

3

EXPERIMENTAL FAMILY ORGANIZATION: AN HISTORICO-CULTURAL REPORT ON THE ONEIDA COMMUNITY*

William M. Kephart

Not long ago the writer had the interesting experience of talking with a woman whose father had been born in the George Washington-Thomas Jefferson period. The woman is a daughter of John Humphrey Noyes, founder of the Oneida Community. Although a number of non-monogamous forms of family organization have appeared on the American scene —e.g., polygyny (the Mormons), celibacy (the Shakers, the Father Divine Movement)—the most radical form remains the group marriage experiment of the Oneida Community.

Subsequent to some correspondence, the President of Oneida, Ltd., invited the writer to spend some time at the site of the Old Community. During the visit, there was opportunity to interview a number of people, including officers of the company, local historians, and persons whose parents had been members of the Oneida group. In addition, the Mansion House Library was opened, which made it possible to examine the unique collection of newspapers, journals, and books formerly published by John Humphrey Noyes and his followers.

Finally, it was the writer's privilege to interview several of the *surviving members* of the Oneida Community. As of the time of the interviews, thirteen members were still living, and while they are all in their 80s and 90s, their minds are sharp, their memories remarkably clear. And when it is remembered that their former leader, Noyes, was living during the time when John Adams, Paul Revere, Thomas Jefferson, and other Revolutionary figures were alive, one cannot help but feel the vital continuum of American history. At any rate, the writer was not only graciously received but was able to compile some significant material, the bulk of which has not heretofore appeared in the literature.

FROM William M. Kephart, "Experimental Family Organization: An Historico-Cultural Report on the Oneida Community," *Journal of Marriage and the Family*, 25, no. 3 (August 1963): 261–271. Reprinted by permission of the National Council on Family Relations and the author.

* Expanded version of paper read at the August 1962, meeting of the National Council on Family Relations, Storrs, Connecticut. The study was facilitated by a grant from the University of Pennsylvania Committee on the Advancement of Research. Although not included herein, an extensive list of bibliographical materials is available. Interested persons may write the author.

By way of background, it should be mentioned that the Community was founded in 1848 on the old Indian lands along the Oneida Creek in central New York State. John Humphrey Noyes, founder and long-time leader of the group, was a graduate of Yale Theological Seminary, although his theological views and Perfectionist philosophy had proved too heretical for the people of Putney, Vermont, where he had been preaching. Noyes' theology revolved around spiritual equality which, as he interpreted it, included both the economic and sexual spheres. In the Kingdom of God, all persons were to love and to share equally—a so-called Bible communism. Noyes gained some adherents, and in Putney the little group of Perfectionists actually started to practice what they preached. Predictably, however, there was little future for the group in an area that had been close to the heart of Puritanism, and Noyes and his followers were eventually run out of town.

Reassembling at Oneida, New York, they constructed a large Community Mansion House, and by expanding their efforts were able to increase the size of the group to several hundred members. And for many decades the Oneida Community sustained one of the most unusual social experiments the world has ever seen. Economic communism, group marriage, scientific breeding, sexual equality—it couldn't happen here, but it did! Indeed, the Community flourished until around 1880, after which a business enterprise (Oneida, Ltd.) was set up and the stock apportioned among the members. It is hoped that the following remarks will shed some light on this very remarkable historico-cultural episode, one which—for some reason—has been neglected by both historians and sociologists.

SOCIAL ORGANIZATION
AND FAMILY FUNCTIONS

What was there, in the elements of social organization, which successfully held the Community together in the face of both internal problems and external pressures? To begin with, much of the communality of action derived from the fact that the entire membership was housed under one roof. The original communal home was built in 1849, but because of the increase in members it was replaced in 1862 by a spacious brick building known as the Mansion House. In subsequent years, wings were added as needed. The building still stands, in its entirety; in fact, during my visit to Oneida, I stayed at the Mansion House and can attest to the fact that it is a striking architectural form, internally as well as externally. Noyes helped both in the planning and in the actual construction, and while sociologists might question the extent to which physical structure influences social organization, the Mansion House would seem to be a case in point.

Although each adult had a small room of his own, the building was designed to encourage a feeling of togetherness, hence the inclusion of a communal dining hall, recreation rooms, library, concert hall, outdoor picnic area, etc. It was in the Big Hall of the Mansion House that John Humphrey Noyes gave most of his widely-quoted home talks. It was here that musical concerts, dramas, readings, dances, and other forms of socializing were held. Community members were interested in the arts, and were able to organize such activities as symphony concerts, glee club recitals, and Shakespearian plays, even though practically all the talent was home grown. Occasionally, outside artists were invited, but on a day-to-day basis the Community was more or less a closed group, with members seldom straying very far from home base. What might be called their reference behavior related entirely to the group. The outside community was, figuratively and literally, "outside," and was always referred to as the The World. It was this system of *integral closure,* sustained over several decades, which served as a primary solidifying force.

Standard reference works make much of economic and sexual communism as being the definitive features of the Oneida Community. As adduced from both interview and documentary materials, however, it would seem that the *communality of action* and the utilization of integral closure were, from a sociological view, paramount. And, of course, it was the Mansion House itself which served as the structural base for practically all Community activity. Insofar as the Perfectionists were concerned, the totality of their existence lay within the walls of the Mansion House. The building was designed to encompass and facilitate this totality pattern, and from all accounts it served its purpose well.

Most of those interviewed were unable to separate the Old Community from the Mansion House. In their minds the two had become one, a fusion of the social and the structural, which, again, underscores the pervasiveness of the physical setting. Even today the building serves as a kind of community center. Most of the surviving members live there, and a good many of the direct descendants live within a block or two; in fact, as the descendants themselves age, they are likely to move into the Mansion House to spend their remaining years. In the words of one of the informants:

> We all love the old place. Many of our folks lived there, and most of us played there as kids. We know the building down to the last brick and board. It's odd, so many of the people who moved away seem to come back when they get older and live in the Mansion House. It's because they had such good times and such happy memories.

It should not be thought that life in the old Community was a continual round of entertainment. The Oneidans built their own home, raised their own food, made all their own clothes (including shoes!), did their own laundry, ran their own school, and performed countless other collective tasks. The performance of these necessary communal chores apparently served as a basic part of the congelation process. To be more specific, one of the interviewees stated that:

> As children we loved to visit the various departments they used to have: the laundry, the kitchen, the fruit cellar, the bakery, the dairy, the dining room, the ice house, the tailor shop—they even had a Turkish Bath in the basement. The thing is that small groups of people worked side by side in most of these places, and they were able to talk with each other as they worked. Many of the jobs—in the kitchen and bakery, for example—were rotated. It's hard to explain, but my mother used to tell me that no matter how menial the job was, they were so busy talking to each other that the time always flew. It was this sort of thing, year after year, that gave rise to a kindred spirit.

Again, from a "family" perspective, it was this *functional partitioning*—the execution of economic tasks through primary group involvement—which helped to explain the success of the Oneida Community. Virtually all of their activities were designed to accentuate the *we* rather than the *I*, and the economic sphere was no exception. Special abilities were recognized; indeed, wherever possible, occupational assignments were made on the basis of individual aptitudes. But at one time or another most of the work had to be rotated or shared, and so it was with Community life in general. The roles of the members were made crystal clear, and whether the activity in question was social, economic, sexual, or spiritual, the Oneida Perfectionists invariably turned against the *culte du moi* in favor of what to them was a selfless collectivism.

Human nature being what it is, of course, there were inevitable lapses on the part of certain members. Role conflicts sometimes did occur, and it was to counteract any tendency toward selfishness or ego-involvement that the much-publicized system of Mutual Criticism was inaugurated. Although details varied over the years, the general system involved a member who evidenced signs of personal aggrandizement being brought before a committee of peers who, frankly and objectively, attempted to pinpoint his social malfeasance. None of the persons talked with had undergone Mutual Criticism inasmuch as they were too young at the time. (Children were not included in this part of the Oneida program.) From all reports, however, the system of Mutual Criticism was well received. None of those interviewed could recall hearing of any adverse comments; in fact, it appears that as the membership increased, the system came to be applied not only to deviants but to any one who was seriously desirous of self-improvement. The following three comments[1] appeared during 1871–1872 in the *Oneida Circular,* the Community's weekly newspaper:

---

[1] Harriet M. Worden, *Old Mansion House Memories* (Kenwood, Oneida, N.Y.: privately printed, 1950), pp. 15–16.

> I feel as though I had been washed; felt clean through the advice and criticism given. I would call the truth the soap; the critics the scrubbers; Christ's spirit the water.
>
> Criticism is administered in faithfulness and love without respect to persons. I look upon the criticisms I have received since I came here as the greatest blessings that have been conferred upon me.
>
> However painful, we have seen it yielding the peaceable fruits of righteousness to them who have been exercised thereby—I am confident, moreover, that instead of producing enmity and grudging, the criticisms that have been performed have increased the love and confidence of the members toward each other.

Although children were not subjected to Mutual Criticism, the meaning of group primacy was impressed upon them in a variety of ways. For instance, an episode was reported as occurring around 1850 involving all the girl children. Prior to this time there had been several large dolls which, like all material things in the Community, were shared. Some kind soul thought it would be helpful if each of the girls had a doll of her own, and this policy was put into effect. However, it developed that the youngsters began to spend too much time with their dolls, and not enough on household chores, Bible reading, and Community matters in general. Accordingly, on a specified occasion, all the girls joined hands in a circle around the stove, and one by one were persuaded to throw their dolls into the fire. For the rest of the Community's existence, dolls were never allowed in the nursery.

Adults, too, were subject to self-imposed deprivations whenever they felt the group welfare threatened, and by present-day standards "group welfare" was given a most liberal interpretation. Several of the informants, for example, mentioned dietary and other restrictions that were adopted over the years. Although the Perfectionists ate well, meat was served sparingly, pork not at all. Lard was not used for shortening. Alcoholic beverages were prohibited, as were tea and coffee. Smoking also came to be taboo. The reasoning behind these prohibitions is not always clear, but presumably the Oneidans were dead set against *informal distractions* of an "anti-family" nature. Thus, dancing and card playing were permitted, since they were regarded as social activities, while coffee-drinking and smoking were condemned on the ground that they were individualistic and appetitive in nature. One of the interviewees made the following points:

> I imagine the prohibitions were pretty well thought out. They didn't just spring up, but developed gradually. I know there were some differences of opinion, but the main thing was that certain practices were felt to be bad for group living. They believed that coffee-drinking was habit-forming, and that people looked forward to it too much—and this would

somehow weaken Community ties. Remember, they were trying to create a spiritual and social brotherhood, and they spent much more time in the art of developing relationships than we do. They had to. After all, hundreds of them were living together as a family, and they worked at it day after day. They were successful, too, for they held together for almost two generations without a major quarrel.

The followers of John Humphrey Noyes were hard-working, well-behaved citizens, among whom crime and delinquency were virtually unknown. Because of this, they were generally respected by the surrounding community and by most every one else who came into actual contact with them. Nevertheless, the Oneidans were different. They knew it and The World knew it: in fact, this *secular differentiation* reinforced what I have called their system of integral closure and thereby served as another binding factor in the interest of group solidarity. By way of illustration, the Oneida women wore a very distinctive attire: in a period of floor-length skirts the Perfectionist ladies wore short ones (knee length) with loose trousers or "pantalettes" down to the shoes. I was shown some of the original dresses, and my impression was that they would create quite a stir even today. How must they have been viewed by outsiders 100 years ago! Moreover, all the Oneida women bobbed their hair, a custom which the Community instituted in 1848—and which was not introduced into The World until 1922 (by dancer Irene Castle). At any rate, it is easy to see why secular differentiation of this kind strengthened group identity. The following comment is illustrative:

> Your asking of sociological questions about what held the Community together reminds me of something my aunt used to tell. The Old Oneidans kept pretty much to themselves, but during the summer months they would sometimes permit visitors. Some Sunday afternoons whole trainloads of visitors would come. They were served picnic-style on the lawn of the Mansion House. I think they were charged $1.00 for the whole thing. Of course, the visitors couldn't get over the way the Oneida women dressed, and they kept staring. My aunt always felt that the way outsiders always looked at them and talked about them had a great deal to do with their feelings of closeness.

Another measure which apparently helped to integrate Community membership was their widely-publicized system of economic communism. Personal ownership of wealth and private property of any kind were taboo, down to and including children's toys. Several of the informants mentioned the fact that in the early days of the Community the Oneidans had rough going; in fact, around 1850 their agricultural economy was in such poor shape that it was necessary for them to sell their watches in order to make ends meet. Fortunately, one of their members developed a steel trap, the manufacture of which involved a secret process of spring tempering. Demand for the traps proved great, and before long it was commonplace for the entire Community to turn out in order to meet the deadline for a large order.

From 1855 on, the Oneidans were without financial worry; in fact, when they broke up around 1880, the treasury showed a balance of some $600,000, no small sum for the period in question. (It was this money which was used to form a joint stock company, which organization today is known as Oneida, Ltd., Silversmiths.) But whether the Community was struggling for survival, as it was during the early period, or whether it was able to reap a financial harvest, as it was during later years, available evidence suggests that collectivistic endeavors, coupled as they were with the other measures described herein, tended to strengthen intracommunity bonds.

A final force which served to unite the Perfectionists was their religion and their spiritual devoutness; indeed, it would not be far from the mark to say that the Oneida Community was basically a religious organization. Their social, economic, and sexual beliefs all stemmed from the conviction that they were following God's word as expounded by John Humphrey Noyes. Following the so-called preterist position, Noyes preached that Christ had already returned to earth and that redemption or liberation from sin was an accomplished fact. It followed, therefore, that the spiritual world was autonomous, free, and quite independent of the temporal order. From this perspective, it is easy to see why Noyes was often antagonistic to temporal or "external" law. The essence of his religious teachings, incidentally, can be found in *The Berean,* a lengthy volume which has been called the Bible of the Oneida Community. Contents of *The Berean* range from the semimystical to the philosophically profound, but in many areas the teachings are heretical, especially when seen in the light of midnineteenth-century religionism.

Because of heresy, Noyes' license to preach had been revoked earlier in Vermont, but following revocation the scope and dogmatic intensity of his preachings increased. Nevertheless, his Oneida followers continued to believe passionately in his religious pronouncements, and any attempt to understand the conjoint nature of the group must take this factor into account. One informant, who had been born into the Community, put it in these words:

> Their religion was different and they were well aware of it. They were also a very devout group. The combination of difference and devoutness made them feel close to one another. Today, you go to church on Sunday, but it doesn't make you feel any closer to the rest of the congregation. Things were different in the Community. Religion brought them together. It wasn't just on Sunday, either—it was part of their everyday living. As a result, the atmosphere was much

more spiritual than anything you'd find today, outside of the religious orders.

What was the net result of all of the above measures? From what was said, it appears that the Oneidans were able to maintain a remarkably cohesive form of family and social organization. Conformity was maintained through a patterned series of social controls which, contrary to the usual system of imposure, actually emanated from *within* the membership. As a result, normative interaction was stable enough, over the years, to debar the cliquishness and factionalism which seem to characterize so many of the smaller religious bodies. Those interviewed were nearly unanimous in their belief that the old Oneida Community was an effectively organized, well integrated, and happy group. The following three comments speak for themselves:

> I was a child in the old Community, and I can tell you that they were a happy group. They used to meet nightly in the Big Hall to socialize, discuss problems, etc. The outside world had their get-togethers on Saturday night. We had ours every night, and it was something to look forward to. Of course, I was only a child at the time—they disbanded before I was 10—and children like to glorify their childhood. Still, when anybody asks me about the old days, my dominant memory is one of contentment and happiness.
>
> I was too young to remember much. But as I grew older and asked my relatives about the Community days, their faces would light up. My own folks were "come outers"; that is, they thought the thing had gone on long enough and weren't too sorry when the group broke up. But even they loved to talk about the "old days" and how much they missed them. They were wonderful people and they had wonderful times.
>
> I was not born in the old Community, although many of my relatives were. But from the way they all talked about life in the Mansion House, they were living life to the fullest. They were able to combine the spiritual, the economic, and the social, and make it really work. At the very end there was some bitterness—about who should take over the leadership— but that's another part of the story.

Sexual Practices

Although their family and social organization were unique, it was the Community's bizarre sexual system which attracted national and international attention. Just as Mormonism is invariably linked with polygyny, so the Oneida Community seems destined to be associated with group marriage. John Humphrey Noyes believed neither in romantic love nor in monogamous marriage, such manifestations being considered selfish and smacking of possessiveness. He taught that all men should love all women and that all women should love all men, and while no attempt was made to impose this reciprocality on The World, group marriage (or "Complex Marriage," as it was called) continued throughout the whole of the Community's existence.

Sex relations within the group were reportedly easy to arrange inasmuch as the men and women all lived in the Mansion House. If a man desired sexual intercourse with a particular woman, he was supposed to make his wish known to a Central Committee, who would convey his desire to the woman in question. If the latter consented, the man would go to her room at bedtime and spend an hour or so with her before returning to his own room. No woman was forced to submit to a sexual relationship which was distasteful to her, and the committee system presumably afforded her a tactful method for turning down unwelcome suitors. It was understood by all concerned that their sexual latitude did not carry with it the rights of parenthood. Only the select were permitted to have children, a point which will be discussed later.

The above facts relating to the sex practices of the Oneidans are those generally contained in texts and encyclopedic references. Many of the really significant sexual questions, however, have never been raised, let alone answered. To what extent did the women refuse sexual requests? Did men and women tend to form more-or-less permanent pairs or was there, in fact, a system of group marriage? Did women initiate sexual requests or, as in The World, was it the men who invariably took the initiative? Was the committee system really used by the Oneida males, or was this merely a formality which was easily by-passed? Did not the women of the Community have difficulty in adjusting, sexually, to a large number of different partners? Was not the factor of male jealousy a problem? And so on. In brief, group marriage is such a rare phenomenon on this earth that ethnographers have sometimes questioned its very existence. Apparently this system of matrimony has too many inherent disadvantages to prevail as a dominant societal form. Contravening a wealth of historical and cross-cultural evidence, therefore, how were the Oneidans able to adjust to group marriage so successfully over a relatively long period? Or were there problems that simply never came to light? One of those interviewed made the following remarks:

> I grant the questions are of interest to family scholars, but look at it from our view. If somebody came to you and asked questions concerning the sex life of your parents and grandparents, you'd have a tough time answering. The same with us. When the old Community broke up, there was a natural reluctance to discuss sex. Former members didn't discuss their own sex lives, and naturally their children and grandchildren didn't pry. I often wish the old people had had a regular system of marriage. Then we wouldn't have had such bad publicity—most of it incorrect or misleading. If it weren't for

the sex part, the Oneida Community might have been forgotten long ago.

One of the company officers supplied the following interesting, if sad, information. During the decades of the Community's existence, many of the Oneidans were in the habit of keeping diaries. (Diary-keeping was evidently much more common in the nineteenth century than it is today.) Some of the Perfectionists also accumulated bundles of personal letters. After the Community broke up, and as the members died over the years, the question arose as to what to do with all these documents. Since so much of the material was of a personal and sexual nature, since names were named, and inasmuch as the children and the grandchildren of these "names" were still living, it was decided to store all the old diaries, letters, and other personal documents in the vaults of Oneida, Ltd. A few years ago a company officer—who happened to be one of the informants—received permission to examine the material in order to see what should be done with it:

> I went through some of the stuff—old diaries and things—and a lot of it was awfully personal. Names and specific happenings were mentioned—that kind of thing. Anyway, I reported these facts to the company, and it was decided that in view of the nature of the material, it should all be destroyed. So one morning we got a truck—and believe me, there was so much stuff we needed a truck—loaded all the material on and took it out to the dump and burned it. We felt that divulging the contents wouldn't have done ourselves or anybody else any good.

Thus went a veritable gold mine of pertinent information! There can be no doubt that the burned material would have shed much light on the sexual patterns of the Oneida Perfectionists. As it is, to reconstruct the operative functionings of group marriage would be a most formidable task; indeed, substantive answers to many of the sex questions may never be found. From the company's viewpoint, of course, the destruction of the above-mentioned documents was understandable. Oneida, Ltd. is not in business to further the cause of socio-historical research, and irrespective of how much the material may have benefited sociologists, there was always the possibility that the contents might have proved embarrassing to the company or to some of the direct descendants.

This diary-burning episode has been mentioned in some detail not only to bring the historico-cultural picture up to date but to point out why it is that for all the uniqueness of their system, next to nothing is known of the actual sex practices of the Perfectionists. The present study may shed a little light on the subject, but it should be kept in mind that like most other Americans of the period, the old Oneidans did not openly discuss sexual matters, so that the children and grandchildren interviewed were probably less informed on this subject than on any of the others that were discussed.

One of the questions asked was whether the factor of male jealousy did not make itself felt. The answer appears to be in the negative. As one of the interviewees put it:

> I don't think it was much of a problem. Certainly the old folks, when they talked about the Community, never made any issue of it. Their religious teachings emphasized spiritual equality, and their whole way of life was aimed at stamping out feelings of envy and jealousy. Also, with so many women to choose from, why should a man experience feelings of jealousy? Once in a while a man and woman would be suspected of falling in love—"special love" they called it—but it happened infrequently. When it did, the couple were separated. One would be sent to Wallingford, Connecticut— we had a small Community branch there for a while.

Although respondents were agreed that the men readily adjusted to a plurality of women partners, they were generally silent on the question of how the Oneida females adjusted to a variety of male partners. It is unfortunate that so little information was available on this point, for this issue—in my opinion, at least—is a crucial one. In effect, the Oneida women were encouraged to have sex relations with a variety of men, but were not supposed to become emotionally involved with any of the men with whom they were having these relations! The American woman of today tends to emotionalize and romanticize her sexual experience, and it would be hard for her to have any empathetic understanding of the Oneida system, wherein neither romance nor monogamous love were supposed to play any part in the sex act. As for the Oneida women, themselves, one can but conjecture. If they were indeed gratified by sexual variety, all human experience would be in for a contradiction. And yet—given the prevailing social system and their religious orientation—who is to say just what feminine feelings really were. In the absence of the diary material, it is problematical whether this question will ever be fully answered.

One thin clue was the belief by four of the interviewees that at least in terms of overt behavior the female refusal rate was not high. The company officer who had examined a small portion of the material-to-be-burned reported that there was nothing therein to indicate that female refusal was a problem. Another male respondent stated that he had been informed by an old Community member that the latter "had never been refused." Two female interviewees had been told by an older woman member that the refusal rate was probably low. Most of the informants, however, had no specific information to offer, and evidence on this point seems likely to remain fragmentary.

The question whether the Oneida women ever took the initiative in requesting sexual relations drew a generally negative response. Several interviewees reported that they knew of some coquetry on the part of certain women, but that they had never heard of anything more direct. Two of the older female respondents stated that there was one known case where a woman went to a man and asked to have a child by him. In this instance, however, the implication is not clear, inasmuch as the Perfectionists differentiated sharply between sex for procreation and sex for recreation. All reports considered, it seems doubtful whether Oneida females were any more disposed to assume the role of active partner than were females in society at large.

That the Perfectionists institutionalized sexual freedom is a matter of record; in fact, the term "free love" appears to have been coined by the Oneidans around 1850. At the same time, certain sexual rules—some written, some unwritten—were developed, and consensus was strong enough to effect optimal conformity. Oneidans were enjoined to act like ladies and gentlemen at all times. Coarse behavior, vulgar or suggestive language, overt displays of sexuality—such behaviorisms were not tolerated. As a matter of fact, the evidence available suggests that sexual activity was not openly discussed within the Community, and it is doubtful whether the subject of "Who was having relations with whom?" ever became common knowledge. It was said, for instance, that one male member who became too inquisitive on this score was literally thrown out of the Community, an act which represented the only expulsion in the group's history.

The extent to which the committee system was utilized is not clear. Officially, male members were supposed to get permission from the Central Committee, or at least from the Chairman of the Committee (usually an older woman), before having sexual relations with a given female, but several of the persons interviewed had reservations on this point. The most pointed response was the following:

> Well, I've thought about the committee business, and I've talked with some of the old folks about it. I'm inclined to think it was kind of a formality that declined with the passage of time. Perhaps in the beginning it was adhered to. Also, it may have been that the first time a man and a woman had relations a go-between was consulted, but I doubt whether further relations called for any formal permission. Of course, in order to have children, committee approval was needed, but from the strictly sexual view I think it was considered pretty much private business.

The Eugenics Program. A vital component of the Oneida sexual system was the eugenics program, usually referred to as Stirpiculture. Noyes had been impressed with the writings of Darwin and Galton, and from the very beginning had decided that the Community should follow the principles of scientific propagation. Accordingly, he requested the Perfectionists to refrain from having children until such time as adequate financial resources were built up, and published accounts make much of the fact that during the 20 years it took to achieve economic self-sufficiency the Oneidans were successful in their efforts at fertility control. The type birth control used was *coitus reservatus,* sexual intercourse up to but not including ejaculation. Male orgasm was permissible only with women who had passed menopause; in fact, it was with this group of females that the younger men were supposed to learn the necessary ejaculatory control. After the twenty-year period, 53 women and 38 men were chosen to be parents, or stirps, and the eugenics program was officially inaugurated. During the ensuing ten years, 58 children were born into the Community, after which period the Perfectionists disbanded.

So much for the published accounts. From the information which could be pieced together, these accounts are somewhat inaccurate. To begin with, some children *were* born into the Community prior to 1869, the year the eugenics program was started. The technique of *coitus reservatus,* therefore, was not 100 per cent effective, though in view of its rather bizarre nature it seems to have worked reasonably well.[2]

It should also be pointed out that several children were born after the eugenics program had started who were *not* the offspring of stirps. Understandably, a number of the women who had failed to be chosen as prospective parents were still desirous of having babies, and a few reportedly did their utmost to achieve motherhood. Mentioned, for instance, was a passage in one of the burned diaries in which a man, referring to his sexual activities with a particular woman, make the remark, "She tried to make me lose control." In spite of some marked exceptions, however, those who were not chosen as stirps seem to have accepted their lot without question.

The actual criteria and methods for selecting the stirps have never been revealed. It is known that committees were set up to make the selection, but what standards they used is something of a mystery. Noyes served on the committees, and it would seem that it was he who largely decided which of the Perfectionists were qualified for parenthood. It was said that Noyes, himself, fathered a dozen children, so that evidently he was not adverse to self-selection.

[2] It should be mentioned that in the minds of the Perfectionists the system was by no means bizarre. *Coitus Reservatus* was looked upon not only as an effective method of birth control but as a means of *emotionally elevating* sexual pleasure. Interestingly enough, in Aldous Huxley's best-selling *Island* (New York: Harper & Row 1962), *coitus reservatus* is the method used by the Utopian society of Pala: "Did you ever hear of the Oneida Communty?" Ranga now asked. "Basically, *maithuna* is the same as what the Oneida people called *coitus reservatus.* . . . But birth control is only the beginning of the story. Maithuna is something else. Something even more important. "Remember," he went on earnestly, "the point that Freud was always harping on . . . the point about the sexuality of children. What we're born with, what we experience all through infancy and childhood, is a sexuality that isn't concentrated on the genitals; it's a sexuality diffused throughout the whole organism. That's the paradise we inherit. But the paradise gets lost as the child grows up. Maithuna is the organized attempt to regain that paradise" (pp. 86–87).

Whatever the criteria used, and whatever the relative contributions of heredity and environment, the Stirpiculture program was apparently a success. As a group, the children born of selected parents led a healthy and vigorous life. Their death rate was reportedly lower than that of the surrounding community;[3] in fact, as mentioned earlier, thirteen of the Stirpiculture children are still living, a figure substantially greater than actuarial expectancy. Interviews revealed that a number of the children had achieved eminence in the business and professional world, several had written books, and nearly all had in turn borne children who were a credit to the community.

It might be well at this point to clear up a misconception relative to the child-rearing program of the Community. It is true that the children were not raised by their parents. Infants were under the care of their mothers up to the age of 15 months, but thereafter were moved to the children's section of the Mansion House. And while the youngsters were treated with kindness by their parents, the Community made a conscious effort to play down feelings of sentimentality between parents and offspring, the feeling being that Perfectionists should treat all children as their own, and vice versa.

It is not true, however, that the child rearing system was one of impersonality. Children were shown ample affection and kindness, and they apparently enjoyed the zest of group living; at least, all those interviewed felt certain that childhood in the Old Community was a happy and exhilarating experience. As one of the "children" put it:

> Well, I remember one little girl always wanted her mother. She'd stand outside her window and call to her, even though the mother wasn't supposed to answer. Other than that particular case, all the children seemed happy enough. Everybody was good to us. You know you were loved because it was like a big family. Also, there were so many activities for the youngsters, so many things to do, well—believe me—we were happy children. Everybody around here will give you the same answer on that!

Perhaps the most puzzling aspect of the Oneida eugenics system is why there were so *few* children born. The Stirpiculture program ran for a little over 10 years, and all-told nearly 100 men and women were involved. In view of the relatively high birth rate which prevailed in the U.S. during the 1870s, the fact that these chosen Oneidans produced but 58 children is most difficult to understand. The method of *coitus reservatus,* practiced by the Oneida males for so many years, may have had an unaccountable effect on fertility, though this would seem a far-fetched explanation. It is possible that the answer lies in the method of stirp selection. It was said that at

[3] H. H. and G. W. Noyes, "The Oneida Community Experiment in Stirpiculture," *Eugenics, Genetics and the Family,* 1 (1932): 374–386.

least two different committees were involved, and there may have been some internal disagreement. It is also possible that there was some sexual incompatibility between certain of the male and female stirps, though this is pure conjecture. In any event, the low birth rate among the Perfectionists is surprising in view of the apparent success of the program.

JOHN HUMPHREY NOYES:
CHARISMATIC LEADERSHIP

From his writings and information provided by people who knew him, John Humphrey Noyes was undoubtedly a very remarkable man and a charismatic leader of the first order. In fact, he was much more than an extraordinary leader. He was the indispensable man. His followers were a hard-working, devout group, among whom there were any number of intelligent and able men and women. But in the last analysis they were— followers. Throughout the many decades of Perfectionist existence, no effective leadership ever emerged other than that of Father Noyes. The ultimate outcome, of course, was predictable: when Noyes resigned, the Community fell apart, torn by internal dissension. It was as though the group had been formed in his image, and as the image faded, the group faded right along with it.

The charismatic qualities of John Humphrey Noyes were in evidence from the very beginning of his career. During the 1830s at Putney, Vermont, he was able to attract followers on the basis of his visionary talents and the strength of his personality—no mean feat when his didactic radicalism is viewed against the backdrop of traditional New England morality. In the 1840s Noyes renounced orthodox medical treatment and declared that for Perfectionists the only true physician was Christ. It was during this period that he allegedly cured a woman who was both crippled and blind.

Whatever the importance of his so-called divine powers, Noyes continued to attract followers through the originality of his thought and his sense of religious dedication, traits which become evident when one examines his social and theological pronouncements. In this connection, he was nothing short of a voluminous writer. In addition to turning out scores of articles and monographs dealing with theology, he was a guiding hand for such publications as *The Witness, The Free Church Circular, The Spiritual Magazine, The American Socialist, The Perfectionist,* and *The Oneida Circular.* One would think that his writings were sufficiently diverse and thought-provoking to have kept historians, theologians, and sociologists busy for many a day, but for some reason his works have come in for little scholarly examination, either of an exegetic or sociological nature.

Although Noyes could count both women and men among his disciples, there is no denying the fact that Oneida womenfolk were strongly attracted to him. It may be that as head of the "family" he presented a strong father image; or it may have been a natural attraction that the platform figure has for so many females; but whatever the reason, the women of the Community paid him undying homage. Those so chosen felt honored to have children by him. Others, it was said, learned shorthand in order that none of his utterances would be lost to posterity. And on his part, Noyes saw to it that the women were accorded not only spiritual but functional equality, as the following remark indicates:

> One thing that most people have overlooked is that Father Noyes delegated a lot more responsibility to the women here than they ever would have received on the outside. Every committee had women on it. It made a difference, too. All the old folks will tell you it made both men and women respect each other.

Like so many charismatic leaders, Noyes had a well of energy which ran far deeper than that of other men. He helped design and build the Mansion House, he performed physical labor in the trap shop, he headed committees, he wrote continually, he traveled widely, and he served as both legislative and judicial head of the Oneidans. It should perhaps be mentioned that his countless organizational duties had no appreciable effect on his sexual prowess. While few details of his sex life have ever been revealed despite the fact that he was the engineer of Complex Marriage, it is common knowledge among the present Oneidans that Noyes fathered a dozen children while he was in his sixties.

In 1877 he resigned, and in 1879 John Humphrey Noyes left for Canada, never to return. The reasons for his leaving have never been made entirely clear. It is true that his health was not good. His voice had failed and he had become increasingly deaf. Also, following his resignation, social organization within the Community had become carious. It seems more probable, however, that the immediate cause of his departure was the fear that he would be charged by the District Attorney's office with committing statutory sex offenses. Actually, the District Attorney never made any legal charges, but had he done so he might have obtained a conviction.

Under the system of Complex Marriage, there was apparently no restriction based on the age factor. It seems likely that some of the Oneida men had been having sex relations with girls who were under the statutory age as defined by New York law. It is also a reasonable certainty that Noyes was one of the men; at least, so several of the informants claimed. Presumably wishing to avoid prosecution and scandal, therefore, he fled to Canada.

Care should be taken, however, not to misinterpret this aspect of his career. Oneida women of all ages revered Father Noyes, and he in turn accorded them full partnership in the Community. When it came to the presumed initiation of younger girls into the sexual rites, Noyes and other senior male members were simply carrying out a stated principle of the Community—in this instance, the principle of *Ascending Fellowship*. Quoting from the Oneida *Handbook,* published by the Community in 1875:

> Oneidans entirely reject the idea that love is an inevitable and uncontrollable fatality, which must have its own course. They believe the whole matter of love and its expression should be subject to enlightened self-control, and should be managed for the greatest good. In the Community it is under the special supervision of the fathers and mothers, who are guided in their management by certain general principles, which have been worked out and are well understood in the Community. One is termed the principle of the Ascending Fellowship. It is regarded as better, in the early stages of passional experience, for the young of both sexes to associate in love with persons older than themselves, and if possible with those who are spiritual and have been some time in the school of self-control, and who are thus able to make love safe and edifying. This is only another form of the popular principle of contrasts. It is well understood by physiologists that it is undesirable for persons of similar characters and temperaments to mate together. Communists have discovered that it is undesirable for two inexperienced and unspiritual persons to rush into fellowship with each other that; it is far better for both to associate with persons of mature character and sound sense.[4]

It cannot be emphasized too strongly that Noyes was an extremely pious man, and in the sexual sphere he was probably convinced that he was fulfilling God's word. And if His word conflicted with man-made law, the latter would have to be disregarded. In this, Noyes was guilty of an error in judgment. A few of those interviewed feel that the error was serious enough to be considered a defect of character. Unfortunately, not enough of the details are known to permit a final verdict.

My own feeling is that Noyes' sexual proclivities played an important part in the total makeup of the man. He had tremendous vigor, a vigor which manifested itself in the spiritual, the mental—and the physical. It can be no coincidence that his Utopian Community included relative freedom of sex expression. Yet to believe that Noyes' life was dominated by sex, in the narrow sense, would be to misunderstand both his nature and the nature of the Oneida Community. John Humphrey Noyes was dominated in life by nothing other than his religious zeal. This factor, taken in conjunction with his wide range of talents and his unflagging energy, leads one to the conclusion that he was, to a remarkable degree, a "most compleat man." In parallel fashion, the Community he founded aimed at being a

---

[4] *Handbook of the Oneida Community* (Oneida, N.Y.: Office of *Oneida Circular,* 1875), p. 39.

spiritual and social organization complete in itself—a so-called society within a society.

Perhaps the most illuminating statement about John Humphrey Noyes was the following, made by a woman whose mother had known the Perfectionist leader quite well:

> I've often wondered about the traits that made him what he was. I just don't know. You might have got an answer 100 years ago. Now, maybe it's too late. I remember asking my mother the same question when I was a young girl. "Why did you live that way? What was there about him?" and I remember her saying, "Don't ask me to explain it. I can't. All I know is that when you were in his presence you knew you were with some one who was not an ordinary man."

Father Noyes died in 1886, though to the very end he retained an active interest in his former flock and in the silverware business, which was then in a period of transition. I was informed that through 1885 he continued to select the bulk of Oneida, Ltd.'s Board of Directors. Thus from the beginning to the end—through all the strife, happiness, and disillusion which formed the sequence of his life—he remained a man seemingly destined to have an irresistible effect upon the lives of other men.

Concluding Remarks

The family field is immeasurably stronger than it was at the close of World War II. The number of substantive areas has increased. Sampling and statistical research have reached new levels of sophistication. Cross-cultural comparisons of family behavior continue unabated. It is somewhat strange, therefore, that the area of historico-cultural research has been by-passed. We do not have graduate students actively working in this area, and neither our textbooks nor our journals give the matter much more than passing reference. I contend that this lack of interest in the socio-historical realm is deleterious to all concerned. Graduate students who have genuine aptitude in this sphere are likely to turn elsewhere for their doctoral work. And in terms of the presumptive and associative inferences which can be drawn from such research, failure to investigate must invariably give rise to blind spots within the domain of family behavior.

As an example of historico-cultural investigation I have attempted to analyze an experimental form of family organization. Other forms are available for parallel study: celibate groups such as the Father Divine Movement and the Shakers; polygynist groups such as the Mormon Fundamentalists (who continue their practice of plural marriage in spite of severe legal obstacles). Still other groups with unique forms of family or social organization would include the Amana Society, the Black Jews, the

Hutterites, the House of David, the Llano Colonies, and the Old Order Amish.

To the best of my knowledge, the present account of the Oneida Community is the first ever to appear in any family journal. Most of the other groups mentioned above have yet to make such an appearance. It would seem, certainly, that they are overdue. Students of the family have made effective use of cross-cultural data, both for teaching purposes and for typologies in theory building. I submit that modern historico-cultural research—as focused, for example, on unique forms of family organization such as those mentioned above—would be similarly effective.

II
THE
FAMILY
IN THE
KIBBUTZ

Spiro's essay is an excellent introduction to the subject of the family on the kibbutz. By raising the question of whether the family exists in this setting, it becomes necessary for him to describe in detail the key aspects of domestic life. We are especially fortunate in having an addendum to the essay in which Spiro reflects on his earlier views and presents a novel way of defining the marriage relationships based on his reanalysis of the kibbutz material.

Family life on the kibbutz is of great importance to the understanding of communal alternatives to the nuclear family, and hence we have devoted an entire section to it. The kibbutz movement is one of the few wide-scale and reasonably unified communal movements that have existed for any length of time. It shows us how an essentially urban, middle-class people, as were the Jews who founded the first kibbutzim, were able to adopt a style of life that, while in line with their philosophy, was nonetheless totally alien to their previous training and experience in terms of work as well as family. The problems they have faced and have found partial and complete solutions for are those that all communal movements must deal with in one form or another.

Communal child rearing is a topic that has been studied in depth only so far as the kibbutz is concerned, and even here much work remains to be done. In their article, the Rabkins not only describe how children are brought up in this setting but also report the findings of studies which have compared kibbutz children with children in noncommunal environments.

On the kibbutz, we see that the nuclear family—whose existence Spiro questioned for this reason among others—

is relieved of virtually all aspects of child care. Parents and their children spend only a few hours of leisure time together each day. This means that *both* parents can work full time. Moreover, the relationships with the children lack many, if not all, of the authoritarian elements that typify such relationships in most societies. Parents are "friends and companions" rather than taskmasters.

Among the many interesting points in this article is the discussion of the personality studies that seem to indicate that kibbutz children do not suffer as a result of having many mothers instead of one. While these results are not conclusive, they suggest that some fears concerning communal child rearing may not be grounded in fact. The children seem to adjust well to kibbutz life, which implies that one of the problems the Moravians among others ran aground on has been resolved by the kibbutzim.

Talmon's is an important paper because it is a rare scholarly attempt to appraise the situation of the elderly in a communal society. Here again we see the kibbutz movement as a source of data; few communal movements last long enough to have to come to grips with the problem of the aged, and of those that have endured little or nothing is known of how they handled it.

In a certain sense, one is surprised that the elderly have as much difficulty in adjusting to retirement as Talmon reports. Most of the financial fears that plague the aged in our society are absent in the kibbutz. Leaving the work sphere does not mean any reduction in the benefits the kibbutz provides for all its members. Yet, the fact that the retirees are nonproductive members of a society that values productivity (direct involvement in agriculture) above all else makes it understandable that giving up one's status as a worker would have a deleterious effect on one's self-concept and sense of self-worth. We should keep in mind, however, that the kibbutz as a type of communal society is unusual in its emphasis on directly productive labor; perhaps other communal societies, which do not place such great stock in this realm, offer their aged members a somewhat less difficult period of adjustment. All of this notwithstanding, the circumstances of the old on the kibbutz are still vastly superior to those faced by their counterparts, particularly the childless and poor, in noncommunal societies.

4

IS THE FAMILY UNIVERSAL?—
THE ISRAELI CASE
Melford E. Spiro

The universality of the family has always been accepted as a sound hypothesis in anthropology; recently, Murdock has been able to confirm this hypothesis on the basis of his important cross-cultural study of kinship. Morever, Murdock reports that the "nuclear" family is also universal, and that typically it has four functions: sexual, economic, reproductive, and educational. What is more important is his finding that no society "has succeeded in finding an adequate substitute for the nuclear family, to which it might transfer these functions."[1] In the light of this evidence, there would be little reason to question his prediction that "it is highly doubtful whether any society ever will succeed in such an attempt, utopian proposals for the abolition of the family to the contrary notwithstanding."[2]

The functions served by the nuclear family are, of course, universal prerequisites for the survival of any society, and it is on this basis that Murdock accounts for its universality.

Without provision for the first and third (sexual and reproductive), society would become extinct; for the second (economic), life itself would cease; for the fourth (educational), culture would come to an end. The immense social utility of the nuclear family and the basic reason for its universality thus begins to emerge in strong relief.[3]

Although sexual, economic, reproductive, and educational activities are the functional prerequisites of any society, it comes as somewhat of a surprise nevertheless, that all four functions are served by the same social group. One would normally assume, on purely a priori grounds, that within the tremendous variability to be found among human cultures, there would be some cultures in which these four functions were distributed among more than one group. Logically, at least, it is entirely possible for these functions to be divided among various social groups within a society; and it is, indeed, difficult to believe that somewhere man's inventive ingenuity should not have actualized this logical possibility. As a matter of fact this

REPRINTED with permission of the author and the American Anthropological Association from Melford E. Spiro, "Is the Family Universal?—The Israeli Case," *American Anthropologist*, 56, no. 5 (October 1954): 839-846, and with permission of the Macmillan Company from "Addendum, 1958," in Norman Bell and Ezra Vogel, eds., *A Modern Introduction to the Family*. Copyright © 1968 by the Free Press, a Division of the Macmillan Company.

[1] G. P. Murdock, *Social Structure* (New York: Macmillan, 1949), p. 11.
[2] *Ibid.*
[3] *Ibid.*, p. 10.

possibility has been actualized in certain utopian communities—and it has succeeded within the narrow confines of these communities. The latter, however, have always constituted subgroups within a larger society, and the basic question remains as to whether such attempts could succeed when applied to the larger society.

Rather than speculate about the answer to this question, however, this paper presents a case study of a community which, like the utopian communities, constitutes a subgroup within a larger society and which, like some utopian communities, has also evolved a social structure which does not include the family. It is hoped that an examination of this community —the Israeli kibbutz—can shed some light on this question.

A kibbutz (plural, kibbutzim) is an agricultural collective in Israel whose main features include communal living, collective ownership of all property (and hence, the absence of "free enterprise" and the "profit motive"), and the communal rearing of children. Kibbutz culture is informed by its explicit, guiding principle, "from each according to his ability, to each according to his needs." The family, as that term is defined in *Social Structure,* does not exist in the kibbutz, in either its nuclear, polygamous, or extended forms. It should be emphasized, however, that the kibbutzim are organized into three separate national federations, and though the basic structure of kibbutz society is similar in all three, there are important differences among them. Hence, the term *kibbutz,* as used in this paper, refers exclusively to those kibbutzim that are members of the federation studied by the author.[4]

As Murdock defines it, the family is a social group characterized by common residence, economic cooperation, and reproduction. It includes adults of both sexes, at least two of whom maintain a socially approved sexual relationship, and one or more children, own or adopted, of the sexually cohabiting adults.[5] The social group in the kibbutz that includes adults of both sexes and their children, although characterized by reproduction, is not characterized by common residence or by economic cooperation. Before examining this entire social group, however, we shall first analyze the relationship between the two adults in the group who maintain a "socially approved sexual relationship," in order to determine whether their relationship constitutes a "marriage."

Murdock's findings reveal that marriage entails an interaction of persons of opposite sex such that a relatively permanent sexual relationship is maintained and an economic division of labor is practiced. Where either of these behavior patterns is absent, there is no marriage. As Murdock puts it:

> Sexual unions without economic cooperation are common, and there are relationships between men and women involv-

---

[4] The field work, on which statements concerning the kibbutz are based, was conducted in the year 1951–52.

[5] Murdock, *op. cit.,* p. 1.

ing a division of labor without sexual gratification . . . but marriage exists only when the economic and the sexual are united in one relationship, and the combination occurs only in marriage.[6]

In examining the relationship of the couple in the kibbutz who share a common marriage, and whose sexual union is socially sanctioned, it is discovered that only one of these two criteria—the sexual—applies. Their relationship does not entail economic cooperation. If this be so—and the facts will be examined in a moment—there is no marriage in the kibbutz, if by marriage is meant a relationship between adults of opposite sex, characterized by sexual and economic activities. Hence, the generalization that, "marriage, thus defined, exists in every known society,"[7] has found an exception.

A kibbutz couple lives in a single room, which serves as a combined bedroom-living room. Their meals are eaten in a communal dining room, and their children are reared in a communal children's dormitory. Both the man and the woman work in the kibbutz, and either one may work in one of its agricultural branches or in one of the "service" branches. The latter include clerical work, education, work in the kitchen, laundry, etc. In actual fact, however, men preponderate in the agricultural branches, and women, in the service branches of the economy. There are no men, for example, in that part of the educational system which extends from infancy to the junior-high level. Nor do women work in those agricultural branches that require the use of heavy machinery, such as trucks, tractors, or combines. It should be noted, however, that some women play major roles in agricultural branches, such as the vegetable garden and the fruit orchards; and some men are indispensable in service branches such as the high school. Nevertheless, it is accurate to state that a division of labor based on sex is characteristic of the kibbutz society as a whole. This division of labor, however, does not characterize the relationship that exists between couples. Each mate works in some branch of the kibbutz economy, and each, as a member (*chaver*) of the kibbutz, receives his equal share of the goods and services that the kibbutz distributes. Neither, however, engages in economic activities that are exclusively directed to the satisfaction of the needs of his mate. Women cook, sew, launder, etc., for the entire kibbutz, and not for their mates exclusively. Men produce goods, but the economic returns from their labor go to the kibbutz, not to their mates and themselves, although they, like all members of the kibbutz, share in these economic returns. Hence, though there is economic cooperation between the sexes within the community as a whole, this cooperation does not take place between mates because the social structure of this society precludes the necessity for such cooperation.

[6] *Ibid.*, p. 8.
[7] *Ibid.*

What then is the nature of the relationship of the kibbutz couple? What are the motives for their union? What functions, other than sex, does it serve? What distinguishes such a union from an ordinary love affair?

In attempting to answer these questions, it should first be noted that premarital sexual relations are not taboo. It is expected, however, that youth of high-school age refrain from sexual activity; sexual intercourse between high-school students is strongly discouraged. After graduation from high school, however, and their election to membership in the kibbutz, there are no sanctions against sexual relations among these young people. While still single, kibbutz members live in small private rooms, and their sexual activities may take place in the room of either the male or the female, or in any other convenient location. Lovers do not ask the kibbutz for permission to move into a (larger) common room, nor, if they did, would this permission be granted if it were assumed that their relationship was merely that of lovers. When a couple asks for permission to share a room, they do so—and the kibbutz assumes that they do so—not because they are lovers, but because they are in love. The request for a room, then, is the sign that they wish to become a "couple" (zug), the term the kibbutz has substituted for the traditional "marriage." This union does not require the sanction of a marriage ceremony, or of any other event. When a couple requests a room, and the kibbutz grants the request, their union is ipso facto sanctioned by society. It should be noted, however, that all kibbutz couples eventually "get married" in accordance with the marriage laws of the state—usually jut before, or soon after, their first child is born—because children born out of wedlock have no legal rights according to state law.

But becoming a couple affects neither the status nor the responsibilities of either the male or the female in the kibbutz. Both continue to work in whichever branch of the economy they had worked in before their union. The legal and social status of both the male and the female remain the same. The female retains her maiden name. She not only is viewed as a member of the kibbutz in her own right, but her official registration card in the kibbutz files remains separate from that of her "friend" (chaver)— the term used to designate spouses.[8]

But if sexual satisfaction may be obtained outside of this union, and if the union does not entail economic cooperation, what motivates people to become couples? It seems that the motivation is the desire to satisfy certain needs for intimacy, using that term in both its physical and psychological meanings. In the first place, from the sexual point of view, the average chaver is not content to engage in a constant series of casual affairs.

[8] Other terms, "young man" (bachur) and "young woman" (bachura), are also used in place of "husband" and "wife." If more than one person in the kibbutz has the same proper name, and there is some question as to who is being referred to when the name is mentioned in conversation, the person is identified by adding, "the bachur of so-and-so," or "the bachura of so-and-so."

After a certain period of sexual experimentation, he desires to establish a relatively permanent relationship with one person. But in addition to the physical intimacy of sex, the union also provides a psychological intimacy that may be expressed by notions such as comradeship, security, dependency, succorance, etc. And it is this psychological intimacy, primarily, that distinguishes couples from lovers. The criterion of the couple relationship, then, that which distinguishes it from a relationship between adults of the same sex who enjoy psychological intimacy, or from that of adults of opposite sex who enjoy physical intimacy, is love. A couple comes into being when these two kinds of intimacy are united in one relationship.

Since the kibbutz couple does not constitute a marriage because it does not satisfy the economic criterion of marriage, it follows that the couple and their children do not constitute a family, economic cooperation being part of the definition of the family. Furthermore, as has already been indicated, this group of adults and children does not satisfy the criterion of common residence. For though the children visit their parents in the latter's room every day, their residence is in one of the children's houses (*bet yeladim*), where they sleep, eat, and spend most of their time.

More important, however, in determining whether or not the family exists in the kibbutz is the fact that the physical care and the social rearing of the children are not the responsibilities of their own parents. But these responsibilities, according to Murdock's findings, are the most important functions that the adults in the family have with respect to the children.

Before entering into a discussion of the kibbutz system of collective education (*chinuch meshutaf*), it should be emphasized that the kibbutz is a child-centered society, par excellence. The importance of children, characteristic of traditional Jewish culture, has been retained as one of the primary values in this avowedly antitraditional society. "The parents' crown" is the title given to the chapter on children in an ethnography of the Eastern European Jewish village. The authors of this ethnography write:

> Aside from the scriptural and social reasons, children are welcomed for the joy they bring beyond the gratification due to the parents—the pleasure of having a child in the house. A baby is a toy, the treasure, and the pride of the house.[9]

This description, except for the scriptural reference, applies without qualification to the kibbutz.

But the kibbutz has still another reason for cherishing its children. The kibbutz views itself as an attempt to revolutionize the structure of human society and its basic social relations. Its faith in its ability to achieve this end can be vindicated only if it can raise a generation that will choose to live in

[9] M. Zborowski and E. Herzog, *Life Is with People* (New York: International Universities Press, 1952), p. 308.

the communal society, and will, thus, carry on the work that was initiated by the founders of this society—their parents.

For both these reasons the child is king. Children are lavished with attention and with care to the point where many adults admit that the children are "spoiled." Adult housing may be poor, but the children live in good houses; adult food may be meager and monotonous, but the children enjoy a variety of excellent food; there may be a shortage of clothes for adults, but the children's clothing is both good and plentiful.

Despite this emphasis on children, however, it is not their own parents who provide directly for their physical care. Indeed, the latter have no responsibility in this regard. The kibbutz as a whole assumes this responsibility for all its children. The latter sleep and eat in special children's houses, they obtain their clothes from a communal store; when ill, they are taken care of by their "nurses." This does not mean that parents are not concerned about the physical welfare of their own children. On the contrary, this is one of their primary concerns. But it does mean that the active responsibility for their care has been delegated to a community institution. Nor does it mean that parents do not work for the physical care of their children, for this is one of their strongest drives. But the fruits of their labor are not given directly to their children; they are given instead to the community which, in turn, provides for all the children. A bachelor or a couple without children contribute as much to the children's physical care as a couple with children of their own.

The family's responsibility for the socialization of children, Murdock reports, is "no less important than the physical care of the children."

> The burden of education and socialization everywhere falls primarily upon the nuclear family. . . . Perhaps more than any other single factor collective responsibility for education and socialization welds the various relationships of the family firmly together.[10]

But the education and socialization of kibbutz children are the function of their nurses and teachers, and not of their parents. The infant is placed in the infants' house upon the mother's return from the hospital, where it remains in the care of nurses. Both parents see the infant there; the mother when she feeds it, the father upon return from work. The infant is not taken to its parents' room until its sixth month, after which it stays with them for an hour. As the child grows older, the amount of time he spends with his parents increases, and he may go to their room whenever he chooses during the day, though he must return to his children's house before lights-out. Since the children are in school most of the day, however, and since both parents work during the day, the children—even during

10 Murdock, *op. cit.*, p. 10.

their school vacations—are with their parents for (approximately) a two-hour period in the evening—from the time the parents return from work until they go to eat their evening meal. The children may also be with their parents all day Saturday—the day of rest—if they desire.

As the child grows older, he advances through a succession of children's houses with children of his own age, where he is supervised by a nurse. The nurse institutes most of the disciplines, teaches the child his basic social skills, and is responsible for the "socialization of the instincts." The child also learns from his parents, to be sure, and they too are agents in the socialization process. But the bulk of his socialization is both entrusted, and deliberately delegated, to the nurses and teachers. There is little doubt but that a kibbutz child, bereft of the contributions of his parents to his socialization, would know his culture; deprived of the contributions of his nurses and teachers, however, he would remain an unsocialized individual.

As they enter the juvenile period, preadolescence, and adolescence, the children are gradually inducted into the economic life of the kibbutz. They work from an hour (grade-school students) to three hours (high-school seniors) a day in one of the economic branches under the supervision of adults. Thus, their economic skills, like most of their early social skills, are taught them by adults other than their parents. This generalization applies to the learning of values, as well. In the early ages, the kibbutz values are inculcated by nurses, and later by teachers. When the children enter junior high, this function, which the kibbutz views as paramount in importance, is delegated to the "homeroom teacher," known as the "educator" (*mechanech*), and to a "leader" (*madrich*) of the interkibbutz youth movement. The parents, of course, are also influential in the teaching of values, but the formal division of labor in the kibbutz has delegated this responsibility to other authorities.

Although the parents do not play an outstanding role in the socialization of their children, or in providing for their physical needs, it would be erroneous to conclude that they are unimportant figures in their children's lives. Parents are of crucial importance in the *psychological* development of the child. They serve as the objects of his most important identifications, and they provide him with a certain security and love that he obtains from no one else. If anything, the attachment of the young children to their parents is greater than it is in our own society. But this is irrelevant to the main consideration of this paper. Its purpose is to call attention to the fact that those functions of parents that constitute the *conditio sine qua non* for the existence of the "family"—the physical care and socialization of children —are not the functions of the kibbutz parents. It can only be concluded that in the absence of the economic and educational functions of the typical family, as well as of its characteristic of common residence, that the family does not exist in the kibbutz.

It is apparent from this brief description of the kibbutz that most of the functions characteristic of the typical nuclear family have become the functions of the entire kibbutz society. This is so much the case that the kibbutz as a whole can almost satisfy the criteria by which Murdock defines the family. This observation is not meant to imply that the kibbutz is a nuclear family. Its structure and that of the nuclear family are dissimilar. This observation does suggest, however, that the kibbutz can function without the family, because it functions as if it, itself, were a family; and it can so function because its members perceive each other as kin, in the psychological implications of that term. The latter statement requires some explanation.

The members of the kibbutz do not view each other merely as fellow citizens, or as coresidents in a village, or as cooperators of an agricultural economy. Rather they do view each other as *chaverim,* or comrades, who comprise a group in which each is intimately related to the other, and in which the welfare of the one is bound up with the welfare of the other. This is a society in which the principle, "from each according to his ability, to each according to his needs," can be practiced, not because its members are more altruistic than the members of other societies, but because each member views his fellow as a kinsman, psychologically speaking. And just as a father in the family does not complain because he works much harder than his children, and yet he may receive no more, or even less, of the family income than they, so the kibbutz member whose economic productivity is high does not complain because he receives no more, and sometimes less, than a member whose productivity is low. This principle is taken for granted as the normal way of doing things. Since they are all *chaverim,* "it's all in the family," psychologically speaking.

In short, the kibbutz constitutes a *gemeinschaft.* Its patterns of interaction are interpersonal patterns; its ties are kin ties, without the biological tie of kinship. In this one respect it is the "folk society," in almost its pure form. The following quotation from Redfield could have been written with the kibbutz in mind, so accurately does it describe the social-psychological basis of kibbutz culture.

> The members of the folk society have a strong sense of belonging together. The group . . . see their own resemblance and feel correspondingly united. Communicating intimately with each other, each has a strong claim on the sympathies of the others.

> The personal and intimate life of the child in the family is extended, in the folk society, into the social world of the adults. . . . It is not merely that relations in such a society are personal; it is also that they are familial. . . . the result is a group of people among whom prevail the personal and categorized relationships that characterize the families as we know them, and in which the patterns of kinship tend to be extended outward from the group of genealogically connected

individuals into the whole society. The kin are the type persons for all experience.[11]

Hence it is that the bachelor and the childless couple do not feel that an injustice is being done them when they contribute to the support of the children of others. The children *in* the kibbutz are viewed as the children *of* the kibbutz. Parents (who are much more attached to their own children than they are to the children of others) and bachelors, alike, refer to all the kibbutz children as "our children."

The social perception of one's fellows as kin, psychologically speaking, is reflected in another important aspect of the kibbutz behavior. It is a striking and significant fact that those individuals who were born and raised in the kibbutz tend to practice group exogamy, although there are no rules that either compel or encourage them to do so. Indeed, in the kibbutz in which our field work was carried out, all such individuals married outside their own kibbutz. When they are asked for an explanation of this behavior, these individuals reply that they cannot marry those persons with whom they have been raised and whom they, consequently, view as siblings. This suggests, as Murdock has pointed out, that "the kibbutz to its members *is* viewed psychologically as a family to the extent that it generates the same sort of unconscious incest-avoidance tendencies" (private communication).

What is suggested by this discussion is the following proposition: although the kibbutz constitutes an exception to the generalization concerning the universality of the family, structurally viewed, it serves to confirm this generalization, functionally and psychologically viewed. In the absence of a specific social group—the family—to whom society delegates the functions of socialization, reproduction, etc., it has become necessary for the entire society to become a large extended family. But only in a society whose members perceive each other psychologically as kin can it function as a family. And there would seem to be a population limit beyond which point individuals are no longer perceived as kin. That point is probably reached when the interaction of its members is no longer face-to-face; in short, when it ceases to be primary group. It would seem probable, therefore, that only in a "familial" society, such as the kibbutz, is it possible to dispense with the family.

ADDENDUM, 1958

This is, quite obviously, an essay in the interpretation, rather than in the reporting of data.[12] After rereading the paper in 1958, I realized that the

[11] R. Redfield, "The Folk Society," *American Journal of Sociology*, LII (1947): 297–301.

[12] For a report on the kibbutz and its family relations, see Melford E. Spiro, *Kibbutz: Venture in Utopia* (Cambridge, Mass.: Harvard University Press, 1956), and *Children of the Kibbutz* (Cambridge, Mass.: Harvard University Press, 1958).

suggested interpretation follows from only one conception of the role which definitions play in science. Starting with Murdock's inductive—based on a sample of 250 societies—definitions of marriage and family, I concluded that marriage and the family do not exist in the kibbutz, since no single group or relationship satisfies the conditions stipulated in the definitions. If I were writing this essay today, I would wish to explore alternative interpretations as well—interpretations which, despite Murdock's definitions, would affirm the existence of marriage and the family in the kibbutz. Hence, I shall here very briefly outline the direction which one alternative interpretation would take.

The kibbutz, it should be noted first, does not practice—nor does it sanction—sexual promiscuity. Each adult member is expected to form a more-or-less permanent bisexual union; and this union is socially sanctioned by the granting of a joint room to the couple. The resulting relationship is different from any other adult relationship in the kibbutz in a number of significant features. (1) It alone includes common domicile for persons of opposite sex. (2) It entails a higher rate of interaction than is to be found in any other bisexual relationship. (3) It involves a higher degree of emotional intimacy than is to be found in any other relationship. (4) It establishes (ideally) an exclusive sexual relationship. (5) It leads to the deliberate decision to have children. These characteristics which, separately and severally, apply uniquely to this relationship, not only describe its salient features but also comprise the motives for those who enter into it. The couple, in short, viewed either objectively or phenomenologically, constitutes a unique social group in the kibbutz.

What, then, are we to make of this group? Since economic cooperation is not one of its features, we can, using Murdock's cross-cultural indices, deny that the relationship constitutes marriage. This is the conclusion of the foregoing paper. In retrospect, however, this conclusion does not leave me entirely satisfied. First, although we deny that the relationship constitutes a marriage, it nevertheless remains, both structurally and psychologically, a unique relationship within the kibbutz. Moreover, it is, with the exception of the economic variable, similar to those distinctive relationships in other societies to which the term marriage is applied. Hence, if I were writing this paper today, I should want to ask, before concluding that marriage is not universal, whether Murdock's inductive definition of marriage is, in the light of the kibbutz data, the most fruitful, even for his large sample; and if it were agreed that it is, whether it ought not to be changed or qualified so as to accommodate the relationship between kibbutz "spouses." Here I can only briefly explore the implications of these questions.

If the stated characteristics of the kibbutz relationship are found in the analogous relationship (marriage) in other societies—and I do not know that they are—it is surely apposite to ask whether Murdock's definition could not or should not stipulate them, as well as those already stipulated.

For if they are found in other societies, on what theoretical grounds do we assign a higher priority to sex or economics over emotional intimacy, for example? Hence, if this procedure were adopted (and assuming that the characteristics of the kibbutz relationship were to be found in the marriage relationship in other societies) we would, since the kibbutz relationship satisfies all but one of the cross-cultural criteria, term the kibbutz relationship "marriage."

Alternatively, we might suggest that Murdock's definition of marriage, as well as the one suggested here, are unduly specific; that cross-cultural research is most fruitfully advanced by means of analytic, rather than substantive or enumerative, definitions. Thus, for example, we might wish to define marriage as "any socially sanctioned relationship between non-sanguineally-related cohabiting adults of opposite sex which satisfied felt needs—mutual, symmetrical, or complementary." A nonenumerative definition of this type would certainly embrace all known cases now termed "marriage" and would, at the same time, include the kibbutz case as well.

In the same vein, and employing similar definitional procedures, alternative conclusions can be suggested with respect to the family in the kibbutz. Although parents and children do not comprise a family, as Murdock defines family, they nevertheless constitute a unique group within the kibbutz, regardless of the term with which we may choose to designate it. (1) Children are not only desired by kibbutz parents, but, for the most part, they are planned. (2) These children—and no others—are called by their parents "sons" and "daughters"; conversely, they call their parents—and no other adults—"father" and "mother." (3) Parents and children comprise a social group in both an interactional and an emotional, if not in a spatial, sense. That is, though parents and children do not share a common domicile, they are identified by themselves and by others as a uniquely cohesive unit within the larger kibbutz society; this unit is termed a *mishpacha* (literally, "family"). (4) The nature of their interaction is different from that which obtains between the children and any other set of adults. (5) The rate of interaction between parents and children is greater than that between the children and any other set of adults of both sexes. (6) The psychological ties that bind them are more intense than those between the children and any other set of adults of both sexes.

Here, then, we are confronted with the same problem we encountered with respect to the question of kibbutz marriage. Because the parent-child relationship in the kibbutz does not entail a common domicile, physical care, and social rearing—three of the stipulated conditions in Murdock's definition of family—we concluded that the family does not exist in the kibbutz. But, since parents and children comprise a distinct and differentiated social group within the kibbutz, I am now not entirely satisfied with a conclusion which seems, at least by implication, to ignore its presence. For, surely, regardless of what else we might do with this group, we cannot simply ignore it. We can either perceive it, in cross-cultural perspective, as a unique group, and invent a new term to refer to it, or we can revise Murdock's definition of family in order to accommodate it.

Should the latter alternative be preferred, it could be effected in the following way. The stipulation of "common residence" could be qualified to refer to a reference, rather than to a membership, residence; and this is what the parental room is, for children as well as for parents. When, for example, they speak of "my room" or "our room," the children almost invariably refer to the parental room, not to their room in the communal children's house. If, moreover, the educational and economic functions of the family were interpreted as responsibilities for which parents were either immediately or ultimately responsible, the kibbutz parent-child unit would satisfy these criteria as well. For, though parents do not provide immediately for the physical care of their children, neither do they renounce their responsibility for them. Rather, they seek to achieve this end by working jointly rather than separately for the physical welfare of all the children—including, of course, their own.

Similarly, though the parents have only a minor share in the formal socialization process, they do not simply give their children to others to be raised as the latter see fit. Rather, socialization is entrusted to specially designated representatives, nurses and teachers, who rear the children, not according to their own fancy, but according to rules and procedures established by the parents. In short, though parents do not themselves socialize their children, they assume the ultimate responsibility for their socialization. Interpreted in this way, the relationship between kibbutz parents and children satisfies Murdock's definition of family.

To conclude, this addendum represents an alternative method of interpreting the kibbutz data concerning the relationship between spouses, and among parents and children. I am not suggesting that this interpretation is necessarily more fruitful than the one adopted in the paper. Certainly, however, I should want to examine it carefully before concluding, as I previously did, that marriage and the family are not universal.

5
CHILDREN OF
THE KIBBUTZ
Leslie and Karen Rabkin

What is believed to be essential for mental health is that the infant and young child should experience a warm, intimate and continuous relationship with his mother (or permanent mother-substitute—one person who steadily mothers him), in which both find satisfaction and enjoyment." Very few professionals in child development, or parents, disagree with the mothering concept that John Bowlby expresses. Precisely for this reason, it is valuable to examine a society in which a different image of child rearing prevails. That society is the kibbutz—in Israel—where the child is entrusted to more than one mothering figure.

The remarkable and revolutionary living experiment that is the kibbutz has been in existence in Israel for more than 60 years—and more and more, kibbutz values are cited in debate about the American system of child-rearing. Current concern over the needs of disadvantaged children, particularly poor blacks from broken families, makes us wonder whether collective child-rearing could be a part of the solution. George Albee and others who theorize about new community models say we need group socialization for disadvantaged children.

More than 200 kibbutzim dot Israel. Although their total membership of about 80,000 is only 3 percent of the country's population, the kibbutzim have contributed a disproportionate share of the nation's military and political leaders. One-third of the officers in Tzahal (Israel's army) are kibbutzniks and nearly 60 percent of a recent class of air-force pilots were kibbutz-born. Most well-known Israeli figures live in or were born or reared in kibbutzim. Among them are former Prime Minister David Ben-Gurion, the late Levi Eshkol and General Moshe Dayan, who was born in the first kibbutz, Deganyah Aleph, on the bank of the Jordan River. (Dayan's parents left the kibbutz, however, joined the more family-centered *moshav* movement, and reared him there.)

The kibbutz is a voluntary, predominantly agricultural collective settlement of community-owned property (except for a few personal belongings) and of collective economic production and child care. The kibbutz motto is: from each according to his abilities, to each according to his needs. The emphasis on cooperation means, of course, that kibbutz ideology rejects

FROM Leslie and Karen Rabkin, "Children of the Kibbutz," *Psychology Today*, 3, no. 4 (September 1969): 40–46. Copyright © 1969 by Communications/Research/ Machines/Inc. Reprinted by permission of Communications/Research/Machines/Inc., and the authors.

certain basic ideas of our own social system—the importance of private property, private enterprise and family child-rearing.

The kibbutz grew out of the desire of a group of young, turn-of-the-century, Eastern European Jewish intellectuals to found a new and democratic society in what was then Palestine. They had experienced the dying years of the Russian Czarist regime, with its brutal anti-Semitism, and were fired by the Zionist dream for Israel; they wanted a society free of the prejudice that closed the world they had left behind, dedicated to full social and political equality. The promise of the Russian Revolution that a decadent society would be remade inspired the kibbutz founders and strengthened their Utopian ideals.

Kibbutz founders rebelled against the double standard for men and women and the traditional structure of the Jewish family. Wife and child had been subservient to the husband and father, and the division of labor confined the woman to the home, excluding her from the community's social, cultural and economic life.

To counter the double standard, kibbutz founders took dramatic steps: they based their marriage relationships on consent instead of on legal contract; they established communal kitchens, dining rooms and laundries to free the women from household chores and give them full roles in the economic and social life of the kibbutz. Kibbutz founders also created a system of collective education to free the mother from the responsibilities of child-rearing and to tie the child more closely to the group.

For 18 months, in 1967 and 1968, we lived in a kibbutz and studied child development. Our kibbutz (we'll call it Kiryat Yedidim) is like many others in this small country. It nestles in a valley at the foot of a mountain range in northeastern Israel, reclaimed by its founders from swamp water and Bedouins.

About 400 adults—the number includes those who are away for army service—and 250 children make up the Kiryat Yedidim community. Our kibbutz, which spreads over 2,500 acres, produces cotton, citrus, olives, carrots, onions, potatoes and several types of fodder. The farming is highly mechanized. A dairy flourishes, thanks to an especially productive crossbreed of Dutch and Arab cattle; poultry thrives on a large scale; fish ponds specialize in carp, an Israeli favorite; and flowers flourish in hothouses.

The village radiates from a communal dining hall, which also shelters weekly movies, community meetings and celebrations. Stretching out in front of the dining hall is a well-landscaped lawn, the work of four full-time gardeners and a source of great community pride. Children's houses stretch out to the west of the dining room. To the south and east are the fields. Behind the dining hall is a handsome new social club and library where people drink coffee, talk and read the papers.

Houses vary from one-room units with community bathrooms—used only by unmarried persons—to new two-room apartments, each with bathroom and kitchen, which house nearly all members over 30. Also, there is a variety of older housing with private baths, kitchens and porches. Usually four living units make up a building, the newest being two-storied. The rooms are pleasantly furnished. Paths connect all the houses and living areas. Many people use bicycles to get around, but most move about on foot. Jeeps and tractors transport nearly everyone to work.

The children of Kiryat Yedidim live and take their meals in their own quarters, sleeping from earliest infancy without adults. Two night watchmen circulate from one of the children's houses; a switchboard hooked to microphones in each house alerts the watchmen when a child is in distress. Specially trained female kibbutz members (*metapelet;* plural, *metaplot*) provide care, socialization and education. The *metaplot* are mostly young women, 21 to 35. A few older women work with school children; all of the married *metaplot* have children of their own. Several hours a day and on most holidays the child visits his parents, who become friends and companions.

When the newborn baby arrives from the hospital, usually after three days, he is placed in a nursery with five other infants. The old but freshly painted nursery building is divided into three wings, each containing entry hall, kitchen and two rooms. Outside is a porch where cribs sit during mild weather. Beyond that is a lawn where mothers play with their infants during visits. Inside, a few pictures decorate the bright, airy rooms; rattles, teething rings, brightly colored decorations are attached to the cribs; mobiles hang overhead. (There are no pacifiers; the belief is that infants should be self-reliant—in this case on their own thumbs—as early as possible.) The open structure permits visual and verbal interaction among the babies.

The mother, who is relieved of work for six weeks, visits as often as necessary to feed her baby. Israelis prefer breast-feeding but do not pressure mothers about it. As the baby is weaned, the mother resumes her work halftime, adding an hour a month, and the *metapelet* takes over part of the solid feeding.

By about nine months, the mother is making only short visits. Until the infant is 18 months old, mothers get daily half-hour work breaks for visits. The infant house, always open and flexible, can meet special needs of mother and child. A woman who has severe anxiety over separation from her baby is allowed to sleep in the infant house. The *metapelet* and the woman in charge of the education program counsel the mother in this crisis. While the *metaplot* are responsible for satisfying the infants' needs, parents spend several hours daily with their children; these are periods of affectionate interplay—parents generally avoid disciplinary or other training situations. Children quickly begin to anticipate these evening parental visits, and the visiting remains a source of gratification long beyond childhood. (One recent kibbutz graduate, commenting on the psychological distance between parents and children during high-school years, told us, "No, you don't go to see your parents so much—you're busy with your group, studies, activities—but they *are* always good for chocolate.")

After a year, the child joins five of his peers in a toddlers' house. Usually two groups of six live in a building. Nurses prepare breakfast and snacks in the buildings but bring hot things for lunch and dinner from a central children's kitchen. The children play with clay, blocks, toy cars and tractors, balls, rattles, picture books, cans for sand and water, wagons and doll furniture. Outside are a sandpit, swings, slide, and crawl-through barrels.

In the toddlers' house the child encounters a new *metapelet* and new physical surroundings. The socialization process begins in earnest. He learns to interact with peers, to dress and feed himself and starts toilet training (between the fifteenth and eighteenth month; it usually ends by age three). Warmth, affection and permissiveness characterize the care in these sensitive areas. Nurses stress independence and praise those who eat with spoons and dress themselves. The child, of course, learns a number of routines, dictated by group needs, that will be expected of him all his life—meals at certain times, designated play periods and places, and a definite bedtime—but an effort is made to balance the need for order with the child's individual needs.

Kibbutz education is designed to lay the foundations for group identification. As Shmuel Golan, the late theoretician of collective education, wrote: "[a] . . . feature of collective education that represents a positive value from the child's earliest years is the feeling of belongingness that it fosters—a feeling of being an essential part of, and rooted in, a society of his peers."

We noticed that a sense of *we* and *they* emerges very early. Children support their group against others, exclude out-group members from play, and show concern when a member is absent. The group expects him to share objects in the children's house, but not something he brings from his parents. The child who shares is praised lavishly.

When the children are between the ages of three and four, a nursery teacher—*ganenet*—takes charge of their social and intellectual development. A group of six moves to a new building—the kindergarten—and joins two other six-member groups. The enlarged group—a *kvutza*—remains the nexus of the child's life until high school.

At this stage the *ganenet* prepares the ground for real intellectual training. She divides playtime into free and structured sessions, the latter sometimes referred to as work. As one *ganenet* explained, "What the children do freely, that's play, but anything I give them to do—that is, anything organized—is work." The *ganenet* places special emphasis on sensory training— the aim is to enhance the child's ability to use his senses to explore the world. Sheila and Michael Cole (he's on the faculty of University of California, Irvine) noted a similar emphasis in Russian nursery schools [*Psychology Today* (October 1968)], though the kibbutz approach is less formal. Kibbutzniks spend many kindergarten hours building things, painting, dancing and playing games. They also grow their own flowers and vegetables and tend animals. From the time they can walk, the children visit the various work settings—the kitchen, fields, gardens, the garage, where they smell, touch, hear and taste the adult world, and equally important, see their parents at work—closing the gap, somewhat, between adult and child worlds.

After a year or two in kindergarten, the children reach a transitional class in which they embark on basic intellectual training—word-recognition, reading and mathematical concepts. Akin to our kindergarten, the transitional class stresses readiness activity.

At about seven, the child enters grammar school. Here he commences full-scale learning and encounters youngsters both older and younger than he. They devote an hour a day to work assignments, all age groups working together. They clean tables in the dining room, arrange their rooms and cultivate a vegetable garden. The teachers are well-trained graduates of the kibbutz movement's own teacher's college. Classroom instruction, based on the project method, is highly informal. Children call the teacher by her first name; there are no examinations or grade marks and passing is automatic.

The project method, kibbutz educators believe, permits a deep, integrated approach to learning. We watched children in a project study transportation development, build models and ride a variety of vehicles. In the process, they learned some history, economics, geography and some elementary mechanics. At the end of the study period, they made exhibits.

Kibbutz education integrates the child's learning with his surroundings, through nature studies and projects that focus on animals, weather and the kibbutz itself. The children camp out and hike to mountains and fields. Kibbutz founders come to tell tales of the pioneer days. Kibbutz children develop a sense of belonging that deeply impressed us, the kind of involvement in their world wanted in American schools by such social critics as Paul Goodman.

In the spring of his last year in grammar school, the child enters the youth movement with which the kibbutz is affiliated—an important and symbolic move that locks the child more securely into the kibbutz. At about 12, when he has finished the sixth grade, the young kibbutznik enters the combined junior-senior high school (*mosad*). This wider society—composed of 300 children from several kibbutzim and the nearby city—involves significant change for him. For the first time he meets important male figures other than his father. They are teachers and youth group leaders (*madrichim*) who guide his moral and ideological growth. His group, after being together for seven years, breaks apart; members go into new groups that include children from outside the kibbutz.

Now the student experiences a greater physical separation from parents and kibbutz, along with a new, strange freedom—institutional patterns are much less rigid. He begins to work in the kibbutz economy—one and a half to three hours a day, depending on age—alongside the adults. By the time he graduates from high school, he will have had enough work experience to choose work that most interests him.

Through sustained, all-encompassing contact in the peer group, the children identify with and depend on the group. Until the age of 18, life varies only slightly for both sexes. Boys and girls sleep in the same room and until the end of grammar school shower together and use the same toilets. (In the beginning they showered together until age 18, but not now.) Not surprisingly, youngsters brought up in close proximity feel like siblings and rarely intermarry. As the kibbutzniks put it: "How can you marry someone you sat next to on the potty?"

Until the end of high school, children are not kibbutz members; they belong to the children's society, which is a microcosm of the regulatory and social agencies of the kibbutz. The children's society elects a student council, plans social programs, punishes troublemakers and helps plan curriculum. After high school, students are elected to kibbutz membership, then leave to serve their compulsory army duty.

Behavioral scientists and educators are interested in kibbutz life because it is a way of life purposely, totally and willingly built around the principles of community and cooperation. And infant care, socialization and the education of children all reflect a determination to abolish family-centeredness and create an atmosphere in which parents and children can maximize love and affection.

Kibbutz educators believe that collective education reduces parent-child conflict for several reasons: (1) the child, supported by the kibbutz, is economically independent of his parents; (2) equality of the sexes eliminates the patriarchal family system; (3) the importance of the nurse allows the child to love someone other than his parents; (4) because nurses handle the primary discipline, the daily visits of parents and children can take place under ideal conditions; (5) jealousy and anger that have to be repressed in the family can be expressed in the kibbutz because the child can find more legitimate objects of aggression among peers; and (6) the collective framework shields the child from overprotective or domineering parents who might block his efforts to become independent.

The results of planned socialization are not easy to evaluate but many professionals, influenced by Bowlby, believe that multiple mothering creates many emotional problems among children. Children raised in institutions often lack stimulation and maternal warmth. These professionals fear that this may also be true of kibbutzniks.

Albert Rabin, of Michigan State University, did a study comparing kibbutz infants and infants reared in the *moshav,* the Israeli communal settlement that retains a private family structure. His results with the Griffiths Infant Scale suggest that kibbutz infants are somewhat less socially responsive than *moshav* infants, but he felt it was due more to the comparatively large number of infants who are under a single nurse's care than to the mother's limited contact with the child. Nevertheless, Rabin's findings support the idea that kibbutzniks are emotionally deprived.

In a more recent and larger study, however, Reuven Kohen-Raz, of

Jerusalem's Hebrew University, who used the more carefully constructed Bayley Infant Scales of Mental and Motor Development, found that kibbutz infants at one, six and 12 months show higher overall achievements than Bayley's U.S. sample. Even when they were compared with infants of highly educated parents in private Israeli homes, kibbutz babies consistently performed better. At the least, this should quiet pessimists who claim that collective child-rearing retards the intellectual development of infants.

Interestingly, when Rabin compared 10-year-olds, older adolescents and young army men from the kibbutz with a *moshav* group, he found indications of higher intellectual achievement and personal adjustment among the kibbutzniks. Rabin concluded: "The facts are that kibbutz child-rearing was designed to raise new kibbutz members, and is quite effective in doing so."

Anthropologist Melford Spiro, of the University of California at San Diego, studied Kiryat Yedidim a generation ago. We followed up his work because the stability of the kibbutz population and Spiro's unpublished data lend dimensions to our study. When Spiro studied the kibbutz in 1951, the oldest kibbutz-born child was 28 and only about a dozen were over 21, but he concluded that the individual reared through collective education is "an efficient, productive and functioning adult. He is an adult with a sense of values and a conscience that assures the implementation of these values. He is motivated to carry on the basic features of kibbutz culture—its collective ownership, distribution according to need, agricultural work, collective child-rearing and its devotion to esthetic and intellectual values."

We have only begun to analyze the result of our study but they already confirm Spiro's impressions. One must, as David Rapaport noted, "pay a price . . . in the coin of developmental crises and pathology" for any system of socialization. And, despite the fact that kibbutzniks call childhood a "Garden of Eden," there *are* crises in collective education. For example, moving a child from one dormitory to another often creates insecurity. Also, kibbutzniks undergo stress when they try to balance their need to be individuals with the need to conform to the group. We hope our study results will illuminate the meaning of these crises in personality development.

Meanwhile, we can sum up the kibbutznik: he is a healthy, intelligent, generous, somewhat shy but warm human being, rooted in his community and in the larger Israeli society. He shows no sign of the emotional disturbance we would expect from a violation of our ideal mother-child relationship.

What can we learn from the kibbutz experience? Can we integrate collective education into our social and economic structure? Is it a panacea for educating the poor? We think not. We cannot translate this socialization system into American terms. To do so we would need a basic overhaul of the goals of our society. To release children into our individualistic, competitive society after rearing them collectively, emphasizing cooperation and responsibility for one's group, would be too much of a psychological jolt. Nor is kibbutz education based on cutting parental ties, a notion implicit in many proposals for using the kibbutz model with poor children. The child may suffer painful and destructive conflicts unless he sees the family and the collective as allies and collaborators.

But we see other possibilities. Bruno Bettelheim once asked: "Is it possible that the privatization of so much of modern middle-class life is not the consequence but rather the cause of human isolation from which modern man suffers and which the kibbutz way of life has tried to counteract?" The kibbutznik has a deep sense of belonging to his kibbutz and his country. The privatization of our family life may counter this belongingness. We may find that if we expose our children to meaningful group experiences in early life, we will give them a sense of integration in something beyond their family, enabling them to identify with the community and the nation.

The need for an exclusive mother-child relationship overconcerns so many mothers who need to work or to study that no matter how competent the substitute caretaker, they feel that the child inevitably suffers psychologically from these separations. Alberta Siegel, "The Working Mother: A Review of Research," suggests that a mother's employment can have a positive, stimulating effect on a child's development. Knowledge that the multiple-mothering of the kibbutz has no long-range ill effects should enable us to see the problem from another angle. Incidentally, the fact that the father is at home and with the child a great deal in the kibbutz is another matter for our matricentric society to reflect upon.

But these are *our* problems. Meanwhile, the kibbutz continues to develop and refine its way of life, and incidentally to provide a fascinating counterpoint to the family life and education that we so completely take for granted.

6

AGING IN ISRAEL,
A PLANNED SOCIETY*

Yonina Talmon

This paper analyzes the influence of ideological and structural factors on the process of aging and elucidates the limitations and potentialities of planning in this sphere. It is based on an examination of the process of aging in collective settlements in Israel.[1] The collectives have solved many of the basic and most persistent problems of aging. Aging members enjoy full economic security. Communal services take care of them in case of ill health or infirmity. Retirement from work is gradual and does not entail an abrupt and complete break from work routines. Aging members are not cut off from community life. Social participation serves as an alternative avenue of activity and provides respected substitute functions. In many cases it compensates the aging member for his gradual loss of competence and status in the occupational sphere. What is most important, grown-up children are expected to live in the community founded by their parents. Parents are able to maintain close and constant relations with their children without losing their independence. Elderly and old people are thus spared much of the insecurity and isolation, the futile inactivity and dependence entailed in aging.

The focus of the analysis is on the main ideological and structural sources of strain and on an examination of the institutional mechanisms by which the collectives cope with problems of the aged.

Analysis in this paper is based on a research project conducted in one of the four federations of collectives.[2] The number of collectives in our sample

FROM Yonina Talmon, "Aging in Israel, A Planned Society," *American Journal of Sociology*, 67, no. 3 (November 1961): 284–295. Reprinted by permission of the University of Chicago Press.

* Enlarged version of a paper read at the International Gerontological Congress, San Francisco, 1960. This research was partly supported by a grant from the research council of the Federation of Labor.

[1] The main features of collective settlements (*Kvutzot* or *Kibbutzim*) are: common ownership of property except for a few personal belongings and communal organization of production and consumption on an equalitarian basis. All income goes into the common treasury, each member getting a very small annual allowance for personal expenses. The community is run as a single economic unit and as a single household.

[2] The project was conducted by the Research Seminar of the Sociology Department of the Hebrew University. Mrs. R. Bar-Joseph took an active part in the initial planning. A. Etzioni assisted me in direction of the project in its first stage. The other main research assistants were: E. Ron, M. Sarell, and J. Sheffer. M. Sarell and E. Cohen took over from Mr. Etzioni in the second stage. The main research

is twelve, or one in six of all the collectives affiliated with the federation. The project has combined sociological and anthropological field methods. The data obtained from the questionnaires, from various types of interviews, and from the analysis of written materials were examined and carefully interpreted by direct observation. We did intensive and systematic field work in the collectives in the sample.

Our initial project dealt with aging primarily within the framework of the developmental cycle of the family and its effects on intergenerational continuity. We were able to deal with other aspects of aging by doing additional research. Documentary material of various sorts, concerned with aging, which appeared in the last five years, was subjected to systematic content analysis. Some of the hypotheses derived from the initial project and from the additional analysis of publications were put to further test in a subsample of two collectives.[3]

SOURCES OF STRAIN

The ambivalent position of old age in a future-oriented and youth-centered society[4] is one of the main sources of strain of aging in the collectives. The founders had dissociated themselves from Jewish traditional life and had rebelled against the authority of their elders, most members having been trained in radical non-conformist youth movements whose values and patterns of behavior have had a decisive and indelible influence on communal life. The original revolutionary ideology was reinforced by the personal experience of rebellion. All this glorified youth as full of potentialities, free, and creative, and emphasized discontinuity.

The appearance of the second generation in time naturally brought to an end the disrupting of intergenerational ties. Children are expected now to settle in the collective founded by their parents and to continue their life work there; the family of orientation is no longer considered an external and alien influence. The continuity of the collective depends on intergenerational continuity, and the second generation is called upon to be responsible for maintaining and developing the heritage of the first.[5]

assistants were: U. Avner, B. Bonne, U. Hurwitz, and Z. Stup. Special thanks are due to Mrs. R. Gutman-Shaku who assisted in collecting the data and preparing this paper for publication. I wish to thank E. Cohen, R. Baki, and R. Gabriel for their help.

[3] Part of the qualitative data was presented elsewhere. See Y. Talmon-Garber, "Social Structure and Family Size," *Human Relations*, XII (1958): 121–146, and Y. Talmon-Garber, "Occupational Placement of the Second Generation," *Megamoth*, VIII (1957): 369–392 (in Hebrew).

[4] Cf. F. R. Kluckhohn, "Dominant and Variant Value Orientations," in C. Kluckhohn and H. A. Murray, eds., *Personality* (New York: Knopf, 1953), pp. 342–357.

[5] A fuller analysis of this change may be found in Y. Talmon-Garber, "Social Structure and Family Size," *op. cit.* See also M. Sarell, "Continuity and Change—the Second Generation in Collective Settlements," *Megamoth*, XI (1961): 32–123 (in Hebrew).

This new ideology of continuity is just beginning to take root. It is, as yet, of only secondary importance because the collective movement, constantly seeking reinforcement from the youth movements, relies on youth-centered appeal and continues to preach rebellion and discontinuity. Since this spirit predominates, aging is looked on as a process of steady decline, a gradual fall from grace.

The central position accorded to work and the exceptionally high evaluation of productivity lead to the same effect. The founders of the collectives have undergone a process of voluntary de-urbanization and proletarization which reversed the traditional Jewish hierarchy of occupational prestige. Retraining for hard physical labor and settlement on the land were imperative for survival in the difficult conditions of settlement. Strenuous work, a dire economic necessity, has become much more than that: it has been endowed with deep meaning and dignity and invested with a quasi-religious seriousness, as an important instrument for the realization of social and national ideals as well as an ultimate value in itself. The idealized figure of a farmer-pioneer tiller of the soil has become one of the main symbols of personal redemption and of national revival.

Work and productivity, in all collectives, has become a compelling drive.[6] Absence from work, even for a legitimate reason, engenders feeling of discomfort and a sense of guilt; an individual who shirks his work responsibilities is severely criticized. The position of a lazy or incompetent worker is precarious, regardless of his other accomplishments and achievements. The position of any member in the collective is determined primarily by his devotion to his work and the excellence of his performance, and those engaged in physical labor in agriculture enjoy highest prestige.

Retirement from work is gradual. Aging members are not suddenly relieved of their major social function but undergo a steady and cumulative decline in occupational status. Inevitably, as they lose their capacity for hard work and find it increasingly difficult to excel in their tasks, they gradually become part-time workers and are eventually transferred to lighter tasks, sometimes in a less arduous nonagricultural occupation. If an aging member happens to hold a managerial position he relinquishes it in due time, for most work branches require a full-time manager. Old people often wander from one work assignment to another, doing odd jobs here and there.

Aging members thus gradually cease to be self-supporting, and grow more dependent on communal institutions and require more services. Even though most have earned their keep in many years of hard and devoted work, they cannot face declining productivity without misgivings: the constant emphasis on productivity and self-maintenance discourages any too easy adjustment to growing dependence. Moreover, unlike dependence

---

[6] See M. Spiro, *Venture in Utopia* (Cambridge, Mass.: Harvard University Press, 1956), p. 17.

on a state pension or on an old-age insurance scheme, dependence on the collective is not neutral and anonymous. The aging member sometimes experiences it as a direct personal dependence on his fellow members. No wonder, then, that many of the elderly refuse to make use of their right to part-time work and continue to work full time as long as they possibly can.

The objective need for hard productive labor and the ideological emphasis on it in agriculture put elderly members at a considerable disadvantage. Moreover, the constantly changing rationalized and mechanized economy of the collectives puts a premium on up-to-date specialized training, with which long experience gained during many years of practical work often cannot compete. Inasmuch as long experience engenders rigid adherence to routine and hampers adjustment to new techniques, it is a liability. Elderly people are thus severely handicapped. Younger people, stronger and more flexible, are often better trained and more up to date.

Paradoxically, the emphasis on equality, another important value, further harasses elderly members. Social status in the collective is a function of ability, not of age: young people enjoy social equality with their elders, and there are few symbols of deference. Aging members have no claim to vested positions; their contributions in the past do not entitle them to special consideration, and they are judged on their merits.

The fear of losing one's position in the occupational sphere is a major source of insecurity of the aged and a cause of much anxiety and discontent. Analysis of self-images of aging members and of the stereotypes employed to describe old age indicate clearly that retirement is crucial in heightening the awareness of the onset of old age. Many members defined the reduction of their hours of work as the beginning of the end.[7]

Gradual retirement spares the workers the shock of an abrupt and total loss of their major social function and enables them to adjust to retirement stage by stage. Moreover it enables the community to utilize the productive capacities of all members fully and spares aging members the long period of involuntary idleness. It should be stressed, however, that full retirement at a fixed age has one important advantage over gradual retirement.[8] Complete retirement constitutes a clear-cut break; gradual retirement spares the worker a major crisis, but at the same time subjects him to difficult and recurrent changes, a long process of continuous reorientation and readjustment.

---

[7] Z. Smith Blau, "Changes in Status and Age Identification," *American Sociological Review*, XXI (1956): 198–203; B. S. Philips, "A Role Theory Approach to Adjustment in Old Age," *American Sociological Review*, XXII (1957): 212–217.

[8] On the influence of full retirement at a fixed age on morale see E. A. Freedman and R. J. Havighurst, *The Meaning of Work and Retirement* (Chicago: University of Chicago Press, 1954); see also C. Tibbits, "Retirement Problems in American Society," *American Journal of Sociology*, LIX (1953): 301. Most researchers emphasize the grave difficulties entailed in adjustment to total retirement. There is, however, some evidence that these difficulties are overstressed. See G. F. Streib, "Morale of the Retired," *Social Problems*, III (1955–1956): 271–280.

The rivalry between old and young can be fully analyzed only when viewed against the wider ramifications of the relationship between successive generations. The second generation is expected to stay in the collective founded by their parents. This pattern of familial continuity enables the parents to maintain close contacts with their children, but it engenders considerable strain in the occupational sphere. Occupational opportunities are rather limited in the collective. Members of the second generation have to compete directly with the first generation for the available jobs.[9] As members of the collective they are in free competition with the older generation, a competition in which the most suitable candidate usually wins— and the better worker is more often than not the younger.

The fear of blocking the channels of advancement often leads to a policy of early replacement of older members by younger, even if the aging workers are more suitable and more qualified for their job. The anomalous age distribution and incomplete generational structure of the collectives are of utmost importance in this matter. The founders of a collective are usually young people, of the same or similar age and unattached. At this initial stage there are no aging parents and no young children in the collective. When additional groups and individuals join the founders at different stages of community development the age distribution becomes more varied. When the one-generation structure becomes two-generational, a number of old parents will be found in most established collectives. These parents live in the collective and enjoy the status of "member's parent" but do not as a rule become full members: they are marginal, and the generation structure remains for a considerable time truncated and incomplete. It is only when the original founders become grandfathers and grow old that the collective develops into a full-scale three-generational structure.

The uneven and discontinuous age distribution and the incomplete generational structure have many repercussions on the process of occupational allocation. Adolescents born in the collective begin to come of age when all members of the first generation are still in possession of their full working capacities and hold most jobs which require specialized skill and experience. The process of taking over is a prolonged one: in collectives which have ceased to expand and have not evolved special mechanisms to speed up the taking-over process, the restriction of occupational opportunities is felt very keenly. Any attempt of the aged to hold on to their positions limits the occupational choices open to the second generation. The young people resent being hemmed in and being unduly restricted. They become restless and in some cases leave their parents' collective in search of better openings. Thus severe and protracted blocking of avenues of occupational mobility endangers intergenerational family continuity.

Our material indicates the growing importance of parent-children rela-

---

[9] On a similar problem in primitive societies see M. Gluckman, *Custom and Conflict in Africa* (Oxford: Basil Blackwell, 1955), pp. 56–57.

tionship in the process of aging. The center of gravity often shifts to the familial role: in many cases it is more important than the substitute functions provided by participation in public affairs. At first this seemed surprising. The family in the collectives has delegated most of its functions to the community,[10] and members' needs are provided by communal institutions. The main socializing agencies are the peer age-group and the specialized nurses, instructors, and teachers. Children are partly segregated from their families, mutual and direct dependence between parents and children being restricted. Since only very few primary familial roles have been left to the family, it seemed reasonable to expect the family to be of only secondary importance. Paradoxically, this limitation of functions seems to have a beneficial effect on family relations: insofar as the family has ceased to be the prime socializing agency it escapes, to some extent, the inevitable ambivalence felt toward agents of socializations, for parents do not have to perform the two-sided role of ministering to their children's needs, on the one hand, and thwarting their wishes, on the other. Parents do not carry the main responsibility for disciplining their children and can afford to be permissive, all of which limits the areas of potential conflict. Since occupational allocation is not familial, it does not affect the relationship between parents and children, and occupational rivalry between generations does not penetrate the family nor disrupt its unity. Moreover, it is mainly within the family that both parents and children have intimate relations, unpatterned by their position in the community and are free from routine duties; only in the family do they get love and care which they do not have to share with many others.

To the elderly, the gradual withdrawal from the occupational sphere enhances the importance of the family. Curtailment of outside activities brings about a concomitant decline in the number and intensity of outside contacts, but they may seek solace and emotional security in their relationship with their children. Grandchildren thus become a major preoccupation, especially with aging women.

Elderly people render their children many small but important services. Although children are looked after mainly by communal institutions the need for aid is not completely satisfied. Children come to their parents' flat after work hours, and the parents look after them during the afternoon and take them to the children houses at night and put them to bed. But if they are very tired after a day's work, the parents may find it difficult to cope with their children without some rest. Parents who have a number of young children will find the afternoon noisy and hectic, and now grandparents may be a great help. They take their grandchildren for walks. They help with older children after the birth of a new baby. They take over the care of children when their parents go on vacation. Whenever either

[10] Cf. Y. Talmon-Garber, "The Family in Collective Settlements," *Transactions of the Third World Congress of Sociology* (Amsterdam: International Sociological Association, 1956), IV, 116–126.

parent is absent from the collective attending refresher courses for specialized training or seminars of advanced studies, the grandparents replace the parent and compensate the children for the temporary separation. They help regularly, but do so especially during emergencies.

Grandparents' needs are provided for by communal institutions. But they, too, often need help, especially when they are incapacitated or very old. But children visit their parents regularly and help with the nursing during illness. They bring in food from the communal kitchen to their parents' flat whenever the parents are unable or disinclined to eat in the communal dining hall, and they carry the parents' clothes to and from the communal laundry. These small domestic and personal services grow very important when the parents are old or infirm; they are indispensable when there is only one widowed and very old parent left.

It should be stressed that the services that children render to their parents are on the whole not very irksome or time-consuming, being auxiliary functions. The old parents' primary needs are provided for by the collective so that they retain to the very last a semi-independence. In the support and care of aged relatives the children only supplement collective institutions. Their limited liabilities and duties do not, in most cases, interfere with their normal life routines. The curtailment and limitation of obligations seem to reinforce rather than weaken family relationships. As a rule, it does not undermine the sense of responsibility toward old parents; quite the contrary; the children are able to help spontaneously and generously. The relationship is free of the feeling of resentment and of the sense of guilt engendered by too heavy responsibilities.[11]

The ties between aging parents and children are, thus, firmly based on reciprocal services, on a constant give-and-take of small but significant and continuous services. During the first and middle stages of aging, services flow mainly from parents to children, who receive more help than they give. It is only during the last stages of aging that the asymmetrical exchange is reversed in favor of the parents, but it seldom becomes completely one-sided. Only in cases of long-term infirmity do aged parents impose severe strain on their families.

The importance of the interrelation between parents and children can be clearly demonstrated by examining the problems of aging of unmarried and childless members, on the one hand, and of parents whose children have left the collective on the other hand. Needless to say, we do not find here the extreme isolation and bitter loneliness found elsewhere.[12] Old people remain full members of a cohesive community and continue to participate in its life. Their diminishing participation in the occupational sphere may be partly counterbalanced by enhanced participation in com-

[11] See P. Townsend, *The Family Life of Old People* (London: Routledge & Kegan Paul, 1957), pp. 164–165, and L. Rosenmayer, "Der alte Mensch in der sozialen Umwelt von Heute," *Kölner Zeitschrift*, Heft IV (1958): 642–657.

[12] Townsend, *op. cit.*, pp. 166–182.

munal affairs. They are surrounded by friends and neighbors. Yet in spite of all these benefits and substitute functions, most of those who have no children living nearby in the same collective feel very lonely and discouraged, especially so if they have no other relatives in the collective.

Increasing age enhances the importance of geographical proximity and daily face-to-face contact.[13] The aged find it increasingly difficult to get about and visit their relatives who live elsewhere; they need daily care and company. The social and health services and their friends and their neighbors take on some of the functions of children, but this substitute aid can not completely fill the gap. Old parents have no qualms about accepting personal services from their children since the relationship is based on reciprocity and deep affection, but they feel unhappy if they have to trouble a nurse more often than do other old people. Accepting aid from neighbors occasionally, they regard it as not quite right to depend on them for regular services, and they are not completely at ease even with very close and old friends.

Some of the childless old members attach themselves to the family of a friend or a neighbor, as additional or substitute grandparents. This creates a basis of common interest and cooperation and enables them to accept the help offered not as a favor but as part of a mutually satisfactory relationship. In some cases the problems are solved by bonds of enduring friendship and mutual aid between two old and childless people. These alternatives offset certain of the difficulties but they do not entirely replace the family.

Relations with children who live in the same collective are essential to the well-being and happiness of the aged. The services that they render to their children give them a hold on life, and the help extended to them by their children is not just a fulfillment of professional duty or a personal favor but a reciprocation of past services and a reaffirmation of a diffuse and comprehensive lifelong loyalty, a recurring symbolic expression of attachment and affection.

There is thus a marked contrast between the interests of old members in the occupational sphere and their interests as members of families. As workers they would like to slow up replacement of old workers by younger ones. But as parents they want their children to achieve their occupational aspirations without delay and press for their assignment to desirable and important jobs as soon as possible. Thus parents pay the price for family

---

[13] See E. Litwak, "Geographic Mobility and Family Cohesion," *American Sociological Review*, XXV (1960): 385–394. Litwak advances the hypothesis that close relations with kin can be maintained in spite of distance or of breaks in face-to-face contact. However, his sample did not include people over forty-five years of age, and he himself noted that older people might vary significantly in this respect. His analysis of patterns of geographical mobility of extended families indicates a tendency to move closer together in the later stages.

continuity by undergoing difficulties in the occupational sphere, for family continuity can be maintained only at the cost of early replacement.

A smooth process of aging entails both disengagement and reengagement. It depends primarily on a smooth retirement from work, a successful reorientation to civic and domestic relationship, and, in addition, to leisure activities.[14] The elderly, having more free time, are often at loss how to use it and need advice. Life in the collectives is work-centered: work for many was an all-absorbing and often deeply satisfying activity. They had little time and perhaps no great need to develop hobbies. Retirement creates a void not easily filled, and their main problem is to find a new balance between work and social participation on the one hand, and study and recreation, on the other.

We must take into consideration the overemphasis on planning which is typical of recently founded revolutionary societies. Consciously or unconsciously, the members assume that all human problems can be solved by comprehensive social reorganization. Sooner or later they learn that social planning cannot cure all ills. It very often involves the sacrifice of certain ends in the interest of others, and in the course of solving a problem, new ones often are engendered. Schemes which favor one subgroup may cause serious difficulties to other subgroups. Emphasis on one institutional sphere may entail strains in adjoining spheres. Gains in one sphere may be offset by minor or major losses in others. Members of the collectives are surprised and deeply disappointed when it becomes obvious that total social planning leaves many problems unsolved and even causes new and unforeseen strains; they are easily discouraged and prone to be impatient. Even those who in the process of aging seem well ordered and well balanced very often feel defeated. In many cases we found a considerable discrepancy between our evaluation of the degree of adjustment achieved by an elderly member, on the one hand and his own self-evaluation, on the other.[15] We found that many of the aged tended to underrate advantages and overrate disadvantages: many took the amenities provided by the community for granted and magnified their difficulties.

The overemphasis on planning has yet another important consequence: the aged tend to rely on organizational changes rather than on ideological reorientation and personal resocialization. They do not fully realize the need for a deliberate cultivation of flexibility in role,[16] hence a certain

---

[14] See L. C. Michel, "The New Leisure Class," *American Journal of Sociology,* LIX (1954): 371; also R. J. Havighurst, "The Leisure Activities of the Middle Class," *American Journal of Sociology,* LIII (1957): 152–162.

[15] The investigator assessed the degree of adjustment by extent of participation in the main institutional spheres, basing his examination on a set of fixed indicators. His judgment in each case was compared with the self-assessment by the elderly person.

[16] R. Havighurst, "Flexibility and the Social Roles of the Retired," *American Journal of Sociology,* LIX (1954): 309.

rigidity and failure to undertake long-range preparation for the inevitable change.

The importance of structural position is clearly expressed in the differences between aging men and aging women in the collectives.[17] We were led by our data to expect that women find it more difficult to adjust to aging than men. Climatic conditions, hard labor, and the negative attitude toward beauty care contribute to a comparatively early onset of aging. Most elderly women drift away from agriculture and child care to service institutions, such as the communal kitchen and laundry, where work is often hectic and full of tension or monotonous and boring and of low prestige. Women, we find, are less inclined than men to participate in communal affairs, and few manage to find a suitable substitute role in this sphere. Most seek comfort in their relationship with their kin and usually cling to their familial roles more than do the men. However, since activities in the family are limited they cannot in most cases fully compensate the women for withdrawal in other spheres. Women tend to engage in leisure pursuits more than men, but there is as yet little systematic cultivation of them in the collectives. Thus women in the collectives apparently have less chance to achieve a balanced and well-ordered old age than men,[18] and we therefore expected them to be more critical of the collective than were aging men.

This hypothesis was examined in our inquiry in the subsample of two long-established collectives. The sample included half of all the members above fifty years of age: the average age of the women was fifty-seven, while that of the men was fifty-eight. The respondents were asked to evaluate the position of aging members in the collective. Table 1 indicates the difference between the statements of men and women.

TABLE 1
Attitudes of Aging Members and Aging Parents of
Members Toward Their Positions in Collective

Group	No.	Appreciative of Collective (percent)	Critical of Collective (percent)	Very Critical of Collective (percent)
Aging Members:				
Men	42	31	45	24
Women	39	18	44	38
Total	81	25	44	31
Parents of Members	33	67	24	9

[17] For a more detailed analysis of the position of women in the collectives see: Y. Talmon-Garber, "Sex-Role Differentiation in an Equalitarian Society," 1959. (Mimeographed.)

[18] Men have a more difficult adjustment to aging than women in working-class families (see P. Townsend, op. cit., chap. vi). There is little comparative material on retirement of women and its effect on their adjustment to aging.

As shown here, fewer women than men have an unqualified favorable evaluation of the position of aging people in the collective and more women are very critical of the collective. When asked to compare the position of aging men and aging women about 70 percent of the women and 62 percent of the men felt that women have a more difficult time than men: only 6 percent of the women and 10 percent of the men stated the reverse.

The connection between the system of values and the strains entailed in aging is conclusively demonstrated by comparing members' parents who are only quasimembers with elderly people who are founders of the collective and full members in it. Members' parents do not serve on committees; they are partly isolated and do not participate as much as full members in the collective's social life. Moreover, many do not fully identify themselves with the collective and find it difficult to get used to its way of life. On the face of it, one would expect quasimembers to be less adjusted than full members who have more substitute functions and are better integrated in the collective. Analysis soon revealed, however, that members' parents are on the whole, much happier and more contented than the others. Many, indeed, describe their life in the collective in glowing terms.

By contrast, aging members are much more aware of the disadvantages. Their praise of the collective is guarded and qualified and they will always point out the need for further planning and reorganization. Table 1 also shows these differences. Members' parents in the sample are older than aging members: their average age is about sixty-four. They numbered fourteen men and nineteen women.

Members' parents, it is seen, who are in a less advantageous position in the collective, express a markedly more favorable evaluation of the position of aging people in the collective than the better situated and more privileged aging members. This seemingly paradoxical finding can be accounted for only if we take into consideration the ideological and structural position of the two groups. Members' parents are not imbued with the prevalent faith in youth, work, and productivity, and being marginal they are less susceptible to the pressure of public opinion. Having come to the collective after, or near, retirement they are grateful for the possibility to work part time and do not regard this as a comedown. As they do not set their hopes high, they are easily satisfied and enjoy many of the amenities of aging in the collective without suffering from the concomitant strains. But the aging members, who are an integral part of the system and adhere to the dominant values, find it much more difficult to avoid the inherent pressures and strains.

REDEFINITION OF POLICY

The collectives tended at first to disregard the spreading discontent among their aged and ignored the symptoms of strain. Those who voiced resentment and pressed for change were usually regarded as incorrigible malcontents. The increasing number of aging members in the long-established collectives and their persistent criticism have gradually brought about a growing awareness of their problems.

The fact that the collectives are not rigidly doctrinaire and that their structure has remained fairly flexible and dynamic is of crucial importance. The collective movement has recently started to develop supplementary institutional mechanisms which cope, to some extent, with the inherent difficulties of aging in it. Some of these mechanisms develop as spontaneous adaptations to a changing situation; others evolve as indirect and unintended consequences of planning in other fields. In addition, there crop up proposals and specific plans which deal directly with the rights and duties of the aging. All the federations of collectives are now engaged in a critical appraisal and reorganization of their schemes, and there is a constant and tireless groping for new solutions.

As indicated, tension mostly develops in the occupational sphere. Consequently, efforts of reorganization are directed mainly toward careful reassessment of the policy of gradual retirement. One of the main problems is the absence of generally accepted and explicit norms of retirement. There is no clear definition of the age of retirement or of the right to progressive reduction of work hours; each collective deals with retirement in its own way and considerable individual variation is the rule even within one collective. Their rights and duties being undefined, the aging are hesitant to apply for partial retirement even when they need it very badly. The federation is now developing flexible standards to guide the collectives. The federation does not aim at uniformity: the individual collective is to be allowed some variation within the accepted framework and may adopt the common standards to its special conditions and to the special needs of its aging members.

The systematic increase of suitable employment opportunities[19] is yet another subject of the planned redefinition of policy. The federation has set about reorganizing the existing work branches and recently a research institute to undertake a thorough job analysis of all work branches. This research sets out to identify the skills, knowledge, and abilities required in each job and to sort out those that, after certain modifications, can be successfully filled by the aging.

An increase of possibilities of employment and a considerable improvement of the position of aging members has been achieved by dividing some of the work branches into subunits and intrusting the elderly with responsibility in some of them. Older people resent being gradually deprived of initiative and authority and find it difficult to work under the supervision of a much younger worker. But the pattern of subdivision retains for them

19 W. Donahue, ed., *Earning Opportunities for Older Workers* (Ann Arbor: University of Michigan Press, 1955), pp. 159–245. Cf. also J. T. Drake, *The Aged in American Society* (New York: Ronald Press, 1958), pp. 100–181.

a measure of responsibility and independence, while the partial segregation of old and young workers limits potential conflict. Not all branches are amenable to such a subdivision but many efforts are made to give the aged as much independence as possible. Quite a number of old members work on their own. The bedridden and the house-bound get work which they can perform whenever they feel like it. Placement of them is slowly becoming more selective and personal.

The development of new work branches in the collective and the employment of the aged in jobs outside the community have widened considerably the opportunities of old people. Many collectives have developed light industries and crafts which mainly employ the aging members. Moreover, a considerable number of the aged find suitable employment in local and country-wide organizations. They work outside the communities and return home every day or every weekend. They keep part of their salary for their personal needs but most of it goes to the collective. There has lately developed a system whereby each established collective adopts a newly established one and sends a number of its members as social and agricultural instructors, and a certain number of elderly members volunteer for this job. The young and inexperienced members of the newly established collectives profit from the experience and knowledge of the older persons and treat them with respect. The instructors, for their part, serve as a living link between the two communities and feel that they are making a real contribution toward the development of the movement; it gives them a new lease on life.

Continuation of employment and successful adaptation to a new job often depend on available possibilities of training. The federation has a program of refresher courses and retraining seminars. Many aging members have discarded a nonmanual occupation before joining the collective. If, when they are no longer able to continue their work in agriculture, they want to return to their former occupation, they are able to do so provided that they get systematic retraining. A considerable number of aging members are sent for comparatively long periods of study. Quite a number of them retrain as teachers, librarians, and accountants.

The collectives realize that enhanced social participation is a necessary antidote to the loss of status entailed in gradual retirement and may compensate the aging for the limitation of their occupational opportunities. They consequently conduct a constant fight against the not uncommon tendency to retreat and retire from public life. The collectives nominate aging members to all important committees and exert pressure on them to accept; they are, in fact, overrepresented on most committees. The collectives also nominate aging members to temporary terms of office in the federation and in many other central country-wide organizations. These are mostly elite positions which provide wide scope for activity and initiative. Most of the leaders of the federation and most of its representatives in outside bodies, such as the government, the parliament and the trade unions, are in fact elderly.

The collectives promote both systematic group leisure activities and personal hobbies. They organize study groups and art classes which attract the aging women, especially. The main emphasis is on cultural activities and not on light recreation. Gardening, photography, cultivation of arts and crafts, stamp-collecting, and reading are the most popular hobbies. Development in this sphere is on the whole slow and inadequate.

The reassessment of policy towards aging has brought about a certain redefinition of the division of tasks between the family and communal institutions. As noted above, combined care by communal institutions and by relatives works well except in cases of long infirmity and an early onset of senility. There is, besides, the problem of old people without children or near relatives in the collective. The collectives have tried to solve these problems in different but complementary ways: to develop additional communal services which will supplement the family and delay as far as possible the need for transfer to a hospital or nursing home, and to build up suitable institutions for cases of severe mental and physical deterioration. The collectives put the main emphasis on enlargement of communal services and resort to the institutional solution mainly in cases needing personal care which cannot be dealt with within the framework of the community.

The collectives have started to provide domiciliary services such as special nursing and home care for their aged. Some collectives keep a special nurse or social worker who is in charge of old people in the community. Her main task is to help the families whenever the burden becomes too heavy and to provide substitute aid to old people who have no close relatives in the collective. Even some assistance from the nurse will very often relieve the strain and enable the relatives to carry on with their duties. Domiciliary services defer the necessity of maximum nursing care.

There is some experimentation with new types of dwelling for the aged as well. Some collectives set up old parents in an independent small flat directly adjoining that of their children. Other collectives favor an arrangement of segregation by age. Planners feel that they can provide various services more economically and more effectively when the aged are concentrated in one area, easily accessible to the center. In addition, these planners assert that concentration of people with similar life experiences and perspectives enhances their social interaction.[20]

The Collective Movement is now seriously considering the development of an inter-collective old-age insurance scheme which will pay each member a regular pension on retirement. The pensions are to go to the collective and contribute toward the maintenance of aging members. The scheme will enable retired workers to continue to be at least partially self-support-

[20] I. Rosow, "Retirement Housing and Social Integration." (Mimeographed.)

ing and will enhance their feeling of security and independence.[21] It is hoped that the collectives will be able to put aside part of this money for the development of comprehensive old-age services.

Underlying the institutional reorganization is an ideological reorientation. There is a growing awareness that the basic difficulties inherent in aging in the collectives are directly related to the overemphasis on youth, on work, and on productivity. There are some signs of the emergence of a more balanced, more flexible, and developmental view of life as well as a more realistic conception of the potentialities and limitations of planning.

[21] D. Knani, *Batei Midoth Israel* (Sifriat Poalim, 1960), pp. 165–167.

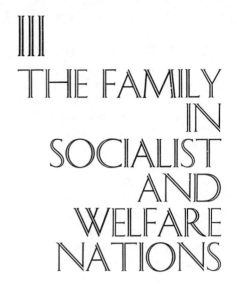

THE FAMILY IN SOCIALIST AND WELFARE NATIONS

In this section we shall look at the family in several social-ist and welfare countries, all of which are committed, to a greater or lesser extent, to modifying the nuclear family. Because the creation of circumstances that permit the full participation of women in the work force is basic to this commitment, child care has been an area of primary con-cern. By providing facilities that allow mothers to work on a full-time basis, the state not only realizes its goal of female employment but also is in a position to socialize children more effectively and to eliminate differential achievement attributable to home environment.

Bronfenbrenner's article serves well as an introduction to this topic because it is concerned with the Soviet Union, a nation that has long been interested in familial modification. In what is perhaps one of the most compre-hensive, though brief, treatments of the subject, Bronfen-brenner delineates shifts in governmental policy from the time of the Revolution to the present. He points out the mistake of those who have seen the Soviets' returning to a traditional family form, and indicates that while the postrevolutionary policy of trying to do away with the nuclear family has been abandoned, it has been replaced by a policy that is still bound to removing most functions from the nuclear family, especially in the sphere of child rearing, but in other areas as well. What Russia has is not a communal family; it is an interesting intermediary form between the nuclear family as we know it and the kibbutz family. In ideal form, if not in reality, however, it is closer to the latter.

The chapter from Jan Myrdal's *Report from a Chinese Village* represents a genre very different from anything included up to this point. Myrdal spent a month late in 1962 living in a northern Chinese village and recording what its people told him about their experiences. Thus, this is not the research report of a social scientist or a philosopher's utopia, but rather a picture of women's life in a Chinese commune drawn from the words of a female member.

In judging the advances China has made in altering family form and the position of women, we must always keep in mind just how far it has had to come. The existence of most married Chinese women prior to the Revolution was little better than that of indentured servants. They were brought into the husband's family for two purposes: to breed and to work. They had virtually no rights. Among the important dimensions of the Chinese communal movement is that it has attempted to recognize the status and rights of women. It provides them with a new degree of independence by paying them for their work. More important is the commitment to the development of equalitarian relations in the home. Husband and wife are both to work and both to bring wages home. What few domestic chores remain are to be shared, and the children are reared communally. To be sure, much of this is more a goal than a reality, but it shows the direction in which Chinese communes are moving.

The succeeding article contains much material relevant for our understanding of alternative family forms. Haavio-Mannila presents data on the social and economic position of women in the Scandinavian countries and in the Soviet Union as well. By distinguishing between the position of women in the economic sphere and the position of women in the domestic sphere, Haavio-Mannila shows how the two need not be directly related. Finnish women have a high degree of economic emancipation but are still subjected to a traditional division of labor at home. Thus, they are doubly burdened; they work and still have major housekeeping responsibilities. So we see that changing the economic opportunity structure for women without at the same time modifying attitudes on housework may create new injustices while eradicating old ones.

Scandinavia should be of particular interest to readers in the United States, for it is these countries that are serving as models of social change for many of today's critics. The changes we are seeing, for example, the beginning of a day care center movement, take their inspiration from Scandinavia.

7

THE CHANGING SOVIET FAMILY*

Urie Bronfenbrenner

At a time when Soviet society appears to be experiencing significant changes, many of them in the direction of greater liberalization, it is particularly important to examine the basic institutions of that society to see whether these too are undergoing similar transformation. If they are, then this development suggests the occurrence of a genuine social change. Conversely, if no modification is evident, one might question the depth and permanence of the broader trend. Finally, if transformation is apparent, but runs counter to the general tendency, one might predict imminent retrenchment or even reversal of policy.

We shall examine one basic institution, the contemporary Soviet family, in an effort to determine what continuities or changes may be observed, both in ideology and actual patterns of living, during the past decade. The primary sources of information are Soviet and Western writings, supplemented by the observations of the author in the course of three visits to the USSR in 1960, 1961, and 1963.

THE SOVIET FAMILY IN ITS FIRST FORTY YEARS

Before turning to the current scene, it is useful to review the developments that have taken place in the Russian family from the early years of the communist regime through the Stalin era. English translations of the basic Soviet documents through 1944 appear in Schlesinger's monograph[1] (1949), which also contains an important interpretive essay. Other treatments, some of them extending up to the current period and dealing with actual patterns of life as well as official policy, include Hindus[2] (1949),

REPRINTED with the permission of the publisher and the author from Donald Brown, Editor: *The Role and Status of Women in the Soviet Union* (New York: Teachers College Press), © 1968.

* This paper is based in part on information gathered in the course of a research project on "Child Rearing in Three Cultures," supported by a grant from the National Science Foundation. The author wishes to express his appreciation to Mrs. Serena A. Weaver for her invaluable assistance in the preparation of the manuscript.

[1] Rudolf Schlesinger, *The Family in the U.S.S.R.*, Vol. I of *Changing Attitudes in Soviet Russia* (London: Routledge & Kegan Paul, 1949).

[2] Maurice Hindus, "The Family in Russia," in Ruth Nanda Anshen, *The Family: Its Function and Destiny* (New York: Harper & Row, 1949), pp. 111–124.

Inkeles[3] (1949), Inkeles and Bauer[4] (1959), Mosley[5] (1959), and Pierre[6] (1960). On the basis of this material, the present writer discerns three major developments in the pre-Khrushchev era.

1. The Attempt to Implement
Communist Conceptions

During the twenty years immediately following the Revolution, the Soviet government sought to bring into being the ideas of the family developed by Marx, Engels, and Lenin.[A] Central to these conceptions was the emancipation of the woman from subordinate status and household chores and her active involvement in economic and political life. To achieve this goal, the government relied principally on two measures: first, it promulgated legislation guaranteeing women equal status in all walks of life, freeing them from traditional marriage bonds by permitting marriage and divorce on an almost casual basis, and granting freedom of abortion. Second, it sought to provide communal facilities for the upbringing of children, as well as for dining, cooking, and performing other household chores.

The inspiration and intent of both of these policies are reflected in two statements, one by Engels and the other by Lenin, which are central to an understanding of communist attitudes toward the family, not only in the 1920s and early 1930s, but, as we shall see, also in the late 1950s and early 1960s.

> . . . the first condition for the liberation of the wife is to bring
> the whole female sex back into public industry . . . and this

---

[3] Alex Inkeles, "Family and Church in the Postwar U.S.S.R.," *Annals of the American Academy of Political and Social Sciences,* CCLXIII (May 1949): 33–44.

[4] Alex Inkeles and Raymond A. Bauer, *The Soviet Citizen* (Cambridge, Mass.: Harvard University Press, 1959).

[5] Philip E. Mosely, "The Russian Family: Old Style and New," in Anshen, *op. cit.,* 2d ed. (1959), pp. 104–122.

[6] André Pierre, *Les Femmes en Union Soviétique* [Women in the Soviet Union] (Paris: Spes, 1960).

[A] Professor Kent Geiger suggested that one reason for the fluctuation of the ideological status of the Soviet family was that Marx and Engels were never able to decide whether the family belonged to the "superstructure" or the "base" of the society. He then pointed out that the confused position of the family in the larger theory of Marx and Engels constituted part of the ambiguous legacy inherited by the Bolshevik leaders. It led in turn to protracted debate during the 1920s about the family and what it should be during the "transition period" as well as in the future communist society. Leaders in the debate were Kollontai and Lunacharski on the left, and Smidovich and Iaroslavski on the right. Lenin had his opinions, tending toward conservatism, but they were hardly canonized and not even published until some time after his death. During the 1920s there was no official line taken by the party about the family. The guiding maxims were two: family life at the moment was a private affair, of no concern to the party; and what it would become in the future was still unclear, a moot question.

in fact demands the abolition of the monogamous family as the economic unit of society.[7]

We are establishing communal kitchens and public eating-houses, laundries and repairing shops, infant asylums, kinder-gartens, children's homes, educational institutes of all kinds. In short, we are seriously carying out the demand in our programme for the transference of the economic and educational functions of the separate household to society.[8]

It is apparent that during the first two decades of Soviet power, the policies of the government toward the family were guided by the communist theory of the withering away of the family as an economic and educational institution. How successful was this attempt?

2. The De Facto Disruption of the Soviet Family

There seems to be general agreement that the measures adopted by the government had comparatively little direct effect as such. Although certain segments of the population, the urban intelligentsia, for instance, wel-comed the liberalization of marriage and divorce, the populace at large continued to adhere to deeply-ingrained traditional customs. The communal facilities were as yet insufficient in quality and quantity to make a significant impact.

Nevertheless, during the first two decades of Soviet power, an appreciable breakdown in the unity and traditional values of the Russian family did take place. What brought about the change was not so much government policy vis à vis the family per se as the broader social and economic crises taking place in the early years of the regime. The chaos and strain of the Revolution and the civil war, the subsequent collectivization, famine, and purges, together with the concomitant mass migration to the new industrial centers, led almost inevitably to the weakening and disruption of the family, both as an economic and as a psychological unit. Husbands, wives, and children were separated geographically, socially, and emotionally by the enforced diversity of their lives. In addition, both the rapidly increasing demands for manpower in the society as a whole, and the decreasing stand-ard of living and value of wages drove increasing numbers of women out of the home into the fields and factories—by 1940, they constituted 38 percent of the total labor force. Finally, family life was further disrupted by heavy and irregular work schedules, for example, the continuous five-day week of the early 1930s with its abolishment of Sunday as a common day off.

It is impressive evidence of the strength of traditional institutions that

[7] Quoted by Schlesinger, op. cit., p. 10.
[8] Ibid., p. 79.

Russian patterns of marriage and family life maintained some stability despite these sweeping changes. For example, Inkeles and Bauer (1959), in their study of some 700 displaced Soviet citizens, found that over 75 percent of their sample had married within the same social class (manual vs. nonmanual workers) and over 85 percent had selected a mate of his own nationality (Russian vs. Ukrainian). More significantly, these percentages showed no appreciable change over marriage dates ranging from 1900 to 1945. Marked increases were observed over this period, however, in the percentages of women working—particularly those of child-bearing age. Even more striking was the consistent reduction in the size of families beginning in the period before the Revolution and persisting through the youngset family members in the sample, who were twenty-five years old or under in 1950. A similar trend is apparent in the only figures on national birth rate available for this period—47.0 for 1913 in comparison to 31.3 for 1940.[9]

Perhaps the clearest indication of serious problems in Soviet family life by the 1930s is found in the sharp turnabout in party and government policy that occurred in the mid-1930s and ushered in what has been called a return to traditional conceptions of the family.

3. Strengthening the Soviet Family

The first omen of the new era was the adoption, in 1935, of a new law making parents legally responsible for the misbehavior of their children. Shortly thereafter, the Soviet press embarked on a propaganda campaign inveighing against laxity and irregularity in sexual relations, condemning abortion, criticizing "light-minded" attitudes toward the family and family obligations, and glorifying the virtues of motherhood and fatherhood. Then in 1936, the government promulgated a new decree declaring abortions illegal, giving special allowances to mothers of large families, extending the network of maternity homes, nurseries, and kindergartens, and introducing stricter regulations in marriage and divorce. These provisions were substantially strengthened and extended eight years later in the Family Law of 1944, which stipulated that only registered marriages had the force of law, outlawed paternity suits (thus creating a factual state of illegitimacy, while freeing the man from legal or economic liability for children born out of wedlock), increased subsidies to mothers beginning with the third child, conferred decorations on those having five or more children, required compulsory organization of nurseries and kindergartens in all existing and projected enterprises employing women on a mass scale, levied a tax on all unmarried persons of child-bearing age as well as parents of small families, and finally, considerably complicated divorce procedures

[9] *Narodnoe khoziaistvo SSSR v 1961 godu* [National economy of the USSR in 1961] (Moscow: Gosstatizdat, 1962), p. 28.

by requiring judicial action at two separate levels, instructing the court to inquire into the motives for seeking divorce and to attempt reconciliation of the spouses, and raising fees to an almost prohibitive level.

The emphasis on the importance of the family contained in the new decrees implied a rejection of the earlier ideological commitment to the eventual "dying out" of the family as a major social institution. In fact the recantation took place immediately upon the promulgation of the 1936 legislation. In a commentary on the new laws published in *Pod znamenem marksizma*, the philosophical organ of the Communist Party, a prominent Soviet publicist, Svetlov, attacked a 1929 treatise on the family by a leading Soviet sociologist, Volfsson. Comrade Volfsson, Svetlov charged, was guilty of "crude mistakes and misinterpretations" in asserting that "Socialism brings the end of the family."

> Comrade Volfsson's book says that during the transition period the withering away of the family begins already, with the introduction of communal education of the children, the participation of women in production, the organization of communal feeding, etc. But since the State is temporarily unable to take upon itself these family functions, it is forced artificially to delay this disintegration of the family, to keep this institution in being for a time. During the period of transition, according to Volfsson, the family is rotting, but the State is artificially preserving this ruin, "the State is forced to conserve the family."
>
> Comrade Volfsson considers that the family will be superfluous under socialism because society will completely take over the education of the children, as a result of which process "family functions will become atrophied."
>
> But where did Comrade Volfsson find it that husband and wife will be completely eliminated from child education under socialism? We have already shown above how great a part the new socialist family plays in the education of the children.
>
> . . . This by no means implies that a new family is not taking the place of the old one. We have quite clearly shown above that a new socialist family is taking the place of the old.[10]

It is noteworthy that in a footnote to his own article in the same journal, Volfsson acknowledges his mistake:

> In my book, *The Sociology of Marriage and the Family,* published in 1929, the entirely erroneous thesis is developed that socialism entails the extinction of the family. Considering these ideas harmful I have completely disowned them.[11]

[10] Quoted by Schlesinger, *op. cit.,* p. 346.
[11] *Ibid.,* p. 315 n.

SOME QUESTIONS
OF INTERPRETATION

A number of Western scholars have interpreted the dramatic shift in Soviet policy on the family in the 1930s and 1940s as a return to, and vindication of, an essentially Western conception of the role of the family in society. Confronted by social disorganization, a falling birth rate, and the need for manpower demanded by industrial expansion and the threat and subsequent actuality of war, the Soviet government, so the argument runs, was forced to abandon its revolutionary conceptions of the family and to rebuild the institution in its familiar form. Inkeles, in a much-quoted authoritative analysis published in 1949, describes the Soviet efforts to transfer the functions of child-rearing from the family to society in the following way:

> Soviet experience clearly demonstrated that this could be effected only at the cost of making major and difficult readjustments in other parts of the social system. It also threw into relief the fact that even under conditions of careful planning, there would be many important, unintended and unanticipated consequences generated by such a program of social action. In this case, at least, the costs and difficulties encountered were sufficient to result in abandonment of the effort.[12]

By the late 1940s, the alternative course followed by the Soviet government brought it to a position that Inkeles describes as "very close to that held in many of the states which form Western society."[13] He concludes:

> . . . the development of Soviet policy on the family constitutes a striking affirmation of the importance of that institution as a central element in the effective functioning of the type of social system which is broadly characteristic of Western civilization.[14]

It is the view of the present author, admittedly with the benefit of hindsight, that the foregoing interpretation of the course of Soviet policy during the late 1930s and 1940s is not fully correct. Specifically, it is at least questionable:

1. Whether Soviet acts and statements during this period, when regarded in their entirety, are accurately described as representing an abandonment of the earlier position.
2. Whether the role of the family defined by the new legislation is properly characterized as being "very close to that held in many of the states

[12] Inkeles, *op. cit.*, p. 38.
[13] *Ibid.*, p. 36.
[14] *Ibid.*, p. 38.

which form Western society" or as a "central element" in a social system of the "type . . . which is broadly characteristic of Western civilizations."

These points are raised primarily not as historical issues, but as considerations basic to the main concern of this paper—an understanding of the current status of the family in Soviet society.

Let us first examine the thesis that the role of the family that is revealed in Soviet legislation and public discussion in the period from 1936 to 1944 comes close to Western conceptions. We may take as our point of departure one of the most influential works published during this period, Anton Makarenko's *Book for Parents*.[B] In this volume, which came to be regarded virtually as the Bible of ideal Soviet family life, Makarenko defined the role of the family as follows:

> But our [Soviet] family is not an accidental combination of members of society. The family is a natural collective body and, like everything natural, healthy, and normal, it can only blossom forth in social society, freed of those very curses from which both mankind as a whole and the individual are freeing themselves.
>
> The family becomes the natural primary cell of society, the place where the delight of human life is realized, where the triumphant forces of man are refreshed, where children— the chief joy of life—live and grow.
>
> Our parents are not without authority, either, but this authority is only the reflection of societal authority. The duty of a father in our country towards his children is a particular form of his duty towards society. It is as if our society says to parents:
>
> "You have joined together in good will and love, rejoice in your children and expect to go on rejoicing in them. That is your personal affair and concerns your own personal happiness. Within the course of this happy process you have given birth to new human beings. A time will come when these beings will cease to be solely the instruments of your happiness, and will step forth as independent members of society. For society, it is by no means a matter of indifference what

[B] Discussing this historical development, Professor Geiger said, "Stalin put an end to the debate by completely shutting off discussion at the theoretical level and by initiating the conservative reforms of the years from 1935 to 1944. It is noteworthy that in 'rehabilitating' the family by renaming it a socialist one and calling attention to the importance of child-rearing and parenthood, Stalin had recourse to the aid of Anton S. Makarenko, a pedagogue and youth worker who had little experience with Soviet family life and little knowledge of, or interest in, Marxism, but who was able to dramatize common-sense precepts and to develop a good case on behalf of discipline and order in child-rearing. With good reason, however, there is hardly a reference to Marx or Engels throughout the works of Makarenko, who became on the practical level the foremost Soviet authority on the family."

kind of people they will become. In delegating to you a certain measure of societal authority the Soviet State demands from you the correct upbringing of its future citizens."[15]

It will be recalled that Inkeles based his characterization of the new Soviet conceptions of the family as fundamentally traditional and Western on the fact that the Russian family was once again held responsible for the early care and upbringing of the child. Certainly such responsibility is stipulated in the passage quoted above. But when one speaks of parental functions as being "delegated" and "demanded" by the state, it becomes difficult, in this writer's view, to maintain the position that such a conception comes "very close" to Western views. Yet this same orientation permeates the Soviet interpretation of the 1944 legislation. Witness the following quotation, cited by Inkeles, himself, from an essay on the new law by G. M. Sverdlov, "one of the most prominent Soviet commentators on family law":[16]

> The law takes as its basis the fact that marital and family relations are not only the private concern of individuals, but the concern of the nation as a whole, and aims at regulating these relations in the interests of both the individual and of society as a whole.[17]

Turning next to the question of whether the new Soviet policy represented an abandonment of earlier, more revolutionary conceptions of the family, we must observe first of all that neither the post-Revolutionary, legal liberalization of marriage and divorce nor the writings of Lenin that inspired it were intended to condone moral laxity in marital relations. Witness the following statement of Lenin's views, cited by Clara Zetkin:

> . . . the so-called "new sexual life" of the youth—and sometimes of the old—often seems to me purely bourgeois, an extension of the bourgeois brothels. That has nothing in common with freedom of love as we Communists understand it. You must be aware of the famous theory that in communist society the satisfaction of sexual desires, of love, will be as simple and unimportant as drinking a glass of water.
>
> But will the normal man in normal circumstances lie down in the gutter and drink out of a puddle, or out of a glass with a rim greasy from many lips? But the social aspect is most important of all. Drinking water is of course an individual affair. But in love two lives are concerned, and a third,

---

[15] Anton S. Makarenko, "Kniga dlia roditelei" [A book for parents], *Sochineniia v semi tomakh* [Works in seven volumes], Vol. IV (Moscow: Izdatel'stvo Akademii Pedagogicheskikh Nauk [Academy of Pedagogical Sciences Publishing House], 1957), p. 35. First published in the journal *Krasnaia nov'*, Nos. vii–x, 1937.

[16] Inkeles, *op. cit.*, p. 35.

[17] *Ibid.*, pp. 37–38.

> new life, arises. It is that which gives it its social interest,
> which gives rise to a duty towards the community.[18]

From this passage it is clear that in inveighing against "disorderly sex life" and "a light-minded attitude towards the family and family obligations," the Soviet propaganda and legislation of 1936 were not reversing but rather reiterating a classical communist theme. Moreover, the concluding sentence of the quotation from Lenin highlights the consistency between Lenin's position in the 1920s and that of Makarenko in the 1930s. For both, the family is but the instrument of society and, to use Lenin's phrase, it is the "social interest" which is paramount.

It is from this perspective that one must view the Soviet decrees of 1936 and 1944. And when one does so, he discovers that to characterize the overall aim of the legislation as the strengthening of the family is to confuse means with ends and parts with wholes. Let us recall that, besides stiffening regulations on marriage and divorce, each of these decrees provided incentives for having children, even for unmarried mothers and, what is more, they substantially expanded the network facilities for communal upbringing. The 1936 legislation called for doubling—within three years— the total number of beds in nurseries and tripling the number of places in kindergartens. The Family Law of 1944, as we have already noted, made the provision of such institutions compulsory in all existing enterprises employing women on a mass scale and in all future plans for industrial construction. In short, the same decrees that strengthened the family also strengthened institutions for communal upbringing. The common concern underlying both these measures was the determination of the government, in a period of national crisis, to insure the continuity of Soviet society by maintaining the birth rate and providing for the upbringing of the coming generation. To accomplish this essential end, it exploited both the institutions in the society engaged in the task of child rearing—the family as well as the facilities for communal upbringing.

How did it happen that the regime was now willing to rebuild an institution that it had previously sought to weaken? The answer lies not only in the seriousness of the then-impending crisis, but also in changes that had taken place in the Soviet family itself. These changes are ably documented in the research of Inkeles and Bauer (1959). Working with a sample of Soviet displaced persons, they obtained data on the values of three successive generations of Russians ranging from the pre-Revolutionary through the Stalin period. Their conclusion is best summarized in their own words:

> On the whole . . . we conclude that the pattern of family
> life has changed in directions congruent with the needs and
> demands of the regime. We have the strong impression that
> Soviet parents are bringing up their children pretty much as

[18] Quoted by Schlesinger, op. cit., pp. 76–77.

the regime wants them to. This then is an area in which the regime has won a major victory. . . . We often hear these days the complacent assertion that the strength of a family is proved by the fact that the Soviet regime was finally forced to compromise with it, as it did with religion. Reassuring as this may sound, it can be very misleading. For it is not with the traditional family as it earlier existed that the regime has compromised, and which it has restored to its former standing as a pillar on which the state rests. On the contrary, only the changes in the family that came about over the years, and the fact that in many ways the old family and its value system were transformed and no longer threatened the regime, made the compromise and present truce possible. The regime is no longer fighting the family, it is true, but not because it has been forced to a truce. Rather, the fighting is at an end because in large measure the Soviet family has been captured, and captured from within, by the regime.[19]

It would appear that Svetlow was not entirely wrong in claiming in 1936 that "a new Soviet family is taking the place of the old."

Even though the Soviet family had become "socialized," the fact that by the latter part of the Stalin era it had regained a position of status and value in the Soviet society is of considerable importance. If our analysis is correct, we are confronted at the beginning of the Khrushchev era with a situation in which two institutions hold substantial responsibility for the important task of rearing the next generation, a generation that, according to the gospel of dialectical materialism, would be the first to live under communism.

In this perspective several interesting questions arise about the role of the Soviet family in the Khrushchev and post-Khrushchev era. To whom have the Party and the government entrusted primary responsibility for bringing up the new communist generation: have they regarded the "new Soviet family" as sufficiently imbued with collectivistic values to be able to educate the "new Soviet man," or is this task being delegated to a still more strengthened and expanded system of centers for communal upbringing? Or is the intent to integrate both approaches through a cooperative relationship? Given the growth of both institutions in the pre-Khrushchev era, any resolution of this problem should not be easily achieved. Moreover, if the major factors affecting Soviet policy on the family in the present and future continue to be those that have been most influential in the past, this resolution will be primarily determined not by ideological considerations but by broader social and economic developments. These, then, are the issues on which we focus as we enter upon the final phase of our inquiry into the changing role of the Soviet family.

[19] Inkeles and Bauer, op. cit., p. 230.

NEW DEVELOPMENTS IN
THE KHRUSHCHEV ERA

If one restricts attention to Soviet legislation dealing explicitly with the family, the Khrushchev regime would appear at first glance to have done little to alter the policies of the preceding period. The only significant changes, both occurring in 1955, involved abolishment of the tax on bachelors and parents of small families and the relegalization, but not approbation, of abortion. In line with past developments, both of these reversals of prior Soviet policy appear to have been dictated by practical rather than ideological considerations. With the passing of the war, the extreme pressure for maximizing the birth rate abated, while the resort to "black-market" abortionists apparently resulted in increased rather than reduced medical and economic costs. Accordingly, the Soviet government replaced the legal prohibition by an active propaganda campaign.

It is only when one looks beyond the family itself that one recognizes developments of profound significance for the role and stability of that institution in Soviet society. Although its precursors were apparent earlier, the new era of change may be said to have been ushered in by Khrushchev at the Twentieth Party Congress in 1956, when he announced his educational reform. A central feature of this reform was to be the introduction of new institutions for the communal upbringing of children. The rationale and character of these so-called "schools of the new type" appear in the following excerpts from Khrushchev's report:

> During the Sixth Fixth-Year Plan our country will make a big new step in building up a powerful material and production basis for communist society. But we must also solve the problem of creating the spiritual requisites for completing this historic transition from the lower stage of communism to the higher stage. In this connection I should like to dwell on a question of tremendous social significance relating to the education of our younger generation.
>
> The war left us with a large number of widows on whose shoulders has fallen the difficult task of bringing up children. There are also many families in which both parents work in a factory or office and are able to give only haphazard attention to bringing up their children. In these circumstances, many children are left in the care of relatives or neighbors, and sometimes without supervision at all. A considerable number of children are thus left to themselves, and this not infrequently has serious consequences. Of course, the family and the school were and remain the most important centres of socialist education of the children. But we cannot restrict ourselves to this. . . .
>
> It is evidently desirable to start building boarding schools (some thought should be given to the name) in picturesque suburban localities, in healthy wooded tracts. These schools

should have bright, spacious classrooms, good bedrooms, up-to-date dining halls, well-equipped centers for all kinds of extracurricular activity, creating all the facilities for the all-around physical and mental development of a young citizen of the Soviet land. Children should be enrolled in these boarding schools only at the request of their parents. They will live at the schools, and their parents will visit them on holidays, during vacations or after school hours. Good teachers equal to the high calling of engineers of the souls of the growing generation should be selected for the schools.

The system of fees in these schools should be graded, at least at the beginning. Children whose parents do not earn much or who are burdened by large families should be fully maintained by the state. Parents with higher earnings should pay part of the cost of the education of their children. Finally, some parents could fully cover the outlay made by the state on the education of their children in the boarding schools.

It is difficult to overestimate the immense importance of this system of education. Funds and efforts should not be stinted in this work, for they will be repaid a hundredfold.

We must also get down to solving another big educational problem, that of providing state nursery and kindergarten accommodation for all children of nursery and preschool age whose parents want it. It will take quite some time to solve this problem completely, and we must make a large-scale beginning in the present five-year period. In the rural areas, collective farms as well as government agencies should take part in building and maintaining nurseries and kindergartens. Concern for children and their education is a matter of the people as a whole. Our Soviet society will continue to pay exceptional attention to the communist education of the rising generation.[20]

Three years later, at the Twenty-first Party Congress, Khrushchev made explicit an important economic consideration underlying the new program:

The possibility of educating all children in boarding schools will be opened up in the future and will solve the problem of imparting the communist upbringing to the rising generation. At the same time, millions of women will be released from the household chores of child-rearing and will find productive jobs in the construction of communist society.[21]

[20] Nikita S. Khrushchev, "Otchetnii doklad tsentral'nogo komiteta kommunistich-eskoi partii sovetskogo soiuza" [Report of the Central Committee of the Communist Party of the Soviet Union], *Materialy XX s'ezda KPSS*, [Materials of the XX Congress of the CPSU], Vol. I (Moscow: Gospolitizdat, 1956), 82–83.

[21] Nikita S. Khrushchev, "O kontrol'nykh tsifrakh razvitiia narodnogo khoziaistva SSSR na 1959–1965 gody" [On the control figures of the development of the na-

In private conversations, many Soviet educators and social scientists echoed Khrushchev's views and stressed the psychological and social advantages of communal methods of upbringing. Their principal arguments may be summarized in the following way:

1. Not having received an adequate communist upbringing themselves, many parents lack the qualities of character necessary for proper child-rearing. They are often ignorant of the special technical knowledge and training procedures necessary for furthering the child's physical, mental, and social development.

2. Since families differ in cultural background, unfair advantage is given to some children and disadvantage to others. For example, children of educated parents who have exposed them to books and constructive activities get a head start on their fellows and may progress further in Soviet society; others, who come from deprived homes with parents who offer them little attention, are unduly penalized. The preschool institutions, with their professionally trained staffs, comprehensive equipment, and enriched program, insure an optimal environment for all children.

3. Above all, it is essential that a child be given experience and training in collective living as early as possible, preferably in the first year of life. This cannot be readily accomplished in the family where children are few in number and differ in age. In the nursery they can be organized immediately into groups of age-mates, and given training in sharing and cooperative activity.[22] In this way they learn early to identify themselves with the collective and to subordinate selfish desires to the welfare and productivity of the group.

THE GROWTH OF ENROLLMENTS IN
INSTITUTIONS FOR COMMUNAL UPBRINGING

Following Khrushchev's announcement of the new plan, there began a program of building construction, which led almost immediately to increased enrollments. The rapid rate of growth in preschool institutions since 1956 is reflected in the figures presented in Table 1. During the five-year period from 1956 to 1961, the total number of children six years of age or under who were enrolled in these institutions rose by over two million, compared with a gain of little over 900,000 during the six years immediately preceding (there are no figures available for the intervening

tional economy of the USSR in the years 1959–1965], *Materialy vncocherednogo XXI s'ezda KPSS* [Materials of the special XXI Congress of the CPSU] (Moscow: Gospolitizdat, 1959), p. 51.

22 A more detailed description of these methods and an appraisal of their effects appear in two papers by the author: "The Making of the New Soviet Man," a paper presented at the fiftieth anniversary of the School of Education of the University of Pennsylvania, February, 1964; and "Soviet Methods of Character Education: Some Implications for Research," *American Psychologist*, XVII (1962): 550–564.

TABLE 1
Enrollment in Soviet Institutions for Children
of Preschool Age (in thousands)

Age	1940[a]	1950[b]	1956	1958[a]	1959[a]	1960[a]	1961[a]	Total Population (1959 census)[d]
0–2 years	859.5	776.7	965.0[c]	1,134.9	1,208.4	1,511.2	1,574.2	14,581.0
3–6 years	1,171.5	1,168.8	1,882.0[a]	2,354.1	2,671.1	2,864.1	3,376.2	18,825.0
Total	2,031.0	1,945.5	2,847.0	3,489.0	3,879.5	4,375.3	4,950.4[e]	33,406.0

[a]Cited in *Narodnoye khoziaistvo SSSR v 1961 godu* [National economy of the USSR in the year 1961] (Moscow: Statistika, 1962); pp. 686, 749. In the years 1960–1961 the *yasli* and kindergarten were merged into one preschool institution, the *yasli-sad*. Approximately 251,000 children of 0–2 years, the number cited for 1961 in *Zhenshchiny i deti* (Moscow: Gosstatizdat, 1963), p. 134, have thus been subtracted from the 3–6 year column in 1960 and 1961 and added to the 0–2 year column to make up for the change-over.

[b]Cited in *Zhenshchiny i deti v SSSR* [Women and children in the USSR] (Moscow: Gosstatizdat, 1963) p. 134–135.

[c]Cited in *Public Health in the USSR*, translated from the Russian original (Bethesda, Md.: U.S. Department of Health, Education and Welfare, no date), p. 24.

[d]Cited in *Zhenshchiny i deti SSSR* [Women and children in the USSR] (Moscow: Gosstatizdat, 1961), p. 59.

[e]A recently published source gives the new total for 1962 as 5.6 million and 6.4 million in 1963 (*SSSR v tsifrakh v 1963* [USSR in figures for 1963] [Moscow: Statistika, 1964], p. 192).

years). The sharpest rate of increase has been for infants two years old or under. These have risen by over 600,000 over the five-year period as compared with 183,000 during the preceding six years. Using as a basis for estimate the latest available figures (1959 census) for the total Soviet population at different age levels, we may reasonably infer that, of all Russian children two years of age or under, over 10 percent are now enrolled in preschool institutions. The corresponding percentage for children between three and six years of age rises to 18 percent or higher.

Accompanying the increased enrollments, there have been important developments in the organization of preschool education. Until 1959 the nurseries and kindergartens were separate institutions under different jurisdictions. The former, serving children of two months through three years of age, were under the All-Union Ministry of Health; the latter, designed for ages four through six, were administered by the Ministries of Education of the several republics. In 1959 the Central Committee and the Council of Ministers ordered unification of the two types of institution into single physical units so that children could obtain continuity of care without experiencing a change in setting or personnel. At the same time, administrative responsibility for the new type of combined structure was vested solely in the Ministries of Education of the several republics. Finally, these institutions, called *yasli-sadi* or nursery-kindergartens, were to make available boarding care for children over twelve months old.[23] By 1960, 359,000 children were enrolled in such institutions, 142,000 of them being under three years of age.[24] A year later, these figures had risen to 654,000 and 251,000 respectively.[25]

The new schools have shown a similar growth, which has likewise involved an administrative change. In 1956, the year the program was introduced, there were 56,000 pupils enrolled in boarding schools. In 1958, the new five-year plan called for expansion to provide for 2.5 million children by 1965. By the beginning of the academic year 1960–1961, actual enrollments had increased almost tenfold, to a total of 540,000.[26] In the same year (1960), the Central Committee and Council of Ministers of the USSR announced the widespread adoption of still another school—"the school of the prolonged day." This institution closely resembles the boarding school, the major difference being that children go home at seven in the evening and return the next morning at eight o'clock.[27]

[23] Since breast-feeding is recommended for all children in the first year of life (by·law, working mothers must be granted time off every three and one-half hours for this purpose), the mother ordinarily takes the child home overnight, at least until he is weaned.

[24] These data are taken from *Zhenshchiny i deti v SSSR* [Women and children in the USSR] (Moscow: Gosstatizdat, 1961), p. 157 n.

[25] *Ibid.*, 1963, p. 133 n.

[26] *Ibid.*, p. 163.

[27] For an English translation of Soviet material describing these schools see *Soviet Education*, II, no. 12 (1960): 20–23.

From 1961 on, the enrollment figures published in Soviet sources give only the combined totals for pupils in both boarding schools and schools of the prolonged day. For the academic year 1961–1962, this figure was 1,500,000;[28] for 1962–1963, over 2,000,000.[29] The latter statistic represents more than 4 percent of all children enrolled in Soviet schools during that same year.[30] In reply to a question about the number of children currently attending boarding schools, staff members of the Academy of Pedagogical Sciences cited estimates approaching one million. They also indicated that approximately one-third of all school children were expected to be enrolled in schools of the new type by 1970, and 100 percent by the 1980s.[31]

The actual rate of expansion is likely to depend mainly on the progress of building construction, for there are long waiting lines for every available space in most of these institutions. Although one hears criticisms of the new program, especially from the older generation, most parents are eager to have their children enrolled. Four considerations appear especially relevant:

1. In a society where housing is crowded, wages low, and food prices high (amounting to 70 percent of the family budget), having one's child cared for in an institution has distinct practical advantages. The mother is free to work or to study full-time (thus increasing her immediate or subsequent earning power), there is more space in the apartment, and food costs are appreciably reduced.[32]
2. Over and above economic pressures, many mothers appear genuinely to identify with the communist conception of the woman as an "active participant in productive labor," and hence are motivated to resume work or study as early as possible following the birth of a child.
3. In a nation of working mothers, the nurseries and boarding schools provide a solution for the otherwise difficult problem of providing adequate care for the child while the parents are not at home. The traditional reliance on *babushka* (grandmother) is no longer possible since she too is away at work or going to school.

[28] Cited in *Narodnoe khoziaistvo SSSR v 1961 godu, op. cit.,* p. 676.

[29] Cited in *SSSR v tsifrakh v 1962 godu* [USSR in figures for 1962] (Moscow: Izdatel'stvo "Statistika," 1963), p. 278. In the 1963 edition of *SSSR v tsifrakh,* the number given for the beginning of the 1963–1964 school year is 2.4 million (p. 157).

[30] *Ibid.* For 1963–1964 the corresponding percentage would thus be more than 5 percent.

[31] As a concomitant to the expansion of the program of collective upbringing, the Khrushchev regime developed communal eating facilities. In 1959, the Central Committee and Council of Ministers issued a decree lowering prices in such establishments and prescribing a doubling of their services. (Text in "O dal'neishem razvitii i uluchshenii obshchestvennogo pitaniia" [On the further development and improvement of public "dining rooms"], *Izvestiia,* February 28, 1959, p. 1.)

[32] Although the boarding schools charge modest fees (scaled to income), these are more than balanced by the fact that the institution supplies all food, clothing, equipment, and other material needs.

4. Above all, Soviet parents see the new institutions are offering benefits to the child that cannot be provided by the family or the ordinary day school. These include an enriched diet, special exercises administered by professional personnel, early training in languages, music, and dance, and, especially, the development of skills, working habits, and attitudes that enhance the child's chances of acquiring further education and achieving success in Soviet society. From the Russian point of view, only a selfish parent would deprive his child of the rich opportunities provided by the new program.

A VISION OF THE FUTURE

What will be the consequences for the family of such developments in communal institutions? As if in answer to this very question, a distinguished Soviet academician and economic planner, Stanislav Strumilin, published an essay in 1960 outlining a projection of the future from present trends, with specific attention to the role of marriage and the family in society. His central conceptions are summarized in the following excerpts:

> Under Soviet conditions it is especially noticeable how the lot of the woman worker is being lightened. She can work in one factory, her husband in another, both can eat in a communal dining facility while sending their children to nurseries, kindergartens and boarding schools.
>
> Recognizing that communal forms of upbringing have an unquestionable superiority over all others, we are faced with the task in the immediate years ahead of expanding the network of such institutions at such a pace that within 15–20 years they are available—from cradle to graduation—to the entire population of the country. Every Soviet citizen, upon leaving the maternity home, will be sent to a nursery; from there to a kindergarten maintained day and night; then to a boarding school from which he will enter independent life. . . .
>
> The question arises: will not this kind of early separation of the child from his family be too painful an experience both for parents and for infants who are so dependent on maternal affection?
>
> This question may be answered as follows: the communal organization of upbringing in no sense requires full separation of the child from the parents . . . and surely no one will keep a mother from visiting her children when she is not working, from looking into the children's area, located in the same building in which she works, as often as it is permitted by the established schedule.
>
> The "vitamins of love" are necessary for all children in equal measure . . . but the easiest way to satisfy this need is through the system of communal institutions of upbringing.
>
> The former family is reduced to the married couple . . .

and when these contracted families recognize that it is not sensible to expend so much work on maintaining an independent household just for two people, the family as an *economic* unit having fused with other families and become incorporated into a larger economic collective, will dissolve within the context of the future social commune.[33]

In short, the Soviet people are once again being presented with the prospect of a communist society in Engels' terms, in which the family, as a basic economic and education institution, has withered away. Given the reality of expanding Soviet programs of communal upbringing, is there any possibility that Strumilin's utopian picture may be a realistic one?

LONG LIVE THE SOVIET FAMILY

One line of evidence shedding some light on this question is the public reaction to Strumilin's article. The editors of *Novii Mir,* the popular literary journal in which the essay was originally published, received so many letters from readers that they turned to a prominent psychologist, Viktor N. Kolbanovsky, to summarize the reader reaction and to express his own views on the issues raised. Obviously reflecting opinions expressed in readers' letters, Professor Kolbanovsky challenges Strumilin's position on several counts: he begins by questioning whether it is necessary "to deprive the family of that joy which is given by well-brought-up children."[34] "Already," he points out, "the Soviet work day has been reduced to six or seven hours, and this is only the beginning. . . . When one adds to this the fact that communal services are relieving the family of many household chores, it becomes clear that parents will be having increasing time to spend in bringing up their children."[35] Moreover, the family has certain unique qualifications for this task in the affectional relationship between its members. Finally, "Children would be deprived indeed," Kolbanovsky charges, "if they had to survive solely on miserly 'vitamins of love' without being able to give anything back in return!"[36] He concludes by acknowledging that communal upbringing has its proper and important place in the Soviet way of life, "but this in no sense implies that the family is to be alienated from the process of rearing children. . . . The Party has never considered it possible to supplant the family by society."[37]

[33] Stanislav Strumilin, "Rabochii byt i kommunizm" [The worker's way of life and communism], *Novii Mir,* no. 7 (1960): 206–209.

[34] Viktor N. Kolbanovsky, "Robochii byt i kommunizm," *Novii Mir,* no. 2 (1961): 277.

[35] *Ibid.*

[36] *Ibid.,* p. 278.

[37] *Ibid.*

It is noteworthy that similar views have recently been frequently expressed by Soviet educators and social scientists,[38] Kharchev in 1960 and 1963, Solov'ev in 1962, and Levshin in 1964. At the same time, the popular press reflects both puzzlement and public concern. A columnist discussing salient issues of the day asks: "How shall we be living after five or ten years? . . . Will the family exist under communism, or will families be sending their children to boarding schools?"[39] Similar queries and confusion are reported by the author of an article in *Komsomolskaia Pravda*.[40] A somewhat dramatic article, written by a female observer, appears in *Pravda*. She reports on a visit to a boarding school in Moscow. Under a window, she saw a young mother who, having missed the regular visiting hours, is hoping to catch a glimpse of her son or to hear his voice. Our correspondent finds this incident disturbing:

> Once again my thoughts return to that mother standing beneath the window of the boarding school. I can't get her out of my mind. This is not a bad boarding school. But just the same a mother's heart begins to yearn. Can we really reproach that heart for sentimentality? Of course not. A human being —especially a mother—is so constructed that she longs to warm her own child with her love and to be warmed herself by its side.[41]

An even stronger reaction is reported by Professor Solov'ev in a recent discussion, in book form, of "The Family in Soviet Society" (1962). He quotes a factory worker:

> We have a great need for boarding nurseries, but the fact that my son is becoming alienated from me is so painful that I can't even talk about it. I call him "Sasha, my son." But he just runs away. No! I have to spend at least an hour or two each day with my son. Otherwise it's impossible, otherwise I can't stand it.[42]

[38] Anatolii Kharchev, "Sem'ia i kommunizm" [The family and communism], *Kommunist*, VII (May 1960): 53–63; and "O roli sem'i v kommunisticheskom vospitanii" [On the role of the family in communist upbringing], *Sovetskaia Pedagogika*, V (May 1963): 62–72. See also Nikolai Solov'ev, *Sem'ia v sovetskom obshchestve* [The family in Soviet society] (Moscow: Gospolitizdat, 1962); and A. Levshin, "Mal'chik-muzhchina-otets" [Boy-man-father], *Sem'ia i Shkola* [Family and school], II (1964): 2–5.

[39] G. Mariagin, "U nas na vspol'noi" [On the edge of our land], *Literaturnaia Rossiia*, May 17, 1963, p. 6.

[40] A. Protopopova, "Logika serdtsa" [The logic of the heart], *Komsomolskaia Pravda*, July 7, 1963, p. 2.

[41] E. Kononenko, "Zhivi, rasti, novoe!" [May the new live and thrive], *Pravda*, April 5, 1961, p. 6.

[42] Solov'ev, *op. cit.*, p. 120.

Solov'ev cites the above example as evidence in connection with his point-by-point rejoinder to Strumilin's now famous, if not infamous, essay. Strumilin's arguments, he asserts, testify only to the transfer of certain economic and educational functions of the family. Such transfer, rather than causing the family to fade away, will enable it to flourish. Moreover it is a completely incorrect idea that under communism parents will be "required" to place their children in collective institutions. "In the new Program of our party it is emphasized that children attend such institutions only at the desire of their parents, the desire of the family."[43]

An even stronger case for the family is made in two essays by the prominent Soviet sociologist Kharchev (1960, 1963), who emphasizes the unique, irreplaceable role of parental relationships in developing the emotional life of the child. In this connection he cites results of a Soviet study showing that children brought up exclusively in institutional settings, seemingly under the best physical conditions, risk being deprived of necessary "psychological stimulation."

> By virtue of its specificity, the nonrepeatable nature of the influence of the family on the child, it constitutes an essential factor for normal child rearing. Children brought up without the participation of the family are at far greater risk of one-sided retarded development, than those who are members of family collectives.[44]

Both Solov'ev and Kharchev refer to the attempts of Western sociologists such as Klaus Mehnert and writers, notably George Orwell and Aldous Huxley, to malign communist society by the accusation that it opposes and seeks to eliminate the family as an institution. This accusation, they hasten to point out, is utterly false; testimony to this fact is found in the Program of the Communist Party of the Soviet Union in which problems of strengthening the family are given considerable attention. It was Khrushchev himself who, in his formal report on that Program at the Twenty-second Congress, stated:

> People who say that the significance of the family drops during the transition to communism, and that it disappears with time, are absolutely wrong. In fact, the family will grow stronger under communism. Completely disencumbered of family considerations, family relations will become pure and lasting.[45]

We have it, then, on the basis of the highest authority, that the Soviet family is here to stay.

[43] *Ibid.*

[44] Kharchev, "O roli . . . ," p. 63.

[45] Nikita S. Khrushchev, "O programme kommunisticheskoi partii sovetskogo soiuza" [On the program of the CPSU], *Materialy XXII s'ezda KPSS* [Materials of the XXII Congress of the CPSU] (Moscow: Gospolitizdat, 1961), p. 196.

But the family is not alone. On the basis of the same authority, communal upbringing is also here to stay. In the preceding paragraph, Khrushchev stated:

> The Party attaches importance to the further development of educational establishments—boarding schools, day-care schools, and preschool institutions. Public and family education are not opposed to each other. The family's educational influence upon children should blend with their education by society.[46]

This second theme is equally prominent in the pronouncements of the contemporary professional critics. Each of our champions of the Soviet family in the 1960s—Kolbanovsky, Solov'ev, and Kharchev—emphasize the central importance of collective upbringing in the making of the new Soviet man and the primary responsibility of the family to the larger society.

WHITHER THE SOVIET FAMILY?

These are ideological assertions, however, and we have argued earlier that the major forces determining the actual course of Soviet family life have stemmed not so much from stated policy as from the larger context of social and economic processes and events. What prognosis for the Soviet family would one make from this perspective?

The prospect is somewhat mixed, but one set of factors nevertheless seems to outweigh the other. It is true that certain of the conditions that undoubtedly contributed to the expansion of communal institutions are abating.[c] According to the latest available figures,[47] the excess of 20,000,000 more women than men in the USSR is at least beginning to be reduced, so that in the age-group of thirty-six and under males are actually slightly more numerous than females. The construction of apartment houses has proceeded at a rapid pace,[48] thus relieving crowded living conditions, and, as both Kolbanovsky and Kharchev have stressed, the work day is being shortened, permitting parents to spend more time with their children. At the same time the percentage of women in the labor force has risen slowly but steadily since the mid-1950s and is now at 48 percent.[49] Concomitantly there has been a slight but steady drop in the birth rate: 26.7 in 1950, 25.0 in 1959, 22.4 in 1962—the latest statistics available.[50] Moreover, all of

[46] *Ibid.*

[c] Professor Geiger felt that the actual position of the Soviet family had begun to stabilize and would adjust with the economic progress toward shorter working hours, increase of dwelling space in new apartments and houses, and an increase in "gadgets" to lighten the number of hours of work, shopping, cooking, and cleaning, at home.

[47] *Vestnik statistiki* [Statistical news], 1964, no. 2, 87.

[48] *Narodnoe khoziaistvo* [National economy], 1961, p. 613.

[49] *Vestnik statistiki*, 1964, no. 2, 87–95.

[50] *Vestnik statistiki*, 1963, no. 8, 91.

the tendencies appear to be appreciably more marked in the cities than in rural areas, and it is in the cities that facilities for communal upbringing are primarily located.[51]

Finally, the urban population of the USSR has been growing at a rapid rate: it was 33 percent in 1939, 44 percent in 1954, 51 percent in 1962,[52] and it can be confidently expected to continue. Under these circumstances, we can expect all of the preceding tendencies to be intensified. To state the issue substantially, the forces that tend to separate the family and encourage utilization of communal facilities are those associated with urbanization, and if there is any one trend that is pronounced in Soviet society today, it is this one.

Wither the Soviet family? Will it wither or flourish? It is fitting that our final answer to this question be stated by a Soviet citizen and a woman. She is the same *Pravda* correspondent who could not get out of her mind the memory of a mother waiting longingly beneath the window of her son's boarding school. To allay her anxiety, our lady journalist turns to fantasy:

> And you know what I'm dreaming about? After all, it's all right to dream, isn't it?
>
> A house. . . . In the house families are living. Next door or not far away there is a building in which a boarding school complex is situated. Children from nursery to senior high school age spend their entire day there, but in the evening, when their parents come home from work, they meet with their children. On those evenings when the parents are busy with civic obligations or go to the theater, the children remain in their boarding school. They stay there too when Mother goes to a hospital or travels somewhere in connection with her job. . . .
>
> I know that this is the dream of many and many a mother.
> . . .
> Perhaps, when we are more prosperous, when we build communism, we shall live exactly so![53]

Yes, perhaps, exactly so.

---

[51] See *Public Health in the USSR: A Statistical Handbook* [English translation] (Bethesda, Md.: U.S. Department of Health, Education and Welfare, no date), pp. 24, 92.

[52] *SSSR v tsifrakh v 1962 godu,* pp. 9–10. It should be noted that the figure for 1939 is not exactly comparable to the other figures because of the border changes following World War II.

[53] Kononenko, *op. cit.,* p. 6.

Bibliography

Bronfenbrenner, Urie. "The Making of the New Soviet Man." Paper presented at the fiftieth anniversary of the School of Education of the University of Pennsylvania, February, 1964.

―――. "Soviet Methods of Character Education: Some Implications for Research," American Psychologist, XVII (1962): 550–564.

Geiger, Kent, and Alex Inkeles. "The Family in the U.S.S.R.," The Journal of Marriage and the Family, XIV (1956): 397–404.

Hindus, Maurice. "The Family in Russia," in Ruth Nanda Anshen, The Family: Its Function and Destiny. New York: Harper & Row, 1949.

Inkeles, Alex. "Family and Church in the Postwar U.S.S.R.," Annals of the American Academy of Political and Social Science, CCLXIII (May 1949): 33–44.

―――― and Raymond A. Bauer. The Soviet Citizen. Cambridge, Mass.: Harvard University Press, 1959.

Juviler, P. "Marriage and Divorce," Survey, no. 48 (1963): 104–117.

Kharchev, Anatolii. "Sem'ia i kommunizm" [The family and communism], Kommunist, VII (May 1960): 53–63.

―――. "O roli sem'i v kommunisticheskom vospitanii" [On the role of the family in communist upbringing], Sovetskaia Pedagogika, V (May 1963): 62–72.

Khrushchev, Nikita S. "O kontrol'nykh tsifrakh razvitiia narodnogo khoziaistva SSSR na 1959–1965 godu" [On the control figures of the development of the national economy of the USSR in the years 1959–1965], in Materialy vneocherednogo XXI s'ezda KPSS [Special materials of the XXI Congress of the CPSU]. Moscow: Gospolitizdat, 1959.

―――. "Oh programme kommunisticheskoi partii sovetskoo soiuza" [On the program of the CPSU], in Materialy XXII s'ezda KPSS. Moscow: Gospolitizdat, 1961.

―――. "Otchetnii doklad tsentral'nogo komiteta kommunisticheskoi partii sovetskogo soiuza" [Report of the Central Committee of the Communist Party of the Soviet Union], XX s'ezda Kommunisticheskoi Partii Sovetskogo Soiuza, Vol. I. Moscow: Gospolitizdat, 1956.

Kolbanovsky, Viktor N. "Rabochii byt i kommunizm" [The worker's way of life and communism], Novii Mir, no. 2 (1961): 276–282.

Kononenko, E. "Zhivi, rasti, novoe!" [May the new live and thrive], Pravda, April 5, 1961.

Korolev, Yu. A. "The Integration of Morality and Law in Marital and Family Relations," Current Digest of the Soviet Press, XVI, no. 11 (1964): 10–13.

Kushner, P. I. (ed.). Selo Viriatino v proshlom i nastoiashchem [The village of Viryatino in past and present]. Moscow: Izdatel'stvo Akademii Nauk SSSR [Publishing House of the USSR Academy of Sciences], 1958.

Levshin, A. "Mal'chik-muzhchina-otets" [Boy-man-father], Sem'ia i Shkola, II (1964): 2–5.

Makarenko, Anton S. "Kniga dlia roditelei" [A book for parents], Sochineniia v semi tomakh, Vol. IV. Moscow: Izdatel'stvo Akademii Pedagogicheskikh Nauk [Academy of Pedagogical Sciences], 1957.

Mariagin, G. "U nas na vspol'noi" [On the edge of our land], *Literaturnaia Rossiia,* May 17, 1963, pp. 5–6.

Mosely, Philip E. "The Russian Family: Old Style and New," in Ruth Nanda Anshen, *The Family: Its Function and Destiny,* 2nd ed. New York: Harper & Row, 1959.

Narodnoe khoziaistvo SSSR v 1961 godu [National economy of the USSR in 1961]. Moscow: Gosstatizdat, 1962.

"O dal'neishem razvitii i uluchshenii obshchestvennogo pitaniia" [On the further development and improvement of public welfare], *Izvestiia,* February 28, 1959.

Pierre, André. *Les femmes en Union Soviétique* [Women in the Soviet Union]. Paris: Spes, 1960.

Programme of the Communist Party of the Soviet Union. Moscow: Foreign Languages Publishing House, 1961.

"Prolonged-Day Schools," *Soviet Education,* II, no. 2 (1960): 20–23.

Protopopova, A. "Logika serdtsa" [Logic of the heart], *Komsomolskaia Pravda,* July 7, 1963.

Public Health in the USSR: A Statistical Handbook [English translation]. Bethesda, Md.: U.S. Department of Health, Education and Welfare (no date).

Schlesinger, Rudolf. *The Family in the U.S.S.R.,* Vol. I of *Changing Attitudes in Soviet Russia: Documents and Readings.* London: Routledge & Kegan Paul, 1949.

Solov'ev, Nikolai. *Sem'ia v sovetskom obshchestve* [The family in Soviet society]. Moscow: Gospolitizdat, 1962.

Spravochnik zhenshchiny-rabotnitsy [Handbook for the woman worker]. Moscow: Propizdat, 1963.

SSSR v tsifrakh v 1962 godu i v 1963 godu. Moscow: Izdatel'stvo "Statistika," 1963 and 1964.

Strumilin, S. "Rabochii byt i kommunizm" [The worker's way of life and communism], *Novii Mir,* no. 7 (1960): 203–220.

Vestnik statistiki [Statistical news], no. 8 (1963); no. 2 (1964).

Zhenshchiny i deti v SSSR [Women and children in the USSR]. Moscow: Gosstatizdat, 1961, 1963.

8

LI KUEI-YING, WOMAN PIONEER, AGED 32

Jan Myrdal

I haven't much to tell. I haven't many experiences. I was born into a farming family. I grew up in the country and have never been anything but just a country woman.

We moved to Yenan in 1950. I don't remember anything of our life in Hengshan. But my father, Li Yiu-hua, and my mother say that they worked for a landowner, and that, though they worked hard, they did not have enough to eat. There were six of us in the family when we moved: Father, Mother and four children. Father carried two worn quilts and a felt rug on his back. I walked and walked, and I was so tired that I cried. When we reached Yenan, we still had to work for a landowner. Father worked for Li Hsiu-tang's family. Then he broke new ground for himself up on the slopes. Mother looked after our pig, and I plucked grass.

I don't remember exactly what year that was, but we children worked too. We worked in Father's labor group. He had organized one. When Hu Tsung-nan was coming with his troops, Uncle took us children with him to Ansai. That was a week before the enemy occupied Liu Ling. Father and Mother went somewhere else. In Ansai, we lived with another of Mother's brothers. It was a small village of four or five households. When the K.M.T. troops finally came there, all the villagers were afraid. They hid all the young girls and women. They were put into abandoned caves and the entrances blocked up with bushes and branches. In that way they tried to protect them from the soldiers.

Now all we children were living in Ansai and we ate lots. The soldiers plundered Uncle, too, and he had difficulties. When the guerrillas came that way, he got out some corn and gave it to them; but when Hu Tsung-nan's troops came he didn't give them anything, but hid everything from them.

One day, when the troops came to the village, my little brother and I were ill. We had high temperatures with bleeding at the nose and mouth and diarrhea. Uncle's only child was ill too. One of Uncle's female relations was staying with us in the cave to look after us and Uncle. The woman's husband was a stretcher-bearer for the guerrillas. She was living with Uncle, as she had been left alone in the village. Now she was to look after us children. That is why she was not hidden when the soldiers came. They

FROM Jan Myrdal, *Report from a Chinese Village,* Maurice Michael, trans. Copyright © 1965 by William Heinemann Ltd. Reprinted by permission of Pantheon Books, a Division of Random House, Inc., William Heinemann Ltd., and the author.

stood outside the cave and told us to come out. We replied: "All those who are well are away, it is only we ill ones left." Then they asked what illness we had. "It's catching." At that they took two paces back. Then they said: "Those who are not ill must come out, otherwise we shall shoot." After that Uncle and the woman stepped outside. They did not bother with Uncle, but they took the woman away with them. Two hours later she came back. Her face was quite gray then, and she was quite silent. She just sat and sat and never said a word. That night her husband came. They sat side by side for a while, then they stood up and walked out, in the middle of the night. No one has heard of them since. No one knows where they went. They just walked out into the dark.

In July, we children went back to Liu Ling. Uncle had no more corn to give us and our parents had already returned. Father had moved across to this side of the village. The whole village was in great disorder. Many families had disappeared and their caves were abandoned. Everything had been smashed, cooking stoves, windows, everything had been destroyed. Everyone was depressed and unhappy. We had breakfast, but no dinner. The corn had been growing in the fields, but the troops had cut the maize before it had had time to ripen and used it as fodder for their horses. Sometimes they had set fire to it. At night, the fields would burn. In the end people became quite indifferent. It was as if nothing mattered any longer. No one went out to the fields any more. Not even to the fields high up on the hillside. Nobody worked. People just lay on their backs and slept. It was as if people no longer wanted to live.

In the autumn, there was almost no harvest to get in. We had no hope for the future. That winter Mother and I did washing for the troops. In that way we survived. Father had no work and it was difficult for him. That was the first time in his life he hadn't worked, and he was so upset. He wasn't accustomed to not working.

In March or April 1948, Hu Tsung-nan withdrew. We then had no grain at all. Father went to Lochuan to fetch seed-corn. My two younger brothers were working in the fields although they were very young. Father went back to Lochuan to fetch more corn. This he sold. He carried the sacks on a carrying-pole. He kept on doing this right till the maize could be harvested. Then he stopped carrying grain from Lochuan. The harvest that year was not too bad. I don't remember exactly when it was, but I think it was the year after that that Father organized a labor group for mutual help. In this the families worked for each other and helped each other. Our family was very poor, and I used to go up on to the hill and pluck grass for our pig. I was also supposed to look after the goats and the group's cattle.

In 1951, we were told that the party school in Yenan was having a training course for female ganbus. It was said that as half the population consisted of women, trained women were needed as well. Our labor group for mutual help was now to be turned into a farmer's cooperative. It was

Father who forced that through. It was the first of its kind and it was an experiment. The labor group for mutual help told the party school about me, and I was accepted and sent off to attend the course and study for six months. Ever since I had been small, I had dreamed of being able to learn to read and write. I had dreamed daydreams of becoming a student. Yet when they talked with me and told me that I had got permission to go to the party school, I became worried. Because what could a farm girl learn at school? I was worried about the housework too: the spring sowing was about to start and there was so much that ought to be seen to at home.

When I got to the school, I met a lot of women and men there. After a couple of weeks, I had got accustomed to being in school. The main object was for us to learn to read and write. To begin with, it was rather difficult for me to live a collective life, but afterwards it went quite all right. I decided to learn all that I could. Now that I had managed to get to a school I was not going to lose a minute. I thought of how things were in the new society and how they had been under Hu Tsung-nan's occupation and I promised myself that, when I was finished with the school, I would organize all the women in the village for this new life, and I read seriously.

At the school, I got up as early as in the village. First, we had a lesson of forty minutes, when our homework was corrected. Then, after a short break, we had another lesson, which was either arithmetic or Chinese. At eight o'clock we had breakfast. We usually got steam bread and vegetables. Then we had three lessons of arithmetic and Chinese. We had fifteen minutes' interval between each lesson. Then we had a rest period of one and a half hours. After that a further three lessons of arithmetic and Chinese. Then we had dinner. We used to get steamed millet and vegetables. Once a week we had a meat dish. This, of course, was better food than we were accustomed to at home, but we needed it, because we were working hard and had to learn everything at once. After dinner, we had ninety minutes' prep. After that we did different kinds of personal activities. We did not have any political studies. This was a course at which we were to learn to read. In the evenings we used to sing and discuss things. We learned lots of songs and talked a lot about our home villages and all the things that could be done. We all knew that we must learn to read as soon as possible. Six of us women shared a room. I still see a lot of two of them; they live near by; but I have lost touch with the others. We were free on Sundays. I used to go home to the village then and help in the fields. I was needed there too.

That time at the party school was the decisive time of my life. It was then I realized what I must do with my life. I came back to Liu Ling in July 1951. I could then read and write, and I took part in the autumn harvest and, in the winter, I began organizing the women to study. When I got back, the women said: "We didn't think grown-ups could learn to read and write, but you have." Because of that, the younger women now wanted to learn to read too, and I told them all how good it was to be able to read and write; that she who could read could see; and she who couldn't was blind.

That winter I taught ten women to read and write a hundred characters each. That isn't enough to be able to read a newspaper or such, but it is enough to be able to write simple accounts and receipts and to keep notes. They have gone on with it since, but it has been difficult for them. They can't read much more now after ten years, though I have been working with them the whole time.

I continued studying on my own. I got hold of old books of legends which I read. I swotted up more characters; I read newspapers and began reading simple new stories. In 1952, I married. That was in August and I was very happy. It was a marriage of free will. We had met at the party school and fallen in love with each other. He was attending a different course. When I told Mother that I was in love and wanted to get married, she said nothing at all, but Father said: "If it's so that you really want to, then I don't intend to oppose it."

There were three labor groups in the farmers' cooperative in 1953. Two of men and one of women. I was chosen leader of the women's group. At the meeting, the women said: "She is young and hard-working and she can read." So I thought that, if they had such faith in me, I must show that I was worthy of their opinion of me. That I must work much harder than before. I wanted to get the women as a group moving. I wanted to get them to break away from the past. I was thinking of the time when Hu Tsung-nan had occupied the area. There was a cavalry regiment quartered here in Liu Ling then. Its duties were to track down and capture deserters. They shot the deserters in our potato plot. Every day I used to stand by my cooking stove in the cave and see them shoot deserters down there. I thought then that that must never be allowed to happen again. That we women must all get together to see that it never happened again.

That winter I opened a winter school. We had lessons in the school and in the homes of Shi Yü-chieh and Li Hai-kuei, who had large caves. We helped the women to make shoes and clothes and to improve their agricultural tools. We gave them lessons in feeding poultry and in spinning. We had discussions after the lessons. We tried to get the women to tell us themselves what things had been like before, and how it was now, and how it ought to be in the future. For example, they said: "My feet were bound so that I could not walk. In the old society, a woman was not supposed to go beyond the threshold of her home for the first three years of her marriage. We weren't allowed to eat on the kang, but had to sit on a stool when we ate, and if my parents had decided to marry me off with a cur, then I had to be content with a cur. But now you are allowed to see your husband before you marry, and you can refuse to marry him if you don't like the look of him. The old society was bad and the new is good." We discussed whether women are men's equals or not, and most said: "Within the family, man and woman are equal. We help the men when they work in the fields and they should help us in the house." But many of the older women said: "Women are born to attend to the household. A woman cannot work in the fields. That can't be helped. It is just that men and women are born different. A person is born either a man or a woman. To work in the fields or in the house." We had long discussions. The young ones were all on the side of equality and freedom. It had now become quite usual with our generation for husband and wife to discuss the family's problems and decide about them together. Women now no longer work just in the house; they also work in the fields and earn their own money. But the men of the older generation still say: "What does a woman know? Women know nothing! What's a woman worth? Women are worth nothing!" In such families the men decide everything and their wives say: "We are just women. We are not allowed to say anything."

The first time we women took part as a group in an open discussion was at the meeting about whether or not we should turn Liu Ling Farmers' Cooperative into the East Shines Red Higher Agricultural Cooperative. Officially, we had the same political and economic rights as the men. We were citizens too, so She Shiu-ying and Li Yang-ching asked to speak and stood up in the middle of the meeting and said: "The old women still say that they don't understand things and are just women, and that it is the men's business to decide and that the women should do as the men decide. But we say that we do understand. We are women and we know what this discussion is about. Everything has to progress. We must increase production. It isn't fair to pay a dividend on land. That can mean that a person who works a lot can be paid less than one who works less well. That is not right. We must increase our investment instead, so that we can all increase production and be better off by doing more work. Therefore we must join forces and do away with land interest. That is progress and we stand for that."

Li Ying-teh, who is an old man and Li Hsin-chen's father, then said: "We should not listen to women when it is a question of serious business. They understand nothing. After all, they are only women and ought not to disturb our discussions. We do not need to concern ourselves with what they have said." But my brother, Li Hai-tsai, replied to this: "Why shouldn't we listen to the women? Every other Chinese is a woman. There is a lot of sense in what they've just said about investment and production and land interest and joint effort. I am entirely with them."

We won. Gradually the others were voted down and persuaded and got to agree. I was elected a member of the committee of the East Shines Red Higher Agricultural Cooperative. Besides this, I had three children. We wanted to have three children, so I had a boy in 1953, a boy in 1957 and a girl in 1958.

I joined the party in 1955. There were women party members in the other villages. We often had meetings with them. Then Yang Fu-lien said: "Why don't you join the party? The party needs women ganbus." But I didn't want to join. I said: "I can work just as well for the people without being in the party." "No," Yang Fu-lien said, "you can't. You will do better work if you are in the party." I thought a lot about what she said. Then I went home to my parents and borrowed Father's copy of the party program and read it through. I realized then that I would be able to work better and train myself better if I joined the party. So I sent in an application. Yang Fu-lien and Li Hai-kuei recommended me. This was in the middle of the discussion about the change to a higher agricultural cooperative. My husband had been a party member since 1948 and he had tried to talk me over several times, but I had not listened to him. It carried more weight when other comrades, who didn't belong to the family, talked to me about it.

After joining the party, I studied the party program, the series of articles called "How does a party member serve the people?" Comrade Liu Shao-chi's "How to become a good communist," our party's history and different articles on topical questions. We studied together in the party association and after the studies held discussions. Besides this, we studied on our own. After this, I thought that everything had become more clear and easier to understand. I have become more assured in my work. After studying those questions, I could understand the whole implication of them. If I make mistakes, the others come and tell me and help me to put things right.

In 1958, we formed Liu Ling People's Commune. It was even bigger than the higher agricultural cooperative. It took in the whole of our hsiang. We had only a short discussion before we agreed to it. Most people were convinced from the start, but some, like Kao Kuei-fang, said: "Why cause all this trouble? Why go on altering everything all the time? It's going well as it is. I think it's a mistake just altering and altering." But Wang Yü-lan replied: "What Kao Kuei-fang says is not correct. She is forgetting that production must go on increasing if we are to be better off. The people's commune will provide better possibilities for accumulation. We will be able to carry out more new building works that require capital, and we can have better-arranged social care. We must keep our objective in view the whole time. If we are on our way to Yenan, we can't stop in Seven-mile Village and settle there." The discussion was very short. The introduction of the people's commune did not involve any great changes in our work, It was mostly that it made it possible for us to do without a number of salaried officials, who had previously been in the hsiang administration and who were no longer needed once we were doing the administration ourselves. Besides that, it gave us the ability to carry out works requiring capital, and we set up a proper system for exchanging labor between the brigades. We had heard it said that in different parts of the country they had food and other things free, but that did not sound right to us. At all events, it wouldn't suit us in northern Shensi. We decided not even to discuss the idea. It was never put on the agenda for any of our meetings.

We carried out great irrigation works in the winter of 1958–59. We built terraced fields and were able to do so because we had arranged for exchange of labor between brigades in the people's commune. There was a bad drought in 1959. We had to fight a hard battle with nature. But the 1959 harvest was not bad at all and that strengthened the members in their belief that the people's commune was the right form. We would not have got through that drought without a people's commune.

In the winter of 1959–60 we had a discussion about our work among the women. I sent a proposal in to the committee of the party association for setting up a special women's committee for our work among the women. I told them that, in my opinion, so far I had been the only one working on the women, and that we could not let so important a matter be dealt with like that. It mustn't be left to a few comrades to do the work more or less on their own. The party itself must be responsible, both politically and organizationally. We discussed the matter thoroughly, and in the end my proposal got a majority of votes and went through. The party association decided to set up a labor group for work with women. Ma Ping and I were elected Liu Ling's representatives in the group. This group now has regular meetings. It has representatives from the various villages, and we now plan our work among the women properly.

I was head of the women's organization in Liu Ling from 1955 to 1961. It wasn't a real organization. It automatically comprised all the women in the village. It was one way of activating the women in social work and getting them to develop and accept responsibility and get up at the different meetings and give their opinion. We abolished it in 1961, because it was no longer needed. We had quite enough women then who realized that women can be in the ordinary organization and speak at their meetings. Instead, we formed a women's work group. I was chosen leader of this. We work directly in production.

But the party group for women's work still functions. It has five different tasks: (1) To organize women to take an active part in production; (2) To spread literacy among women and get them to study and take an interest in social questions; (3) To help them do their domestic work effectively and economically, to help them when any economic problem arises in their family; (4) To teach them personal and public hygiene; (5) To give help and advice over marriage or other personal problems of wedded life.

I have already told you about our work in teaching and production. Otherwise, there are no great problems. One gets those mostly with the older people. That goes for marriage: some of the older people do not believe in marriage of free will. "How can a girl run off with the first chap she sees?" the older women ask. We have to talk to them and make propaganda for the new marriage. We have to remind them of how they felt when they were young and how they were made to suffer under the old system of marriage. It isn't so often it ever comes to a real conflict, but we did have a case in 1960.

That was when Tuan Fu-yin's eighteen-year-old daughter, Tuan Ai-chen, fell in love with a boy from Seven-mile Village. But her parents refused to let her marry. They said that the boy was poor and that they wanted to marry her to somebody better off. One evening Tuan Ai-chen came to me and wept and complained. I went with her to her cave and talked with her parents. I said to them: "You have no right to prevent your daughter from marrying, you know that, don't you? Purchase marriage is not allowed in the new society. It is a crime to sell your daughter these days. Before, you could sell your daughter like a cow, but you can't do that any longer." I told them about the things that used to happen in the old days, about girls drowning themselves in wells, of girls hanging themselves and that sort of thing, about all the unhappiness purchase marriage caused. At first, Tuan Fu-yin tried to stand up to me. He said: "I had to pay dearly for my wife. Now I have been giving this girl food and clothes, I have brought her up and she just goes off. It isn't right. I just lose and lose all the time. I must get back something of all the money I have laid out on her. If she can't fall in love with a man who can pay back what she's cost, then it isn't right for her to marry."

I talked a long time with them that evening, and in the end I said: "You don't live badly in the new society. If you ever have difficulties, your daughter and son-in-law will help you. They are not rich, but they won't refuse to help you." Then they replied: "We must think about it." The next time I went there, only the girl's mother was at home. She had thought about it and she now told me her own story. I hadn't known it, otherwise I would have made use of it on the first occasion. She said: "I was sold to Tuan Fu-yin when I was a little girl. I was sold in the same way you sell a goat. But my parents got a lot for me. Tuan's father had to take out a loan. That made them nasty to me. I was forced to work hard so as to make the loan worth while. They were all nagging at me. I can remember how much I used to cry. Now that I think of that, I don't want my daughter to marry someone she can't like." Then she wept. Tuan Fu-yin didn't say anything more. But such cases are rare. It is the only one I remember. Tuan Fu-yin's own sons had been allowed to marry in the new way, of course, because that meant that he did not need to pay anything for his daughters-in-law.

Another thing we have to deal with now and again is that the old women find it difficult to understand that nowadays women laugh and joke with men. They scold their daughters and daughters-in-law and granddaughters for not observing decent behavior. When that happens, we have to speak with the old women about the equality of the sexes. We tell them that, now, a woman is the equal of a man in the family and in society. She does not just look after the home, she also works in the fields. She has to vote and she can be elected. It is obvious that she also talks with men and jokes with them as comrades. We remind the old people about their own bitter youth and keep telling them that as women now are equal, they also have the right to chat and joke. The old people say that they agree we are right. But in their heart of hearts they always feel uneasy and uncertain when they see girls joking with men. But we are patient with the old people. They can't help their attitude. Perhaps not all old women are like that, but most, I'm sure, think it indecent and immoral and shocking that young people talk with each other. The young people, of course, are all agreed. None of the young people think like the old ones on this question. So it will solve itself in time.

We have continued our work with hygiene and public health all the time, especially since 1958, when we formed the people's commune. The public health work was better organized after that. We go to see the women who are pregnant and talk with them about what to do in their pregnancy. We instruct them in the new delivery art and tell them how to look after their infants. Before, a woman had to be sitting straight up and down on her kang three days after having her baby. And you can understand how that must have felt. Now we say to them: "That is all just stupidity and superstition. Lie down with the child beside you and rest. You're not to sit up at all." We tell the women to let themselves be examined regularly and follow the doctor's advice. We instruct them in birth control and contraceptive methods. The women follow our advice because they have found that with the old methods many children died, but with our new scientific methods both mother and child survive.

Birth control is primarily a matter of propaganda. Firstly, many say: "We want to have more children"; secondly, after all birth control is voluntary. We have discussed which contraceptives are best. Personally I find the condom to be the most reliable. They are rather inexpensive too: Thirty-three pieces for one yuan. But there are other methods, too, and certain of the families don't use any contraceptives at all but only simple techniques. A lot of women still believe that they can't become with child as long as they are suckling. And each time, they are as surprised as ever, when they find they are pregnant again. But we are working to enlighten them.

In certain families with lots of children, the women would like birth control, but their husbands won't. In those families the husbands say: "There's not going to be any family planning here!" Then we women go to them and try to talk sense into them. We say: "Look how many children you have. Your wife looks after the household and sees to all the children and she makes shoes and clothes for both you and the children, but you don't think of all she has to do or of her health, but just make her with child again and again. Wait now for three or four years. Then you can have more if you want." Usually, they will eventually say: "If it isn't going to go on all one's life, then all right. But if she's going to go on with birth control for ever, then I'm not having any." In those cases, all goes well and usually they do not decide to have any more afterwards. But in other cases, the husband just says: "No." Then we women speak to him about it every day, till he agrees to birth control. No husband has yet managed to stand out for any length of time, when we are talking to him. Actually, of course,

they know that we are right. They know, of course, that they are responsible. It's only their pride that stands in the way, and we have to tell them
that such pride is false and not at all right. But there are, too, families,
where both husband and wife are agreed that they want to have children
all the time. We can't do anything there. The whole thing's voluntary. The
chief thing is to have a healthy family, and that the mother feels all right.

Since 1958, we have also established a children's day nursery and a
collective dining-hall. These are used in the busiest of the harvest season,
when it is important that as many as possible work, and so the women have
to be relieved of their domestic work for a time. It's the same at the ploughing. Li Hai-Ching is in charge of the collective dining-hall, and Wang
Yü-lan of the children's day nursery. They were elected by the representatives of the labor brigade. Those are positions of trust. During harvest and
ploughing, the women who are pregnant and the old ones with small,
crippled feet do the work in the day nursery and the collective dining-hall.
All the others are out in the fields. It works very well. In that way the
women earn money. They like that. Neither the day nursery, nor the
collective dining-hall is free. But the labor brigade contributes a certain
share of the cost. This, too, was discussed and decided at a meeting of the
representatives. Every child that spends a month in the day nursery entails
a cost of thirty work points, that is to say three days' work. Of this the
child's family pays fifteen work points and the labor brigade fifteen. The
collective dining-hall serves three meals a day. For these, those who eat
there pay seven or eight work points a month and the labor brigade pays
three.

That's how we women work in Liu Ling Labor Brigade. We are making
progress all the time. Every year the labor brigade chooses a few merit
workers. They are given various prizes as a token of appreciation. I have
had a pair of socks, a fountain-pen, a hoe, some notebooks and some
diplomas. In 1960, the women elected me their delegate to a conference
of merit workers that was being held down in Sian. They did that because
I had taught them to read and write. I was very touched by it. I could not
help thinking how they were commending me, though really I had not
done all that I ought to have done. I determined to work even better, seeing
that the women believed in me. I want to solve all our women's problems
here. You see, not all women by any means are aware that they are their
husband's equals. Some still look up to their husbands as in the old days,
before women became free. They suffer because of that, and that they must
be freed from it.

People Say of Li Kuei-ying

She is always clear and sensible. She speaks in a low voice, but she always
knows what she wants, and when she says a thing, then it is so. She does
not like loose talk and she is not much of a one for laughing or joking. One

has no need to be shy with her. One can talk with her about everything and she understands everything. She likes children and children like her, but they have respect for her too. If children are making a noise and fighting and she comes along, they will stop fighting at once. She is like her father, she is unselfish and hard-working and straight and helpful and serious. But she does not condemn and, whatever one discusses with her, she will help over it. She is the sort of person you can discuss your gravest problems with. She helps the women to earn money. If anyone in a family is ill, she organizes the neighbors to help. She is liked and no woman has ever said anything nasty about her. Even the old women respect her. Besides this, she is a good housewife and a good cook.

She studied for six months at the party school, and her husband is a ganbu. All the women admire her, because she has always decided exactly when she is to have children or not have children. Chi Mei-ying said: "I am not like Li Kuei-ying. We too, tried, to be clever and plan, but it went wrong and so I had my last child. Not everyone can be as decided as Li Kuei-ying."

9

THE POSITION OF FINNISH WOMEN: REGIONAL AND CROSS-NATIONAL COMPARISONS

Elina Haavio-Mannila

Cross-cultural variation in the degree of sex role differentiation can be studied on two levels: the behavioral and the attitudinal. Behavior and attitudes usually correspond to each other, but situations may arise when there is discrepancy between them. On the societal level this may indicate a situation in which the generally approved expectations are not realized in the actual practices of people. As a consequence of this discrepancy, legislation and social services—which are dependent on general attitudes as well as on official ideology—may not meet the actual needs of the people.

Comparison of different nations offers an opportunity to investigate on a general level the consistency of expectations and behavior. Behavior can be studied on the basis of official statistics and interview data. Measurement of attitudes gives some information on the normative expectations in a country. In the following analysis the position of women in Finland will be compared with that of the other Scandinavian countries—Sweden, Norway, and Denmark—and the Soviet Union.

The position of women is compared with that of men. It is nowadays customary in Scandinavia to talk about sex roles and not only about the woman's role. The "biased" title of this article has been chosen because we are discussing sex roles mainly from the point of view of women.

Apart from the comparison of these five countries, some wider comparisons between nations will be made. One is based on a worldwide factor-analytic study made by Jack Sawyer, the other on the semantic differential study of ten cultures by Charles E. Osgood.

There are clear regional differences in the position of women inside Finland. Such differences reflect the international comparison of East and West and are thus of interest in this connection.

INTERNATIONAL AND HISTORICAL BACKGROUND

The position of women in any society can be compared with other variables indicating various aspects of the social system and its development. Jack Sawyer has made a factor-analytic study of 82 nations based on 236 social,

FROM Elina Haavio-Mannila, "The Position of Finnish Women: Regional and Cross-National Comparisons," *Journal of Marriage and the Family*, 31, no. 2 (May 1969): 339–347. Reprinted by permission of the National Council on Family Relations and the author.

economic, political, and other characteristics assessed in 1955.[1] The main factors which explained 40 percent of the total variance in the original matrix were size, wealth, and politics. Closely indexing these three dimensions were three variables, among themselves practically uncorrelated: population, gross national product per capita, and political orientation—Communist, neutral, or Western. These three variables sort nations into groups of considerable homogeneity.

Two indicators of the position of women are included in Sawyer's report, published in the *American Journal of Sociology*: the proportion of girls among primary and secondary school pupils and the proportion of female workers in the labor force. The former is mainly correlated with wealth (correlation .65 with gross national product per capita); the latter with politics (correlation—.35 with Western politics). Correlations with the other variables are in both cases very low. In the wealthy nations girls are usually educated, while women in the labor force are a characteristic of the Communist countries.

Finland is a special case as regards the position of women. Women attend institutions of higher education more often than in almost any other country in the world: from 1965 onwards 50 percent of the students at the universities have been girls. Participation in the labor force is also high: in 1960, 48.5 percent of the females over 15 years of age were economically active. Finland is neither wealthy nor communist. Why, then, is feminine participation in both education and the labor force so high? And as regards suffrage, why were Finnish women, as long ago as 1906, the first in Europe and the second in the world to get the vote?

In anthropological studies, theories—for example, functionalist or evolutionary theories—can seldom account for more than part of the distributional facts. After that we must resort to historical-diffusionist theory in an attempt to explain them.[2] The situation of women in Finland does not fit into the general pattern of factors which explain women's position. We have to treat it in the light of its special historical and geographical circumstances.

Historically, Finland was part of Sweden until 1809, when she became an autonomous part of Russia. In 1917 she achieved political independence. Social and cultural ties with the West have been stronger than those with the East. Even under the Russian regime Swedish legislation was kept in force. In eastern Finland the Eastern influence, for example, through the Greek Orthodox religion cannot be disregarded. Cultural diffusion has taken place from both East and West. The Finnish language belongs to the Finno-Ugric group, the same one to which the Estonian and Hungarian languages belong. It is quite different from the Germanic and Slavic

[1] Jack Sawyer, "Dimensions of Nations: Size, Wealth, and Politics," *American Journal of Sociology*, 73 (1967): 145–172.

[2] Robert Marsh, *Comparative Sociology* (New York: Harcourt Brace Jovanovich 1967), p. 65.

languages of the neighboring peoples. Thus separated linguistically from its neighbors and isolated geographically, Finland may be regarded as a cultural pocket characterized by some special features of its own.

To give some basis for comparison, the gross national product of the four Scandinavian countries and Russia in 1965 will be presented:

Sweden	$2,130 per person
Denmark	1,740
Norway	1,620
Finland	1,550
Soviet Union	1,000

Finland is halfway between Sweden and Russia and very close to Norway.

FINDINGS

Cross-National Comparisons

Differences in Behavior. The special position of women in Finland will now be examined from the point of view of formal and informal behavior and of attitudes. As indices of formal behavior, the participation of women in education, occupational life, and politics will be discussed.

At the high-school level of education, the proportions of girls among pupils receiving a general education are fairly similar in the Scandinavian countries and the Soviet Union (Table 1). Only Norway has a low percentage compared with the other countries. Vocational training takes in the highest proportion of girls relative to boys in Sweden and the Soviet Union. It is at the university level of education that the ratio of women to men is higher in Finland than in these other countries. In Norway this percentage is very low.

The proportion of economically active members of the total male and female population can be seen from Table 2. Among women it is highest

TABLE 1

Percentage of Female Students at the Second and Third Level of Education in Scandinavia and the Soviet Union in 1965 (in percent)

Country	Education at the Second Level		Education at the Third Level
	General Education	Vocational Education	
Norway	49	37	22
Denmark	52	28	36
Sweden	55	49	34[a]
Finland	54	37	49
Soviet Union	55[b]	47	43

[a]In 1961.
[b]In 1955.

Source: UNESCO Statistical Yearbook 1965, May-June 1966, pp. 198–265.

TABLE 2

Percentage of Economically Active
Population of Total Male and Female
Population in Scandinavia in 1960
and Soviet Union in 1959

Country	Men	Women
Norway	60.6	17.8
Denmark	63.7	27.9
Sweden	60.9	25.7
Finland	57.5	34.8
Soviet Union	55.8	49.3

Source: International Labour Office, Yearbook of Labour Statistics 1967, Geneva, 1967, pp. 31–40.

by far in the Soviet Union and lowest in Norway. Finland has a much higher percentage of gainfully employed women than the other Scandinavian countries. This situation has already been pointed out and discussed by Harriet Holter.[3]

The political participation of women in parliament and in local government is shown in Table 3. The proportion of women in parliament is highest in the Soviet Union, next highest in Finland, and lowest in Norway. In the local elections in Finland, women have not been as well represented as in Sweden and Denmark, but even here the Norwegians have the lowest percentage. The Soviet Union has a much higher proportion of women than the Scandinavian countries. In the local elections of 1968 in Finland, a campaign was launched by women's organizations to get women in, and their proportion rose to 11 percent.

Participation in voluntary organizations among women is not especially lively in Finland. The percentage of membership among married women in two small towns in Norway and in the whole of Denmark is higher than among the married women in Gothenburg in Sweden, and in the whole of Finland, according to preliminary results obtained from unpub-

TABLE 3

Percentage of Women Among Those Elected in
Parliamentary and Local Elections in Scandinavia
and the Soviet Union (year of election)

Country	Parliamentary Elections	Local Elections
Norway	9.3 (1965)	6.7 (1963)
Denmark	11.2 (1967)	9.7 (1966)
Sweden	13.3 (1964)	12.0 (1966)
Finland	16.5 (1966)	7.9 (1964)
Soviet Union	28.0 (1966)	42.8 (1967)

[3] Harriet Holter, "Women's Occupational Situation in Scandinavia," International Labour Review, 93 (1966): 9–11.

TABLE 4
Median Age at First Marriage
in Scandinavia in 1960

	Men	Women	Difference
Norway	25.7	22.6	3.1
Denmark	24.9	22.3	2.6
Sweden	25.7	22.8	2.9
Finland	24.5	22.6	1.9

Source: Leena Bogdanoff, *Perhe ja avioliitto Poh-joismaissa* (Family and Marriage in Scandinavia), master's thesis in sociology, University of Helsinki, 1967, p. 35.

lished studies made by members of the Scandinavian sex role research group.[4]

In their behavior outside the family, Finnish women are active in acquiring higher education and gainful employment but are not particularly well represented in politics or voluntary organizations.

Data on family relationships in Scandinavia show that the age difference of the spouses is lower in Finland than in the other Scandinavian countries (Table 4). This would suggest a fairly egalitarian relationship between husband and wife in the family. There are no comparative studies from all of the countries examined here. We may only mention some studies in which Finland and Sweden have been compared at the informal level of behavior at home.

In 1966 some 750 interviews were conducted on both sides of the Swedish-Finnish border in the north, and some questions about family life were included. The Finnish families were more traditional in the division of household tasks than the Swedish ones. The Swedish husbands participated more in washing the dishes, preparing food, and cleaning the house. In 60 percent of the Finnish farm families, the wives were solely responsible for the cattle; in only about 30 percent of the Swedish farms was this so. In Sweden the husbands participated more in this job, and outside help was also more often available. Socialization of the children into religion, for example, was in Finland more often done by the mother alone; in Sweden by both parents. Household duties, care of livestock, and education of children were thus conducted in Finland mainly by the wife alone. The modern companionship family was more prevalent in Sweden. Decision-making in the family was in Finland somewhat more often in the hands of the husband, but this difference was small. In both countries the wives more often than the husbands made family decisions.

[4] Barbro Jansson, in Gothenburg, and Johannes Noordhock, in Copenhagen, are members of the Scandinavian sex role research group and have provided information for this report. Data from Norway have been obtained from Biørg Grønseth, "En undersökelse av husmødres sosiale situasion og deres behov for opplysning og veiledning." [Oslo: Institutt for Samfunnsforskning, 1965 (stencil)].

TABLE 5
Time Budgets (in hours and minutes) in Helsinki,
Moscow, and Novosibirsk, by Sex

	Helsinki		Moscow and Novosibirsk	
Type of Activity	Men	Women	Men	Women
Earning and productive activity[a]	7–40	5–57	7–25	6–18
Travel to work			1–52	1–22
Housework and connected activity	1–50	4–41	2–00	5–38
Leisure[a]	6–44	5–09	4–10	2–22
Sleeping[a]	7–46	8–13	8–28	8–14
Total hours	24	24	24	24

[a]In Helsinki travel is included in earning and eating is included in leisure; in Moscow and Novosibirsk, in sleeping.

Source: Data from Helsinki were collected in 1966 by the author from 444 interviewees aged 15–64 representing the total population of Helsinki. Data from Moscow and Novosibirsk have been obtained through University of Tallinn.

Unpublished data from Uppsala and Helsinki give the impression that the division of household tasks is about the same in these two cities.

We may conclude that Finnish wives more often than Swedish ones are in practical charge of their families alone but that their power in family decision-making is at least not greater than in Sweden. The independence of Finnish women can thus be seen in their single-handed performance of household tasks in the family. The Finnish wives have a large amount of work at home even though, as shown above, they often work outside the home.

Time-budget studies from the Soviet Union and Finland show that Finnish women spend less time on housework than Russian women but that men spend about the same amount of time on it (Table 5). Thus the difference between men and women is greater in Russia than in Finland. Furthermore, a comparison of Hungary and Finland revealed that the difference in the amount of time spent on housework by men and women is greater in Hungary than in Finland.[5] These results indicate that in the east European socialist countries the division of labor between the sexes at home is more traditional than in Finland. Finland, on the other hand, may be more traditional than Sweden. Informal sex role behavior thus does not correspond to formal behavior.

Family conditions may be further described on the basis of official statistics. Birth and divorce rates might give some indication of the situation of women in the family.

Until recently the birth rate has been higher in the Soviet Union and

[5] Veronica Stolte Heiskanen and Elina Haavio-Mannila, "The Position of Women in Society: Formal Ideology vs. Everyday Ethic," Social Science Information, 6 (1967): 185.

TABLE 6
Crude Birth Rates in Scandinavia and
Soviet Union in 1950-1966

	1950-54	1955-59	1960-64	1965	1966
Norway	18.7	18.1	17.3	17.5	—
Denmark	17.9	16.8	17.0	18.0	18.4
Sweden	15.5	14.5	14.5	15.9	15.8
Finland	22.8	19.9	18.1	16.9	16.7
Soviet Union	26.4	25.3	22.4	18.4	18.2

Source: *United Nations Demographic Yearbook 1966*, New York, 1967, pp. 217-219.

Finland than in the other Scandinavian countries, especially Sweden (Table 6). Only in the past decade has there been a considerable decline. Thus a low birth rate did not precede women's activity outside the home in Finland.

In Scandinavia the divorce rate, except for the postwar period, has been next to lowest in Finland; it is by far the lowest in Norway (Table 7). In the Soviet Union the divorce rate is higher than in Scandinavia. The lower rate of industrialization in Norway and Finland may be the explanation for a low divorce rate. In the Soviet Union a different legislation may count for the high divorce rate. No clear relationship between divorce rates and position of women can be seen.

The investigation of sex role behavior in Scandinavia and the Soviet Union has given the following results: the formal economic, educational, and political activity of women increases from west to east. In the home the informal division of labor between the sexes is, however, most traditional in the Soviet Union, next most traditional in Finland and least traditional in Sweden.

Differences in Attitudes. We have found some clear differences in the sex role performance between the Scandinavian countries and the Soviet Union. Are these differences reflected in the sex role expectations or norms? If there exists a consistency between public behavior and attitudes, the sex role norms should be more equality-oriented in the east than in the west.

TABLE 7
Divorce Rates per 1,000 Population in Scandinavia
and the Soviet Union in 1936-1965

	1936	1940	1945	1950	1955	1960	1965
Norway	0.35	0.32	0.62	0.71	0.58	0.66	0.69
Denmark	0.86	0.91	1.45	1.61	1.53	1.46	1.37
Sweden	0.45	0.55	0.97	1.14	1.21	1.20	1.24
Finland	0.40	0.36	1.49	0.92	0.85	0.82	0.99
Soviet Union	—	1.10	—	0.40	—	1.30	1.60

Source: *United Nations Demographic Yearbook, 1953, 1961,* and *1966;* and *Vestnik Statistiki* No. 1 (1965), pp. 93-96; and No. 12 (1966), p. 93.

Unfortunately we do not have any information about the general attitudes or public opinion in Russia. We only know that the official ideology is very much in favor of the equality of the sexes. This is reflected in the activity of Russian women outside the home. The "everyday ethic" does not, however, follow this ideology: informal behavior at home is quite traditional.

In Scandinavia there is no clear official ideology concerning sex roles. Especially in Sweden but also in Norway and Denmark, a lively sex role discussion has flourished since about 1960. In Finland this first began in 1965. One may expect the effects of this discussion to be reflected in the attitudes.

An attitude scale constructed by Harriet Holter was used in interviews in two small Norwegian towns [and in] Gothenburg, Sweden and Helsinki, Finland. Originally it consisted of 11 items, two of which were omitted in the Norwegian report. The remaining nine items, with the frequency distributions of the replies, are presented in Table 8.

Among women in Helsinki, the items correlate on the average with a .19 coefficient of correlation. Simple summing procedures will be used to shorten the presentation of further results. An index of attitudes towards woman's role in society is based on the first four items (average correlation .27), and another index on attitudes towards sex roles in the family is based on the next four items (average correlation .19). The last item is left out because the replies are so unanimous. The index is constructed by subtracting the percentage of negative replies from the percentage of affirmative ones—from the point of view of attitudes towards equality of the sexes —and then calculating the average of these scores. Employed and nonemployed wives are treated separately because the Norwegian sample was not representative in this respect.

The most conservative or nonegalitarian attitudes towards women's role both in society and in the family are found in Helsinki as can be seen from Table 9 (a summary of Table 8).

In Finland and Sweden the employed wives are more egalitarian than the nonemployed ones. In Norway the situation is the reverse. In Sweden and Norway the differences in attitudes between employed and nonemployed wives are smaller than in Finland.

In Gothenburg and Helsinki, husbands were also interviewed. In Gothenburg they were the husbands of the interviewed wives; in Helsinki they were a random sample of the population. Table 10 shows that the husbands in Helsinki are very conservative compared with those in Gothenburg. The difference is even larger than in the case of the wives. The only exception is that the Finnish husbands accept women's employment by not demanding that they stay at home. Only 62 percent of the husbands in Helsinki compared to 73 percent in Gothenburg agreed with the item, "In general, women should stay at home and care for the children and the housework."

TABLE 8

Attitudes Towards Sex Roles Among Employed and
Nonemployed Wives in Scandinavia (in percent)

		Employed Wives			Nonemployed Wives		
$(N)^a$		Norway (45)	Sweden (234)	Finland (65)	Norway (53)	Sweden (237)	Finland (36)
Sex Roles in Society							
Women ought to have as good a chance of attaining managerial positions at work as men.	Agree	91	94	82	89	89	81
	Cannot say	5	3	11	7	5	11
	Disagree	4	3	7	4	6	8
		100	100	100	100	100	100
Women in general should not occupy leading positions.	Agree	15	11	15	13	14	11
	Cannot say	23	8	11	22	9	19
	Disagree	62	81	74	65	77	70
		100	100	100	100	100	100
It is the woman's as well as the man's duty to participate in leading and administering society	Agree	83	86	65	84	83	56
	Cannot say	13	7	11	9	9	22
	Disagree	4	7	24	7	8	22
		100	100	100	100	100	100
Women ought to keep in the background when politics are being discussed.	Agree	16	10	11	9	15	28
	Cannot say	15	6	14	11	6	14
	Disagree	68	84	75	80	79	58
		100	100	100	100	100	100

Sex Roles in the Family

Boys as well as girls ought to learn to take care of the home.	Agree	96	98	83	96	96	67
	Cannot say	–	1	9	2	2	14
	Disagree	4	1	8	2	2	9
		100	100	100	100	100	100
In general, men should leave the housework to women.	Agree	26	32	32	62	61	61
	Cannot say	6	2	12	6	5	11
	Disagree	68	66	56	32	34	28
		100	100	100	100	100	100
In general, women should stay at home and care for the children and the housework.	Agree	60	48	52	64	67	58
	Cannot say	22	15	15	6	9	19
	Disagree	18	37	33	30	24	23
		100	100	100	100	100	100
The man has to decide on important matters concerning the family.	Agree	22	21	34	20	21	50
	Cannot say	8	4	12	11	6	6
	Disagree	69	75	54	69	73	44
		100	100	100	100	100	100
In the family the two spouses ought to have an equal voice in important matters.	Agree	92	98	94	96	98	97
	Cannot say	2	1	3	2	1	3
	Disagree	6	1	3	2	1	–
		100	100	100	100	100	100

aIn Norway the sample includes 28–42-year-old married women in middle-income categories in one middle-sized town. In Sweden the sample has been drawn from the total population of married women aged 20 to 59 in Gothenburg. In Finland the sample consists of married women aged 15 to 64 in Helsinki.

TABLE 9
Index of Egalitarian Sex Role Attitudes Among
Employed and Nonemployed Wives
in Scandinavia (Based on Table 8)[a]

Attitudes Towards Sex Roles	Norway	Sweden	Finland
Employed Wives			
In society	+.64	+.78	+.60
In the family	+.35	+.43	+.25
Nonemployed Wives			
In society	+.71	+.71	+.49
In the family	+.40	+.39	+.06

[a]The samples and Ns are the same as in Table 8.

The attitudes of Finnish women and even more of the men are more traditional than those of the Swedes and Norwegians. This does not correspond to the actual situation in economic, educational, and political life, where the Finnish women are more active than women in the other Scandinavian countries. The attitudes are consistent, however, with the division of labor at home, where the Finnish husbands do not participate as actively in household tasks as the Swedish ones. We may conclude by saying that informal behavior—for example, the amount of housework done by men—and attitudes towards equality of the sexes are consistent, but that in Finland there exists a discrepancy between formal participation of women in economic, educational, and political life and general attitudes toward women's power in society and family and toward division of household tasks. Only the behavior and the attitudes related to women's employment are fairly consistent.

Differences Within Finland

In political elections the women of eastern Finland have always been elected more often to the local governmental bodies than those of western Finland. This behavior pattern has long traditions: as long ago as the 1870's, women from the eastern part of the country participated more actively than those from the West in such bodies as elementary school boards. The proportion of women on the committees of voluntary associations as well as in Finland's "Who's Who" is larger in the east than in the west, as I have earlier shown.[6]

There is no similar systematic difference in the employment rates of women in the different parts of Finland. In the rural areas the women of the northern and eastern parts are actively occupied on the farms. In the

[6] Elina Haavio-Mannila, *Suomalainen nainen js mies* (Finnish Woman and Man) Porvoo: Werner Söderström Oy., 1968, pp. 77, 84, and 142.

TABLE 10
Index of Egalitarian Sex Role Attitudes Among
Husbands and Wives in Sweden and Finland

Attitudes Towards Sex Roles		Sweden	Finland
Husband			
	(N)	(471)	(171)
In society		+.63	+.44
In the family		+.18	−.20
Wives			
	(N)	(471)	(101)
In society		+.75	+.56
In the family		+.31	+.13

urban areas it is the industrialized southwestern countries which have the highest proportion of women in the labor force.[7]

If women are active in society in eastern Finland, do men participate in household tasks to make it easier for the women? This is not the case. There seems to be no East-West difference in the amount of housework done by the men in the various parts of Finland.[8]

Attitudes towards sex roles are presented in Table 11, using the same index as before, according to type of community, language group (seven

TABLE 11
Index of Egalitarian Sex Role Attitudes According to
Type and Location of Community and Language
Group Among Men and Women in Finland

Attitudes Towards Sex Roles	Men (N)	Women (N)
In Society		
Helsinki		
Swedish-speaking	+.51 (35)	+.65 (31)
Finnish-speaking	+.35 (194)	+.52 (184)
Rural communes		
Western Finland		
Swedish-speaking	+.17 (43)	+.07 (57)
Finnish-speaking	+.31 (105)	+.43 (95)
Eastern Finland		
Finnish-speaking	+.51 (48)	+.45 (348)
In the Family		
Helsinki		
Swedish-speaking	−.19	+.16
Finnish-speaking	−.22	+.02
Rural communes		
Western Finland		
Swedish-speaking	−.20	−.14
Finnish-speaking	−.07	+.09
Eastern Finland		
Finnish-speaking	−.04	+.19

[7] Unpublished data from the Central Statistical Office, Helsinki.
[8] Haavio-Mannila, *op. cit.*, p. 175.

TABLE 12
Attitudes Towards Women's Participation in Society
According to County and Sex (in percent)

| County (from West to East) | Women Should Be Allowed to Participate ... | | | | |
	Totally Agree	Somewhat Agree	Don't Know	Disagree	N
Men					
Turku and Pori	50	22	17	11 100	72
Häme	65	14	7	14 100	81
Uusimaa	61	15	3	21 100	79
Vaasa and Middle Finland	70	20	5	5 100	86
Oulu and Lapland	71	16	5	8 100	92
Kymi and Mikkeli	70	16	4	10 100	90
Kuopio and North Carelia	74	11	3	12 100	72
All	67	16	6	11 100	582
Women					
Turku and Pori	74	10	11	4 100	70
Häme	76	15	2	7 100	66
Uusimaa	73	18	4	5 100	105
Vaasa and Central Finland	80	13	–	7 100	71
Oulu and Lapland	73	13	7	7 100	55
Kymi and Mikkeli	85	11	–	4 100	48
Kuopio and North Carelia	81	14	3	2 100	42
All	77	14	4	5 100	456

percent of the Finns are Swedish-speaking), and geographical area. Table 12 gives the distribution, by county, of replies to one item measuring attitudes toward women's role in society: "Women should be allowed to participate as much as men in leading and administering society." This item was included in a study based on a random sample of the whole Finnish-speaking population conducted by the Finnish Radio Research Institute in 1968.

Attitudes towards sex roles are most conservative, or nonequality-oriented, in western Finland. The position of women in eastern Finland differs from that in western Finland in two respects: women participate more in active political life, and the attitudes towards equality of the sexes are more egalitarian. In other dimensions no differences were found.

In Helsinki the Swedish-speaking men and women are more egalitarian than the Finnish-speaking ones, but in the rural communes the Finnish-speaking people are more in favor of women's equality (Table 11). This is consistent with the general notion that the Swedish-speaking people in Helsinki are a rather liberal, radical group and influenced in many matters by the Scandinavian community. The rural Swedish-speaking people, on the other hand, are generally considered to be very conservative.

The behavior of the Finnish-speaking women outside the home compared with that of the Swedish-speaking ones is more emancipated: they are more often educated comparably to men, economically more active, and more often have political positions of trust. The Swedish-speaking women are, however, more often members of organizations, especially women's organizations. At home no differences between the language groups in the division of labor between the spouses can be seen.[9]

DISCUSSION

Women in Finland are economically active compared with women in the other non-socialist countries. Their high educational achievements are also notable. They are well represented in parliament, but their participation at the lower levels of politics and in voluntary associations is not exceptionally active. In the family the division of labor between the spouses is more traditional than in Sweden but less so than in Russia. We may conclude that in some formal respects women in Finland are more independent and emancipated in their behavior than women in other Scandinavian countries. However, informal behavior and attitudes towards women's power in society and the family and towards division of the household tasks are more traditional in Finland than in the rest of Scandinavia.

The emancipated behavior of Finnish women is not due to any explicit propaganda but is probably based on old cultural traditions. These are more pronounced in eastern than in western Finland. Some deep-seated tendencies of a matriarchal type may explain this difference. According to George P. Murdock, matrilineal institutions among primitive tribes in general are associated with lower cultural levels:

> The full matrilineal complex was not, however, primitive, but a special adjustment to a somewhat exceptional set of social and economic circumstances on a relatively advanced level of cultural development. . . . The patrilineate and matrilineate represent adjustments to special elaborations respectively in the male and female realms of economic activity. . . . Male-supported societies tend to be patrilineal, female-supported ones matrilineal.[10]

Compared with the other Scandinavian countries, Finland is more "female-supported." Both men and women supported the family, but it is noteworthy that in eastern Finlnad it was earlier customary for the men to spend a considerable part of the year away from home hunting, fishing, trading, and later as lumbermen, while the women had to mind the farm. Because women were present in the town or village, they also could participate in public affairs.

[9] *Ibid.*, p. 177.
[10] George P. Murdock, "Correlations of Matrilineal and Patrilineal Instructions," in George P. Murdock, ed., *Studies in the Science of Society* (New Haven: Yale University Press, 1937), pp. 467–469.

There is no difference between western and eastern Finland in the amount of household duties undertaken by men; the independent position of eastern women in society is not reflected at home. Women in eastern Finland take care of the housework, the agricultural work, and communal politics. This somewhat resembles the present situation in the socialist countries. In the west the situation more nearly resembles the old patriarchal traditions in central Europe and in the Scandinavian peninsula, where especially in the towns women have been tied to their homes and children, and the men have taken care of public affairs outside the home.

In eastern Finland, where attitudes towards women's independence are more favorable and women's behavior outside the home more emancipated than in western Finland, we may speak of an old "matriarchal" tradition. This and the modern radical feminism in the other Scandinavian countries are two quite independent tendencies.

The Swedish-speaking Finns in Helsinki represent the liberal Scandinavian attitudes, but the behavior of women outside the home is not as emancipated as that of the Finnish-speaking Finns. Their status is more like that of the other Scandinavian countries.

The special position of Finnish women according to Osgood's semantic differential is of interest in this connection. The results of the comparative studies of affective meaning conducted by Charles E. Osgood in ten different cultures[11] give Finnish women a rather interesting position: they are rated high on the activity dimension but low on both evaluation and potency dimensions in almost every case. This result is based on the rating of five female relatives (grandmother, mother, sister, aunt, and bride). Among the male relatives (grandfather, father, brother, uncle, bridegroom, and husband), no similar exceptionality could be seen. The other language cultures which were included in the study were America-English, Delhi-Hindi, Greece-Greek, Hong Kong-Cantonese, Japan-Japanese, Lebanon-Arabic, Netherlands-Dutch, Sweden-Swedish, and Jugoslavia-Serbo-Croatian.

According to Osgood's study, Finnish women are thus active, but have low ratings on the potency and evaluation dimensions. What are the implications of these results in the light of the data presented earlier in this article? High ratings on the activity dimension correspond to the actual situation: Finnish women are comparatively active in society. Their low ratings on potency dimensions are reflected in the results, according to which they have not much power in the family, and particularly men's attitudes towards their power in society and the family are negative. Osgood's and my results support each other. They give us a picture of active, hard-working, but not very strong nor appreciated Finnish women.

From the point of view of the family, the position of Finnish women

[11] Charles E. Osgood, "Notes on Atlas Analysis: Example Kinship Concepts" (stencil).

at the present time is difficult. On the formal level women are relatively emancipated, but there are clear difficulties in their position at home; there is no effective child-care system organized by the society, nor do the husbands help very much at home. This situation has been accepted perhaps because the general attitudes towards women's role are traditional. Recently the feminist movement has begun to draw attention to this discrepancy, and plans are being drawn for public measures to lessen the practical strains inherent in the present situation.

IV
THE FAMILY AND THE CURRENT COMMUNAL MOVEMENT

Rosabeth Moss Kanter's "Communes," the first article in this section, does not focus specifically on the family but, it does serve as a bridge between the eighteenth- and nineteenth-century communes we looked at earlier and those of today. Professor Kanter does more than merely describe the two movements; she also attempts to formulate a scheme for understanding why some of the earlier groups succeeded and others failed. As she suggests, the same kind of analysis may be applicable to present-day communes.

One generally thinks of communes as rural phenomena, and for this reason Fonzi's report on the growth of urban communes in Philadelphia is particularly important. With a few insignificant exceptions (for example, a short-lived branch of the Oneida community in Brooklyn) nineteenth-century communes were in rural settings. The fact that not all of those involved in the current communal movement see the city as antithetical to the achievement of their goals shows the degree to which the myth of the evil city has weakened. There are still many who feel that one must live in the country in order to establish proper relations among men and with God, but as this article indicates there is a growing number who do not.

The communes described by Fonzi do not show much in the way of alternative family forms. They may be thought of as transitional structures created by persons who for reasons of ideology or efficiency have rejected the pattern of separate family residence most of us take for granted, and have opted instead for a communal arrangement. In doing this, they still cleave to the integrity of the nuclear unit, in contrast to the group marriages the Constantines describe in this section. But like the persons in group marriages, they have tried to rotate the various domestic tasks so as to create a more equalitarian system. More importantly some have attempted to develop intense, though non-sexual, relationships with their cohabitants. It would seem that if they are successful, these communes will move in the direction of greater intimacy.

Many people associate communalism with the Hippie movement. While the movement may have been a key element in the resurgence of interest in communalism in this century, the diversity of the communes that currently dot the country's landscape suggests that they embody as many differences as similarities. The article by Smith and Sternfield does, however, focus almost solely on communities that might be thought of as Hippie. The majority of the communes they deal with have been in existence for only short periods and thus have not had to face the problem of educating children from birth to adulthood. The findings suggest the course such education may take. The emphasis is on the child's relation to nature and to other persons. Unlike the kibbutz, where conventional academic skills are emphasized despite the fact that the children in likelihood will become agriculturists, children of the Hippie communes are being educated in a naturalistic manner which members hope will insulate them from prevailing cultural values. We see these communes attempting to create future members who will share the value of the founders—something which, as we have seen, is an important element in building an enduring commune.

The Constantines' report is the only available study of a new form of marriage that is beginning to emerge in the United States. While vulnerable to criticism at many points, this work's pioneering character more than compensates for any deficiencies it manifests. In the years to come, social scientists will be increasingly grateful to the Constantines for providing a picture of group marriage in its early stages.

Readers acquainted with the novels of Robert Rimmer (*The Harrad Experiment* and *Proposition 31*) will find much that is familiar in this article, and there is reason to believe that some of those involved in group marriages took their inspiration from his writings. Nevertheless, as the Constantines point out, some of Rimmer's ideas are more realizable in fiction than in fact. A case in point is the problem of working out sexual access to partners within the group. Rimmer suggests weekly rotation, but the Constantines' informants find this robs sex of spontaneity.

All in all, this article offers us insights into a number of problems persons involved in group marriages are facing, and in some cases resolving. The authors emphasize that these marriages are not communes and thus have to be understood in terms of a different set of internal dynamics. This point is worth keeping in mind, but the editor is not sure the distinction is always as clear as the Constantines would have us believe. Where does a group marriage end and a commune begin?

10
COMMUNES
Rosabeth Moss Kanter

"Life together" is the experience of communal living expressed by one founder of a new 30-member commune in Vermont. Like others, she is participating in a renewed search for utopia and community, brotherhood and sharing, warmth and intimacy, participation and involvement, purpose and meaning. Today's utopians want to return to fundamentals. They want to put people back in touch with each other, nature and themselves.

This quest for togetherness is behind the proliferation of communal-living experiments. The ventures vary widely. There are small urban groups that share living quarters and raise their families together but hold outside jobs, and there are rural farming communes that combine work and living. Some are formal organizations with their own business enterprises, such as the Bruderhof communities, which manufacture Community Playthings. Others are loose aggregates without chosen names.

They have been started by political radicals, return-to-the-land homesteaders, intellectuals, pacifists, hippies and drop-outs, ex-drug addicts, behavioral psychologists following B. F. Skinner's *Walden Two*, humanistic psychologists interested in environments for self-actualization, Quakers in South America, ex-monks in New Hampshire, and Hasidic Jews in Boston. Estimates of the number of communal experiments today run to the hundreds. There are intercommunity magazines, newsletters, information clearinghouses and conferences to share experiences, help build new utopias and bring potential communards together.

Now. Today's communal movement is a reawakening of the search for utopia in America that started as early as 1680, when religious sects first retreated to the wilderness to live in community. While experiments in communal living have always been part of the American landscape, only a few dozen survived for more than a few years. Building community has been difficult, and today's communes are heirs to the problems.

I studied nineteenth-century American communities—9 lasted over 33 years; 21 lasted under 16 and on the average less than 3 years—and have gathered information from 20 contemporary communes and from growth-and-learning communities. I then compared successful nineteenth-century utopias with today's anarchist communes and growth-center communities and found that while the growth centers tend to incorporate important

FROM Rosabeth Moss Kanter, "Communes," *Psychology Today*, 4, no. 2 (July 1970): 53–57, 78. Copyright © 1970 by Communications/Research/Machines/Inc. Reprinted by permission of Communications/Research/Machines/Inc., and the author.

features of the nineteenth-century groups that were successful, many of the anarchist communes do not.

Family. Today's communes seek a family warmth and intimacy, to become extended families. A 50-person hippie commune in California, for example, called itself "the Lynch family"; a New Mexico commune "The Chosen Family"; a New York City group simply "The Family."

For some communes becoming a family means collective child-rearing, shared responsibility for raising children. Children and adults in a Vermont commune have their own separate rooms, and the children consider all the adults in the communty their "parents." Other communes experiment sexually to change the man-woman relationship from monogamy to group marriage.

The desire is to create intense involvement in the group—feelings of connectedness, belonging and the warmth of many attachments. How did the successful utopias of the past achieve this?

Intimacy was a daily fact of life for successful nineteenth-century communities. The group was an ever-present part of the member's day, for his fellows were his work-mates as well as his neighbors, and people ate and slept together in central buildings. Many successful communities saw themselves as families and addressed leaders in parental terms—Father Noyes in Oneida, Father Rapp in Harmony.

Exclusive couples and biological families were discouraged through celibacy, free love or group marriage. In Oneida's system of complex marriage, for example, each member had sexual access to every other member, with his or her consent and under the general supervision of community leaders. A man interested in liaison would approach a woman through a third party; she had the right to refuse his attentions. Couples showing an excess of special love would be broken up or forced into relationships with others.

Successful nineteenth-century communities tended to separate biological families and place children in dwelling units apart from their parents, creating instead a "family of the whole." In Oneida children were raised communally from soon after weaning. The heads of the children's department raised the children; they were called "papa" and "mother." Children visited their own parents individually once or twice a week but accepted the community's family life as the focus of their existence.

They also celebrated their togetherness, joyfully in group rituals such as singing, religious services and observance of anniversaries, holidays and other festive occasions.

Group. Many members look to today's communities for personal growth through small-group processes in which members honestly and openly criticize and support one another. T-group interaction or mutual criticism in its various forms can be a primary and essential part of a community's goals. In the Synanon groups, community was first embodied in self-help group sessions for drug addicts and only later grew into the desire to establish a total way of life.

Other communes use group process to work out disagreements, to regenerate commitment, and to create a sense of intimate involvement. A Vermont commune reached a crisis when so many problems accumulated that people asked: *Just what are we doing here anyway?* An extended encounter group was held and the sense of common purpose reaffirmed.

Successful nineteenth-century communities used a variety of group techniques, including confession, self-criticism, and mutual-criticism sessions, to solidify the group and deal with deviance and discontent before they became disruptive. The individual could bare his soul to the group, express his weaknesses, failings, doubts, problems, inner secrets. Disagreements between members could be discussed openly. These T-group-like sessions also showed that the content of each person's inner world was important to the community. Oneidans periodically submitted themselves for criticism by a committee of six to 12 judges and were expected to receive the criticism in silence and acquiesce to it in writing. Excessive introspection was considered a sin, and no matter was too private for mutual criticism.

The Llano Colony, a twentieth-century, socialist utopia, had a weekly "psychology" meeting that one observer described as a combination of "revival, pep meeting, and confessional."

Possibly because they developed such strong group ties, successful nineteenth-century groups stayed together in the face of outside persecution, financial shakiness, and natural disasters. Unsuccessful utopias of the past, on the other hand, did not tend to build these kinds of group relations.

Property. The desire for sharing, participation and cooperation in today's communes extends to property and work. One ideal is to create economically self-sufficient communities, with all property owned in common. The desire for self-sufficiency and control over their own financial destinies leads many communes to form around farms, to attempt to provide for their maintenance needs themselves, to live in simple dwellings and to work the land.

Many of today's communards believe that money and private property create barriers between people. Money should be thrown into a common pot and property should belong to anyone who uses it. This acceptance of common ownership is reflected in the answer of a small child in a Cambridge commune, questioned about who owned a cat. He said, *The cat is everyone's.*

Many urban communes where members work at outside jobs try to operate with common exchequers. The commune has the responsibility to provide for everyone economically. In Synanon's new Tomales Bay city, as in all Synanon houses, goods and facilities are community-owned. Members receive small amounts of "walking-around money."

A common-work community is another important goal of today's groups. Some have their own businesses—agriculture, crafts, toy manufacturing (the Bruderhof), advertising specialties and gas stations (Synanon), schools, film and other media. In the Bruderhof groups, members work at assigned jobs in the household or school or factory, sharing kitchen and dining-room chores. Other communes without money-making enterprises may still expect strong participation in community upkeep.

In most successful nineteenth-century utopias, property was jointly owned and shared, goods equally distributed to all members, and private property abolished. The successful groups all required members to sign over their property and financial holdings to the community on admission. At one point in Harmony's history the leader, George Rapp, even burned the contribution record book.

The successful groups tended to have their own means of support. Generally all members worked within the community. Oneidans, for example, first supported themselves by farming. Because of financial difficulties, they later engaged in manufacturing enterprises ranging from steel traps to silverware. A business board of individual department heads and other interested members regulated the industries. Work was a community-wide affair where possible, and jobs were rotated among members.

Such work arrangements required central coordination; how a member spent his time was a matter of community policy. In unsuccessful communities like Brook Farm, individual members made their own decisions about when and how long to work. The Shakers, on the other hand, instituted a minute-by-minute routine with bells ringing to mark the time.

These property and work arrangements were conducive to a strong community commitment and help account for the successful groups' longevity.

Believers. Often today's communities are founded to implement elaborate philosophies or world views communicated through charismatic leaders. Synanon coalesced 11 years ago around the visions of Chuck Dederich, who formed the community (now numbering in the thousands) on a $33 unemployment check. His personal example and teachings continue to guide the community. Mel Lyman is the central presence for Fort Hill. A number of communes consider their leaders manifestations of Christ, great prophets, or seers.

Many successful nineteenth-century communities had charismatic figures; they were considered godlike, if not actually manifestations of God, and were viewed with awe by members, treated with deference and respect, and accorded special privileges and immunities. In successful communities when the charismatic died his teachings lived on. The Shakers continued to coalesce around Mother Ann Lee after her death, and today the Bruderhof still are translating the teachings of their founder from the German.

The emphasis on a value-based and value-oriented life required an ideological commitment or a set of vows for admony, for example, merely advertised for anyone interested in joining a communal experiment.

Two Kinds. Today's communities differ as widely in structure, values and ideology among themselves as the nineteenth-century ones did. One set of present-day utopias, religious communities such as the Bruderhof and the Hutterian Breathren, have their roots in the traditional communities of the past. But two distinct kinds of groups are emerging as the *now* forms: small anarchistic communes and communities formed around growth centers, of which Esalen, Kairos, Cumbres are examples.

Some of today's communes are small and anarchistic, consisting of 12, 20, to 30 persons. They seek intimacy and involvement, but refuse to structure community life. Everyone does his own thing at his own time. They are concerned with flexibility and mobility, not with permanence. They reject the control of other groups. Many tend to share living arrangements in which members continue to work outside instead of developing self-sufficient communities. Their lack of solid financial bases is a great problem. In addition they report that many jobs within the commune remain undone, many conflicts never get ironed out, and "family feeling" develops only with difficulty.

I find little definable pattern, rule, or group structure in many of today's anarchist communes. In a Maryland commune of 12, one pays nothing to join. Private property remains private, although members report that it is shared freely. Most members have outside jobs and contribute $30 a month each for food and utilities. All work within the community is voluntary. There are no leadership positions. Decisions are made individually.

Some of these communes do try to develop the intimate, T-group-like sessions of the nineteenth-century utopias. But the anarchist groups have a tendency not to do this on a regular or formal basis.

Today's anarchist communes tend to lack integrating philosophies. Many begin with only a vague desire for closer personal relationships and group living in the most general sense.

A member of one short-lived commune talked about its failure: "We weren't ready to define who we were; we certainly weren't prepared to define who we weren't—it was still just a matter of intuition. We had come together for various reasons—not overtly for a common idea or ideal. . . . The different people managed to work together side by side for awhile, but there really was no shared vision."

Anarchist communes tend to be open to all comers at the start. In strong contrast with the successful nineteenth-century communities, some anarchist communes do not make a member/nonmember distinction. A member of a rural California commune that dissolved after a year saw this as one of their problems: "We were entirely open. We did not say no—we felt that this would make a more dynamic group. But we got a lot of sick people. . . . Most people came here just to get out of the city. . . . they had no commitment."

The prospects for most of today's anarchistic communes are dim; they lack the commitment-building practices of the successful communities of the nineteenth century.

Today's growth-and-learning centers on the other hand offer greater prospects for success in longevity, economic viability and personal fulfillment. These groups tend to be highly organized, by comparison with their anarchistic cousins. In their own ways they implement many of the practices of successful nineteenth-century groups.

These 100 or so growth centers—many of them outgrowths of the encountergroup movement—provide temporary communities in which their guests find intimacy and expressive involvement. For their staffs they are permanent communities of total involvement.

Growth-and-learning communities are centered around small-group interaction that generates strong group ties and family feeling. Encounter groups are part of the community life. Lama, in New Mexico, has a group meeting every evening for personal growth and the release of interpersonal tensions. The Synanon game is in many ways the Synanon community's most central activity.

At some communities, family feeling is extended; the community encourages sexual experimentation and acting on physical feelings. While some members may be married, they are not bound by monogamy. Finally, in these communities there is often an abundance of group rituals—from Tai Chi exercises (a Chinese moving meditation that resembles dance) to mixed-media celebrations of important events.

The growth-and-learning communities also tend to have explicit sets of values, integrating philosophies that members must share—from the principles of zazen to humanistic psychology. Members are expected to grow in the community spirit and, as at Synanon, character is the only status.

Some communities have communal living arrangements with minimum privacy. They tend to have stringent entrance requirements: potential members must meet community standards and often must serve long apprenticeships to be accepted.

In the growth-and-learning communities work tends to be communal; a member may lead a workshop then clean the kitchen, sharing responsibility as a growth experience. Discipline through work is a theme at Zen learning centers; a new Synanon member's first job often is to scrub toilets.

These communities also tend to have fixed daily routines and schedules with tasks assigned in advance.

Like the successful utopias of the past, the growth communities have their charismatic figures, from the late Fritz Perls and William Schutz at Esalen to Cesareo Pelaez at Cumbres in New Hampshire.

Growth-and-learning communities, in short, tend to create family-like feeling, to use mutual criticism, to provide a strong sense of participation

Comparison of 9 Successful and 21 Unsuccessful
Nineteenth-Century Communities

	Successful:	Unsuccessful:
	Percentage that adhered to the practice	
Group Relations		
Communal Family Structure:		
Free love or celibacy	100%	29%
Parent-child separation	48%	15%
Biological families not living together	33%	5%
Ritual:		
Songs about the community	63%	14%
Group singing	100%	73%
Special community occasions		
celebrated	83%	50%
Mutual Criticism:		
Regular confession	44%	0
Mutual-criticism sessions	44%	26%
Daily group meetings	56%	6%
Property and Work		
Communistic Sharing:		
Property signed over to		
community at admission	100%	45%
Community-as-whole owned land	89%	76%
Community-owned buildings	89%	71%
Community-owned furniture, tools	100%	79%
Community-owned clothing, personal		
effects	67%	28%
Communal Labor:		
No compensation for labor	100%	41%
No charge for community services	100%	47%
Job rotation	50%	44%
Communal work efforts	100%	50%
Fixed daily routine	100%	54%
Detailed specification of routine	67%	13%

and responsibility, to affirm their bonds through ritual, to organize work communally, to have stringent entrance requirements, and to develop strong values symbolized by charismatic leaders.

In the light of history, the small anarchistic commune does not seem to be stable or enduring, while the growth-and-learning community appears to have much greater prospects. Yet in today's world—a mobile, change-oriented society that is increasingly wary of long-range commitments—there may be room for both kinds of groups. The small, dissolvable, unstructured commune may meet its members' needs for a temporary home and family. The more permanent growth-and-learning center is a place for enduring commitment for those who want a rooted way of life in community.

11
THE NEW ARRANGEMENT
Gaeton Fonzi

Joshua laughed. He giggled. He curled his nose and squealed. This crazy chick was getting to him, nibbling at his ear, nuzzling around behind his neck, blowing her hot breath against his cheek and under his chin. She was all over him, kissing and nibbling and nuzzling and, my God, going after him as if he were . . . *oh, no!* It crosses *her* mind, too:

"*Edible!*" she shrieks. "Hmmmmmmmmmyummmmmm! He's just so *edible!* I'm going to *eat* him!" She plunges back into his neck. Joshua squirms and hunches up his shoulders tight but he can't keep her away. This crazy chick is in there nibbling at this ticklish spot right below his ear and he goes into another fit of giggling.

Communal living for a guy like Joshua is a ball. There are all these long-haired chicks always around committing all types of assaults upon him. He has yet to complain. Although he would probably like a bit more occasion for privacy, Joshua's experience with communal living may one day make him one of the most vocal advocates for the life style. Right now, like most one-year-old kids, he is at a loss for words.

So is his cohabitant, Christina, who is less than three months old. But Joshua and Christina represent something about the newly proliferating style of urban communal living that gives it meaning beyond its immediate social significance. They represent commitment.

"That's exactly what my folks can't understand," says Bob Bair, who is Christina's father. "Their attitude is, well, we can *barely* see it if you and Nancy want to live that way, you're sacrificing yourself. But to raise your daughter in that kind of environment, with all those people and not enough money and no new clothes, that's really an irresponsible thing for a family person to do. My feeling is that it's *necessary* for a family person to live in a commune. It's *necessary* for a child to live around other children and adults right from the start."

Communal living is the inevitable adjunct of the new Counter Culture, the highest affirmation of its basic seriousness and redemptive qualities, the ultimate commitment to it. It is also something far more: It is a search for an alternative to the existing social structure, a search precipitated by young revolutionaries questioning society's basic values.

Questioning, yes! But beyond the rhetoric of revolt. *In vivo!* Questioning

FROM Gaeton Fonzi, "The New Arrangement," *Philadelphia Magazine* (January 1970): 98–104, 126–135. Reprinted by permission of *Philadelphia Magazine* and the author.

with their very *lives*. Life-style revolutionaries *living* their critique of society.

They feel there is much to be critical about, but they believe that society's principal hypocrisies—the ones they are counterpointing their own lives to—are these: That it proclaims a Judeo-Christian ethic and supports the immorality of war. That it produces a glut of consumer goods and permits millions to starve. That it genuflects to the precepts of brotherhood and equal justice while perpetuating inhumanity and injustice.

Historian Theodore Roszak, in *The Making of a Counter Culture*, contends that what is new about the young today is that they have a clear view of American technocracy as coercive, a machine that destroys men's souls as it despoils their landscape and savagely manipulates their lives behind a facade of democracy and freedom. That's why youth is forming "a culture so radically disaffiliated from the mainstream assumptions of our society that it scarcely looks [like] a culture at all."

Communal living is just a disaffiliation from "the mainstream assumptions." One of the common tenets of communal living, for instance, is that conspicuous consumption is a bad bag, that happiness and a meaningful life are not to be found in *things,* but in the cultivation of the self and in an intensive exploration of inner sensibilities with like-minded others.

But *the* principal counter-assumption of communal living is that there is something basically wrong with the very *structure* of society, that man must experiment with new ways of addressing himself to the problems of marriage and family organization, to the character of his friendships and personal loyalties and to the forms of his political participation.

Historically, others have time and again come to the same conclusion and, banding together, have divorced themselves from the constriction of civilization and gone forth to create "new" societies. Communes have formed and faded down through the years, their success not always commensurate with their length of survival. Today, many of the young are again taking that route, some as part of the evolution of the hippie movement. They have fled the crime, police harassment, squalor and disillusionment of the East Village and Haight-Ashbury and set up tepees and log cabins in the woods. They plant crops and chop wood and in their work and isolated togetherness seek meaning and spiritual rebirth. There are quite a few such communes in various parts of Pennsylvania.

What is far more significant today, however, is the increasing number of young people who are taking to urban communal living, not as a means of withdrawing from civilization but as a way of becoming more involved in it. Political activists for the most part, they view communal living as either a useful or necessary form for effectively advancing their counter culture (or "Movement"); or as a viable manifestation of their belief that there *is* an alternative to the present unredemptive structure of society.

"It would have been easier to establish a rural commune," says one member of a West Philadelphia house. "We could have just gone away and built Our Own World type of thing. But we feel different, we feel a responsibility to the way life is here. We want to be relevant to American life and most Americans live in cities. We feel communal living is the answer to many of the urban problems and we want to turn on other people to it. That's why some of us even have jobs in society. We don't want to be isolated. That would lessen our relevancy."

Even among urban communes in Philadelphia, however, there is a tremendous disparity in purpose, structure and the desire to be politically and/or socially relevant. It is difficult to document the limits of that disparity. The media has generally sensationalized communal living as juvenile orgies of free sex and drugs, the result being that some serious communes have decided to veil themselves against outside inquiry. Others are composed of members so alienated from the social mainstream, so polarized into a kind of guerrilla warfare attitude, they automatically bare teeth when strangers approach. (One such commune, at 4711 Warrington in West Philadelphia, refused by consensus to talk with *Philadelphia Magazine*. "It was a political decision," explained one member. "It's just that we're in the Movement and you're not in the Movement.")

If the definition of communal living were given its widest interpretation, the number of communes in Philadelphia would probably reach into the hundreds. Taken in the most constricted sense, the number would drop to a mere handful, perhaps less than half a dozen. There are communes and there are communes. Most urban communal living situations, however, are taking place in (1) crash pads, (2) cooperatives or (3) intentional communities.

The definitions are arbitrary. Crash pads are generally populated by hippie types or teenic boppers on a runaway gig. It's usually a rented apartment financed by someone with a job or generous parents. Friends and strangers "crash" the pad, come and go, stay as long as they like, may or may not kick in to help with expenses or maintenance. Everyone does what he wants and there is little group decision-making. A crash pad is just a place to stay, but some of them do take on the sense of a commune because, in addition to the common dwelling they inhabit (often without any semblance of privacy), the residents do share things and do establish group relationships, sometimes to the point where most of them derive a sense of security from the group.

Cooperatives, on the other hand, are organized living arrangements. The residents share the expense of the dwelling and its upkeep and sometimes subsistence. Decisions are usually made by the group, mostly by majority rule. ("Should we get a plumber to fix the third-floor bathroom this week or should we wait until next week?") A cooperative is practical. It is cheaper than living alone. Common facilities and group cooperation when needed usually made it more convenient. And it has a built-in social advantage, sort of like a fraternity house. Despite such pragmatic considerations, however, it appears that many cooperatives around town have as their generative force a strong political orientation.

Intentional communities, or communes in the traditional sense, may also have a strong political orientation. But, by definition, *intention* is their chief characteristic. "The members of this type of cooperative are attempting to establish in miniature a social system that will allow them to live as they think men should live," a member of a Powelton Village commune has written. "The motivation for a 'prophetic' or 'utopian' community is more than economic or practical. It is to be faithful to a principle, to live according to a life style that one believes in, to revolutionize oneself *and* to provide an example for a revolutionary society."

However neatly definitions can be patted into place, the truth is that most instances of communal living in Philadelphia defy categorization. Groups slide from one form to another, often indiscernibly and without decisive intent. A place called the Backbench, for instance, near Fortieth and Market, originally began as a Quaker Meeting for University City residents. Eventully the ground-floor store of the building was turned into a coffeehouse community center and the two floors of rooms above it became occupied by individuals who helped run the center and others involved in Quaker peace movement activities.

At one point there were seven people living at the Backbench. Each had his own room, except for two couples who had two rooms each. The building was rented for $200 a month and each contributed according to the square footage of the room he or she occupied. (There were three girls and four boys in residence.) The only common rooms were a kitchen-dining area and two baths. Everyone bought his own food and cooked, most times, only for himself. Each took a nightly turn running the coffeehouse.

It was a diverse group (two grad students, a Teacher Corps member, a librarian, a tobacconist, a couple of office clerks) and not all were Quakers, but there eventually developed among them a communal feeling. Soon they discovered that it was cheaper to buy food as a group rather than individually, more convenient to cook and eat together, take turns washing dishes and cleaning up. They began sharing things more freely and eventually came to divide the rent according to income and ability to pay, rather than square footage occupied. Communal spirit developed to the point where when one unmarried couple decided to split, each chose to move into separate rooms rather than leave their friends at the Backbench.

But there was no real commitment to the communal way of life. Individuals eventually moved out for various reasons, new people came and the nature of the place began to change again. Today the Backbench is still a Quaker Meeting and a coffeehouse, but it is far from the type of intentional commune it once seemed headed towards. It probably will keep changing.

Another house that was originally Quaker-sponsored is a place called

Any Day Now. (The name is from the title of a Bob Dylan song.) It is on Baring Street near Thirty-seventh in Powelton Village. (An integrated neighborhood on the fringe of University City and heavy with intellectual types, Powelton probably has more communes per block than any other section of the city. A key factor is the plethora of huge, old, multiroomed Victorian houses in the area, many deteriorating and relatively inexpensive to buy or rent.)

Any Day Now was established initially as a place for draft resisters and their families. Today there are about a dozen people, four couples among them, living in the big three-story house, and almost all are involved in some Quaker action type of activity. The place, however, falls short of even being a cooperative. Each person or family pays $25 a month for maintenance, taxes and utilities, but the house is divided into apartments, most with their own bath and kitchen, which keeps interrelationships at a minimum and communal spirit pretty low.

Around the corner from Any Day Now, near Thirty-sixth Street, there is another large square Victorian house with an open front porch and long narrow front windows. In one of the windows there is a large sign lettered thickly in red: STOP THE TRIALS. This is the Hamilton Street Resistance House. It, too, might be termed a cooperative, but there is such a close, common political orientation among its residents that a certain comaraderie, which comes from more than just living together, has emerged.

There is a sense of ordered neatness to the Hamilton Street Resistance House that hints at its organization. Carefully aligned peace posters decorate the hallway wall. The front living room is freshly painted a stark white, the brick fireplace painstakingly refinished and the Danish modern furniture looks relatively new. On one wall a framed poster, vivid in splashes of bright red and white, bears a quote from Camus: "I should like to be able to love my country and still love justice."

All the residents of the house are in their early 20s, except for a 31-year-old lawyer named Jerry Fenton ("He was our straight-looking front man when we went to get the mortgage") and four-year-old Mark, the son of one of the couples. Jerry and a guy named Mike Griefen, who works at the Draft Resistance office, raised the money to buy the house early last year and everyone living there is kicking in a fourth of his or her income to pay off the mortgage. In addition, everyone contributes $7.50 a week for food.

The members of the Hamilton Street Resistance House may be the most politically active of any commune. "We were careful in choosing people right from the beginning," says Mike, a Penn grad who is currently awaiting trial for his antiwar activities. "We wanted people who were Movement-oriented and committed to radical activity." Adds Ron Whitehorn who originally came from Vermont as a Vista volunteer: "I feel strongly that collectivist forms are necessary to sustain serious political activity. You really can't be a nonstudent radical unless you develop this kind of a base."

The house is usually a beehive of activity, with people coming and going, the telephone ringing, the doorbell buzzing. Its members are so involved in business or political projects outside the house that little attention is turned inward to the nature or structure of the commune. A meeting is held every couple of weeks to reassign household tasks, discuss finances or deal with other house problems that may arise. Nevertheless, there has developed a strong sense of community among the members.

"We've really come to be a kind of extended family," says Josh Markel, a thin-faced bearded youth who also works at the Resistance office. "And to a greater extent than we expected," he adds. "We didn't make any attempt to move in that direction, it just happened."

"Neither did we say that we're going to share our clothes or share the other things that we own, but we do," chimes Susy Knox, a pretty short-haired blonde who was once an airline stewardess. "I don't really think you need a direct commitment to a community for one to develop."

The sense of community comes from living closely with a group of people who share a common political and philosophical viewpoint. The members of the Hamilton Street house feel they must talk freely and honestly to one another about personal problems and individual hangups. Closeness forces conflicts out in the open. "You just can't go ego-tripping around here being pissed off at someone," says Ron. "We all know each other well enough to get down to the nitty-gritty when a problem comes up."

Yet within the house there remain varying degrees of commitment to communal living as a way of life. Eva Gold, a slim young thing with deep brown eyes and long dark hair, admits: "Day to day I don't feel much differently living here than I did when I was living in an apartment. But it's what we're doing together in the long run that's important." Ron, on the other hand, contends, "It's not a temporary frame of mind for most of us. I'm sure life will change at some point, though not in the foreseeable future." Naki Stevens, soft-spoken flaxeny blonde, adds: "Whatever happens, communal living has been a positive experience and we're bound to remember it as such."

The Hamilton Street Resistance House has survived for almost a year without the priority of a unanimous commitment to communal living.

The Joseph House, with the same lack of priority, has been in existence since 1963.

There is a feeling you get when you go into a communal home that emerges from the place itself and from the people who live there and from their relationship to the place and to each other. Like any and probably every other commune, the Joseph House exudes its own particular essence. It also imparts, however, something of the aura—at once depressing, warm, squalid and human—of its very location deep in the black ghetto of North Philadelphia.

The Joseph House was founded by a group of LaSalle students, a man named Tony Gaenslen, who was then head of the Philadelphia Tutorial Service, and Father Clement Burns, who was later to achieve the distinction of being the first Archdiocesan priest to be expelled for his radical civil rights activities. There was a trichotomy in the initial purpose of the house: It was to be a center for a tutoring service for ghetto children. It was to be an impetus to others to commit themselves to social action. And by being a white enclave in a black jungle, it would itself serve to bear witness to the existence of racism.

The house has long since fulfilled its initial mission. It has served over the years as a center for numerous voluntary social action programs. Neighborhood kids swarmed through it by the thousands. Dozens of inspired social activists have lived there for various lengths of time.

Then something happened. The neighborhood itself began to change. Whole blocks of slum houses were torn down and rubble-strewn lots, posted with signs of official promises, spread around the surrounding area. The Philadelphia Electric Company built a new fortress-like sub-station, surrounded by moats of paved parking lots, just across the street from the house, near 8th and Montgomery. Eventually, the pace of the house's activities began to slacken and many of its residents drifted away. At one point, there were only three people left living in the house, the last stirrings of life in an increasingly desolate row of decaying slum homes.

Yet the Joseph House has survived as a commune. Those who left, while no longer involved with the immediate neighborhood, remained active in political and social work and came to meet others attracted to the concept of communal living. Today there are seven people living in the house: Ed Donahue, a paunchy, gray-stubbled refugee from the Catholic Worker settlement in New York, acts as a kind of house watchman; Charlie Butterworth, a lawyer, provides legal counsel for the Philadelphia Peace Center; Mike Inemer works for the Neighborhood Renewal Program; Pauline Chamberlain is a teacher; Sharon Fronz is a social worker; Myra Reichel is a student at the Philadelphia College of Art and Bob Williamson goes to St. Joe's. (The latter is a liberal convert who once won an American Legion Medal for a speech against draft card burners.)

It's a disparate group with a lot in common. All are Catholics, all seem to have a deep spiritual commitment to the religion and yet most are alienated from the organized Church. All have rejected capitalistic materialism as an important objective in life. All are involved in the peace movement to some degree. All would undoubtedly have been attracted to the original concept of the Joseph House, when it was more than just a commune.

Yet the significance of the Joseph House today for those who live there is that it does survive as a commune. It does survive as a place where serious young people, most of them devoting their working lives to social action and doing things they feel need to be done in this world, can come together in the evening with others who feel the same way. They can live with them, eat with them, share their problems with them, survive with them.

"I feel this is an honest attempt at brotherhood, an attempt at actually living it," says Sharon, a soft-eyed, pleasant-faced girl. "And the strength we draw from it we take out with us in our daily lives."

Mike, a bearded, quietly intense young man, tried to explain it. "The basis of all this, I guess, is humanism," he says. "It's the need we all feel to try to keep human. You can lose it so easily today, it's a struggle every day of your life. I think this place, this sense of community we feel here, helps us keep aware of that need."

The nature of the relationships among those who live there is unusually important in the Joseph House because it is almost totally without any formal structure, rules or organization. Everything is based on mutual understanding and consideration for the need of others. There is not even a morning schedule for the use of the bathroom. Some have their own toothpaste, others don't. It all works out. The rent for the house is only a dollar a year, courtesy of a landlord who is happy to have someone living in the place. When food has to be bought or a bill comes due, whoever has the money pays for it.

There are nicer places to live in Philadelphia if one were concerned about the amenities of the good life, modern American style, but no one at the Joseph House seems to be. As houses go, it is not much even to look at. It is a narrow, three-story old row home, its bricks worn and its wood rotting. In front, a couple of sway-backed steps lead to a flaking, faded pink door, a droopy gray curtain hung across its wide window. Inside, the rooms themselves are in pretty good shape, but the wrinkles and wear of age are apparent everywhere. Maintenance is a constant concern in a ghetto house, as is a bit of vandalism and, until Ed came down from New York to act as a house sitter, things had a way of disappearing. Once a whole set of radiators disappeared.

Windows are another problem. They tend to break when rocks are thrown through them. It's nothing significant or malicious, it happens to most of the remaining homes in the neighborhood whether or not people are living in them. It happens because some ghetto kids like to throw rocks and hear the pleasant splatter of breaking glass. So at the Joseph House replacing window panes is a recurring task. One day last month, for instance, Mike spent most of the late afternoon removing window sashes painstakingly cutting glass, fitting the panes and carefully jamming sticky strips of putty into place. It was a messy and tedious job which he didn't relish. When he finished, he scraped the drying bits of putty from his fingers and from under his nails, scrubbed his hands clean and sat down to have dinner. Sharon had baked stuffed green peppers. Mike reached for one, placed it on his plate and, as the first forkfull was about to reach his mouth, the pleasant splatter of breaking glass heralded the arrival of a rock through the rear kitchen window. Mike put down his fork and said something to himself.

The Joseph House has survived because it is there. Far from being just a crash pad, it is something more than a cooperative. While it has come to serve as a kind of spiritual fountain, the very act of communal living providing a reinforcing source for maintaining a basic faith in humanity, there is no real commitment to the place *as* a commune. While all its members may more or less share a common ideological viewpoint, they have directed their commitments to that viewpoint in various ways outside the house. The Joseph House is therefore really not an intentional community. It is not, for instance, what A Family of Peace is.

A Family of Peace may be the closest thing to a true intentional community in Philadelphia. It is located on Baring Street near Thirty-fourth in a big, old, square Victorian-styled twin house. There is a small, slanting front yard that sits above the pavement behind a low stone wall. A wrought iron gate, held closed by a loop of wire that slips over a rounded post, leans drunkenly against the rusty fence that skirts the front yard. The wire can easily be lifted and the low gate pushed aside. The front porch, with its graying wood floor and the paint on its columns crackled and yellow, is an open one. The tall, narrow front doors with their thick glass insets are not usually locked and the second pair of doors in the vestibule is almost always ajar. It is not difficult to get into the house of A Family of Peace. Getting into the minds of its members is something else.

A Family of Peace got itself together only last September, but it is already a cohesive enough unit either to take seriously or not to take seriously. That is something that is important to remember. You can look at it as something of a game that a bunch of irresponsible kids are playing, kids who are much too idealistic, dangerously lack a sense of the realistic and may be more than just a little bit crazy. Or you can view it as a serious effort by a group of sincere people attempting to do something most others are not doing, and that is to make their very lives a true extension of their social, religious and political beliefs. View it one way and it can be dismissed; view it the other and its unsettling significance cannot be dismissed.

The members of A Family of Peace know this, of course, and that is one of the reasons for their communal way of life. For one thing, most are not that youthful, almost all are in their mid-20s and have had a range of traveling and experiences beyond their years. For another, the group includes two married couples, each with a very young child. Both factors make it a communal experiment that is not easily dismissed.

Bob Bair, for instance, who sparked the start of the place, once worked for IBM. In fact, he was with its advanced research facility in New York and was planning a career with the firm. He's 25 now, a slim, casual guy who wears his straight dark-blonde hair close to his shoulders and is usually dressed in a sweatshirt, slacks and sneakers. "You wouldn't believe how straight I was," he says. "I mean, it scares me when I think about it now. Nancy and I were *really* into it. She was working as a private secretary and we were living in this big luxury apartment. With my doctorate I could be easily making over $20,000 a year. Sometimes it causes me to perspire when I think about how close I came."

There was, naturally, an evolution in the thinking of each of the members of A Family of Peace that led to considering communal living as a way of life. For Bob Bair it started when he attended his first Quaker Meeting as an undergrad at Bucknell. "I was a pacifist," he says, "and I decided to become a Quaker because of their whole testimony on war. I had been a Presbyterian, but it didn't make sense to me that you can be pacifist or you can be a general and still be a Presbyterian. I just couldn't take their ambivalence on that. I read the Sermon on the Mount again and the Guy is really making it clear. You've *got* to be a pacifist, He's saying, if you're going to be a Christian."

When he left IBM to get his doctorate in computer science at the University of Pennsylvania, Bob Bair became more involved with Quaker action groups here in Philadelphia and eventually began thinking more deeply about the implications of pacifism of his whole way of life. He had come from a good family, his father was an executive with a major manufacturing firm, and he had grown up comfortably in the middle-class suburb of Greensburg in Western Pennsylvania. He had never lacked for the good things in life. But when a man begins thinking about war and why men kill other men, it can lead pretty far.

"What gave Quakerism its special appeal to me," recalls Bob Bair, "is this very thing they have about simplicity. You don't always see it in Quakers around town who are bankers, but Quakers have traditionally tried to live as simply as possible. To me, that naturally fits in with their attitude toward wars. One of the really great Quakers, John Woolman, said something that really inspired me. He said, 'Let us look into our possessions, our homes and our garments and the things that we possess and see if there is not contained in them the seeds of war.'

"I really think he's right. Wars are really the result of man's possessiveness toward his land, toward his property, toward other people. That's why one of the things we're trying to do in our commune is abolish private property. It's been kind of a nice experience for us. It's something we have to get into. We often find ourselves lapsing back into the traditional ways of thinking. We find ourselves talking about '*my* sweater,' or '*my* coat.' We try to correct each other. 'It's not yours,' we'll say, 'you're just using it.' It's a lot of fun. I mean, *really* sharing everything you've got."

When Bob Bair concluded that possessiveness was what drove man to war and to killing, he decided he had to change his way of living to limit his material possessions and his pursuit of them. He dropped out of graduate school, turned in his draft card (he is still awaiting indictment for that) and he and his wife Nancy gave up their big apartment and became part of the first group to take up residence in the Quaker-founded Backbench coffeehouse commune.

Bob and Nancy, a small, fair-skinned, blue-eyed blonde from his hometown, had married right after he had been graduated from Bucknell. She went to New York with him and when he came to graduate school she got a job as a secretary with IBM here in Philadelphia. Nancy came to Quakerism long after her husband. "I think I realized the depth of the religion," she says, "and it scared me. What disturbs some of the Quakers today about Bob and me and many other young Friends is that we take the religion very seriously."

As both Bob and she became more active in Quaker peace work, Nancy became more uncomfortable with her job at IBM. And as she got deeper into Quakerism her ideas about her style of life began to change also. "I got tired of watching people at the office playing games with each other," she recalls. "I got tired of becoming a different person when I left the house each morning. I got tired of getting dressed up and putting makeup on and wearing heels. I got tired of smiling when I didn't mean it." Then one day, not long after her promotion to the rank of private secretary, Nancy heard a salesman talking to her boss about a computer program for the production of helicopters at Boeing. "All of a sudden," she says, "I realized I was part of the war machine!" That night she went home and told Bob she was quitting her job.

"That," as Nancy puts it, "was the beginning of our simplistic life." When the Bairs first went to live at the Backbench, there was no water, no heat, no electricity and very little money. (Bob eventually began scraping out a living by starting a computer-programmed direct mailing service for local peace groups, something that is still today his only source of income.) But they lived there for more than a year as their commitment expanded. Eventually it extended to what Bob Bair thinks is the inevitable conclusion: the concept of an intentional community where, eventually, the demon of private possession could be abolished.

Today not all the members of A Family of Peace are Quakers, but all believe deeply in the basic humanistic principles common to almost all religions; deeply enough to want to live their lives according to them. "That has got to be one of the priorities of an intentional community," explains Bob Bair. "The members have to agree on an ideology that they would like to see developed and strengthened in their own lives and in the affairs of the community."

The Bairs found two others living with them at the Backbench who were ready to make the commitment to an intentional community: Laura Preston, a tall, long-haired, softly angular, 24 year old Middlebury graduate who had also once been very into the straight life as a buyer for a commercially avant-garde importing and furniture design outlet; and Colin Messer, a quiet, youthful-looking 19-year-old whose father runs a private school endowed by the Mellon family of Pittsburgh.

They were also joined by the Cope family, John, Linda and their son Joshua. John Cope, 25, has straight brown hair that double-arches over his forehead, and a thin, blondish moustache. He comes from a Moorestown, N.J., Quaker family. His father, mother and sister are now in Africa with the American Friends Service Committee. He himself works as an aide at Haverford State Hospital. He was doing alternate service as a conscientious objector in South Carolina when he met his wife Linda. She is 25, a tall girl who wears her long auburn hair tied back and heavy ankle-length skirts. There is a clear-voiced directness about her and certain mystic serenity that bespeaks of her studies and travels through India and the Near East. (She hopes one day to spread the concept of Shanti Sangh, an international brotherhood for peace.)

Joining this initial group later was a 25-year-old Penn grad named Carol Parker, a pretty, quick-smiling girl who once lived the life of an aspiring young doctor's wife in Grand Rapids, Michigan, of all places. "That was the height of possessiveness for me," she says. "Possessiveness of things and people." But she had earlier transferred from a backwater Midwestern college to the urban environment of Penn and had become involved in political and social welfare activities. ("I was concerned. I wanted to do something for people who had no power or rights or dignity.") That planted the seed of discontent that eventually bloomed in Grand Rapids. "I began to feel a spiritual awakening," she says. "I began to feel that my whole life was off base as far as spiritual truth was concerned." That's why she returned to Philadelphia where she met the Bairs and evolved her own commitment toward communal living.

The group paid $12,000 for its late-nineteenth-century three-story house. It was structurally sound but in need of much repair. The money was borrowed on short-term bases from families and friends. ("We actually raised $20 more than we needed," says Bob Bair, "but we didn't want to deal with banks, which make money from the poor and the war.") Now the commune has asked various Quaker Meetings for donations and loans to pay the debt. "Several have responded," says Bob Bair, "because what we're doing is in the Quaker tradition. The early Christians lived in a commune."

On the dining room bulletin board in the house of A Family of Peace there is tacked, amid scrawled notes and due bills, a newspaper clipping, a small item that reports a statement from Harvard psychologist B. F. Skinner. Most communes, Dr. Skinner is reported to have said, are too poorly organized to survive.

If A Family of Peace does not survive, it will not be because it is too poorly organized. Although there is only one "rule," prohibiting illegal drugs in the house, the group is highly structured. All duties, including cooking, dishwashing, shopping and putting the trash out, are rotated among both men and women. Everyone must give half of his or her earned income to the commune. (Most, it is turning out, are giving more). There is an imposed meditation hour before dinner each day. There is a weekly 7:00 A.M. Friday "business" meeting. There is an encounter-like group discussion on Sundays.

Most of the members agree that by the nature of their intention the concerns of the commune must take higher priority than their outside concerns. They also agree that each must accept group pressure or criticism. By banding together, they believe, there is both increased vigilance against personal hypocrisy and group support to give members strength to live according to their beliefs.

There is a definite air of directed introspection about the peace. "Communes, or families, *can* be run without getting into each other's head," says Bob Bair. "When someone feels hurt you *can* ignore it. When someone is depressed, withdrawn or frustrated, you *can* avoid them. But in a commune one must learn when he is inconsiderate, learn what upsets other people, learn when someone needs to be drawn into the group and when he needs privacy. It's time-consuming and sometimes painful to get involved in someone else's personal problems, but if this personal responsibility for each other is lacking, the results have to be disastrous for the community in the long run."

That's what communal living is really all about for the members of A Family of Peace. It is a concentrated attempt to know one another. The concept, they believe, can then be extended infinitely. "We're more oriented toward the expansion of the *idea* of a commune," says Linda. "Everyone may not be living under the same plaster roof, but we're all living under the same sky." Adds Colin: "Our philosophy is openness. I'd like to be able to open my mind and heart to anyone, to any group of people I might be living with."

Of course they are idealistic. They do not claim they are not. Nor do they believe they are unrealistic. They say, in fact, that they are very realistic in facing the problems that living together poses.

On the surface, there are advantages and disadvantages. Communal living is, of course, a less expensive way of life. That is important to most members who have what they term "variable incomes." John's salary from Haverford State Hospital is, at about $90 a week, usually the highest. Colin's, from the Draft Information Center, is about $35. Laura works afternoons as a typist at the *Distant Drummer* newspaper and Carol and Nancy help Bob with his direct mail service. The income contributed to the communal pot usually runs about $150 per week. From that comes expenses for food, house maintenance, car maintenance and insurance (they have a small foreign station wagon and an old panel truck) and a self-insurance hospitalization plan they have instituted. (They refuse to use Blue Cross because they believe it fosters discriminatory hospital care for the poor.)

"Taking half of everyone's income gives us more than enough money to live on," says Nancy, "and it still leaves everyone with something if they want to buy a chocolate bar or some goodies." Shopping is mostly done at the Ninth Street Italian market, brown rice is bought by the hundred-pound bag and day-old bread costs ten cents a loaf from a bakery at Third and Poplar. There is always plenty of food.

Privacy is something else. Each member of the group has his or her own room, the two couples the largest ones, and there is usually a place for a friend or someone who needs it and wants to stay for a while. The two bathrooms are shared. If someone does want privacy, doors can be closed, but no one denies that group living does infringe on complete freedom for the individual to do what he wants when he wants.

"Living by yourself as a hermit would be the maximum in individual freedom," admits Bob Bair. "But as soon as you live even a little close to someone else you've got to take him into account. If someone starts another hermitage near yours, for instance, you've got to be careful that your sewage doesn't go into his well. And there's an awful lot of sewage and wells in a communal house. We've got to be careful not to upset each other's wells, we have to be constantly considerate. But my feeling is that's exactly what our responsibility as humans is. To live as a hermit is easy. Living with others is the real challenge."

Actually, what the members of A Family of Peace are doing is establishing a *love* relationship, the most intense kind of caring for each other, and that is a difficult and delicate thing to do. Especially with married couples involved. "I think all the relationships we establish here are just as important as a husband and wife relationship." says John. "I don't think any one replaces the other, or should."

"Love isn't on a vertical scale," adds Bob. "My love for Nancy is different tnan my love for Laura, but it's the difference between a love for a wife and a love for a sister. That's why sex is in its place here. A sort of natural incest taboo has grown from this kind of love. People living together just naturally begin to consider themselves more brothers and sisters than sexual partners. Sex isn't really important when you consider we're already sharing all our deeply felt emotions with each other, the many aspects of our really private individual selves. Sex relationships are just something physical and superficial compared to the other relationships we've developed."

Says Carol, from her own point of view: "I don't think I can ever be married to one person again. I don't want to possess anyone and I don't want anyone to possess me. Marriage is a beautiful thing, not just something sexual. It's the beauty of a special relationship, of sharing and working together and that's what I think we have here. I feel married to everyone here in this house, both the men and the women."

"I feel, at 24, I've discovered what love is," says Laura. "I feel *this* is a marriage. Perhaps some day I shall want children and perhaps a real group marriage will evolve, but that's something we'll have to spend a lot of time thinking about."

The children of the commune, Joshua and Christina, were, of course, the first to come to be loved easily and openly. Each now shares the private rooms of his and her parents but eventually, it is hoped, there will be a communal nursery. Now, neither of the children lacks for attention. There is always someone picking them up, holding them, patting them, kissing them and tending to their wants. Perhaps they do not have as many frilly things or soft blankets as other babies and perhaps they do not receive as much discipline or often hear the sharpness of a scolding voice and perhaps it will make a difference someday. For now, however, they do not lack for attention. "I don't think of them as someone else's children," says Colin. "I just think of them as children I'm very close to."

"Watching the children together also makes it easier for us," says Linda. "They don't have all these hangups about relating to each other as brothers and sisters. They *know* they're brothers and sisters."

It all sounds rather strange, doesn't it, for young people to be living and talking that way. Just the *effort* of communal living seems to be a misdirection of some sort in this day and age. How do they ever expect to *get* anywhere?

They don't. What they expect to "get" they are already getting and will have whether or not the commune survives. They are getting an enriching and positive experience and a deeper knowledge of themselves and other people. What they expect to "give" is something else.

Laura puts it this way: "I feel a kind of strength when we're together, a kind of force that can be related, almost an electrical charge that other people can *feel*."

Part of the message of A Family of Peace is that whatever is wrong with the world today cannot be solved solely by replacing one economic or political structure with another. It cannot be solved solely through political action or social action or violent or nonviolent resistance. What is needed in the long run, if there is to be a long run, is for people to learn to live together. It is not a new idea, but the only way that it can become more than a verbal ideal is for people to actually *live* together.

It's as sample as that. Yet, for most, the concept boggles the mind and goes beyond the "mainstream assumptions" of historical reality. The members of A Family of Peace know this, of course, and they are not rushing out into a wild proselytizing campaign for communal living. They are, however, whenever the opportunities arise, sending forth soft overtures.

Among the hundreds of thousands of people, for instance, who, as part of the November Moratorium, thundered through the streets of Washington in the biggest mass demonstration in this country's history, there were many who held banners or carried huge signs or posters expressing, in one way or other, the depth and intensity of their motivating concern. Most of the signs were in the strident tone of uncompromising mandates, such as *STOP THE WAR!* or *GET OUT NOW!* They came to be seen by millions of people on television and in news photos around the world. Amid the surging flow of humanity, however, there bobbed one relatively inconspicuous sign with a statement of quiet beseechment. It was carried by one of a small group of people who clustered around it, a group of people who call themselves A Family of Peace. The sign said simply, CARE FOR ONE ANOTHER.

12
NATURAL CHILD BIRTH
AND COOPERATIVE
CHILD REARING
IN PSYCHEDELIC COMMUNES
David E. Smith
and
James L. Sternfield

Where have the Flower Children gone? This question has been raised all over America. The Haight-Ashbury district of San Francisco, once the hip capitol of the world, now is populated by teenage thrill seekers and drug experimenters, disturbed youngsters, motorcycle gangs, and criminals of an extremely violent nature. In a community that was once dominated by the philosophies of love and nonviolence, over thirty murders [were] committed in 1969. The Flower Children have left and the psychedelic philosophy of "Turn on, tune in, and drop out" is no longer practiced in that area of San Francisco.

The national news media, which directed so much time and attention towards publicizing the hippie movement in San Francisco, now focuses on drugs and violence. Marshall McLuhan (1) noted that "the medium is the message," and in accordance with this theory, the majority of American citizens seem to believe that the "psychedelicized hippies" no longer exist.

Nothing could be farther from the truth. In the last two years there has been an increased number of individuals actively participating in the new community philosophy. In addition, these individuals are raising a second generation of youth steeped in the same philosophy. However, the "hip movement" has left centers such as the Haight-Ashbury and moved to self-initiated urban and rural communes.

Because the life style of the hip community is based on the rejection of dominant social values and institutions, one would expect the manner in which the second generation hippie is raised to deviate radically from accepted child rearing practices in the United States.

The purpose of this paper is to define the characteristics of the contemporary psychedelic commune and to analyze the patterns of child birth and cooperative child rearing which are evolving within the framework of these communes. The philosophy underlying these practices will be presented and analyzed. However, this movement is only in its beginning, and the

FROM David E. Smith and James L. Sternfield, "Natural Child Birth and Cooperative Child Rearing in Psychedelic Communes," *Excerpta Medica International Congress Series No. 207* (April 1969): 88–93. Reprinted by permission of Excerpta Medica Foundation, and the authors.

consequences of such practices on the development of hippie children can only be speculative.

The Haight-Ashbury Medical Clinic is a general medical and psychiatric facility located in the Haight-Ashbury district of San Francisco (2, 3). The Clinic has seen over 30,000 patients in two years of operation, including a wide variety of teenagers and young adults and the psychedelic community centered there in 1966–67. As Haight-Ashbury became more violent and involved with methamphetamine abuse (4), most of the psychedelic community left. However, many of the individuals living there, especially mothers in need of pediatric care, still associate with the Clinic and use its free medical services. In addition, many of the physicians on the staff regularly go to various communes to administer medical services and often physicians are called to assist with some problem associated with home delivery and natural child birth. A good deal of the data in this report is based upon patient experiences in the Haight-Ashbury Clinic. In addition, the authors have gone into a number of rural and urban communes in California, Hawaii, Pennsylvania, Ohio, Colorado, and New Mexico in their attempt to gather general impressions. The general areas of investigation are outlined in Table I.

Most of the data for this report is based primarily on patient experience at the Haight-Ashbury Medical Clinic and direct investigation of specific communes in Northern California. This research was not funded and

TABLE 1
Communal Child Birth and Child Rearing Categories of Investigation

Contraception	*Health Habits*
Pill	Diet
Condom	Normal, purchased in supermarket
Other	Natural foods and/or vegetarianism
Marital Status and Conception	Macrobiotics (Zen) and concentrated
Premarital	grain diets
Conjugal	Other, natural food disciplines
Marital	(Ehretism)
Extramarital	
	Pediatrical Care
Obstetrical Care	Use pediatricians and prescriptions regu-
Prenatal	larly
Regular obstetrical care	Use pediatricians in emergency
Infrequent or no obstetrical care	Never use pediatricians
Delivery	*Drug Use—Legal and Illegal*
In hospital with anesthetics	Use of physicians and prescriptions
In hospital, natural birth	Use of self-administered patent
In home, natural birth, physician attending	medicines
In home, natural birth, father and/or	Use of psychedelics, LSD[a]
midwife attending	Use of cannabis derivative[a]
	Other illegal drug use
Education	
Public school system	
Communal	
Private	

[a]Age of initial experience and number of experiences recorded for children.

because of the personal expense involved, communal research outside Northern California occurred only when one of the investigators had professional reasons for visiting an area. The purpose of this paper is not to present all the collected data but rather to present impressions of the various types of communes, and the attitudes within them toward child birth and child rearing. More specific research data will be presented in future papers.

The label 'Psychedelic Commune' was chosen by the authors because it became apparent that the new commune life-style was closely associated with the psychedelic or 'mind-expanding' drug movement which began about 1965 in the United States. Many of the general beliefs of the psychedelic commune, including non-violent behavior, vegetarianism, mysticism such as astrology, and the more natural way of life were in great part related to the psychedelic experiences described by Smith in *LSD and the Psychedelic Syndrome* (5). It became apparent to the authors, however, that the life within psychedelic communes encompassed more than drug experiences. It could be viewed as a response to the popular theme of alienation and dehumanization in American industrial society. The individual in the psychedelic communes felt that while "straight" society was generating more social complexity, they were attempting to make their existence simpler, more harmonious, and natural. The members of these communes felt they had found the answer to psychological survival in the cybernetic age. They not only discussed their philosophies quite willingly but also very often proselytized their new social form.

Commune dwellers tended to be antiintellectual in their belief that democratic theorists, pondering away at mega-issues or esoteric theology in universities and government bureaucracies, were in no way relating to the real needs of the people. Most commune dwellers were apolitical, although "S.D.S." and "Herbert Marcuse" type communes were observed in New York, Berkeley, Los Angeles, Santa Cruz, Long Beach and San Diego. For the most part commune dwellers felt that they should show their philosophies by example rather than rhetoric. Natural food, self-reliance, emphasis on natural surroundings consistently appeared to be major elements of communal life.

Another characteristic of commune life was the trend toward natural, almost primitive techniques of child birth. These deliveries took place in the home and whenever possible, with the assistance of a midwife or a physician. Almost none of the individuals involved in these deliveries were able to give specific reasons for this practice. They dealt in generalities, stating that natural child birth was the centerpiece of their philosophy and that for adults of the psychedelic movement, creating life was the essence of life itself. It seems paradoxical that a subculture known for its drug use would shun drugs during child birth. However, the only drug taken by the mothers during delivery was marijuana, and many of them used no drug at all. Most commune members believed that child birth was supreme experience to be shared with their respective mates, and during the natural child birth the father was always in attendance.

Many commune members voiced dissatisfaction with their own birth, saying that through repeated use of LSD they were able to recall some aspects of their own birth. Natural child birth was viewed as the antithesis of production line maternity wards where mothers were not allowed to share in the birth experiences and where infants were separated immediately from their mothers.

In the commune immediately following delivery, the newborn is brought to its mother to provide continuity in birth. One of the characteristics of child rearing in the psychedelic commune is that the newborn child almost never leaves its mother. It accompanies her everywhere and is raised in a permissive environment.

Birth certificates are often scorned by commune members for the same reasons that production line maternity wards are rejected. The commune people question the entire social process of human certification, arguing that such licensing interfered with basic and natural human processes. Many felt that our system of marriage was ludicrous. It makes love-making illegal without a license issued and sanctioned by the state government. Many couples disregarded the formal marital institution, even though they remained monogamous as man and wife for many years. Similarly they considered the birth certificate to be a method of accounting for an individual by putting him in line for military conscription, social security, taxation, and indoctrination through compulsory public education. Without a birth certificate commune members felt their children would not be subject to the draft, compulsory attendance at school, or the social security system; they would not be on file cards processed and manipulated by machines. The rejection of the birth certificate is an attempt to battle social mechanization in a cybernetic age. Although most of these young people in the psychedelic communes were Caucasian and of middle-class American backgrounds, they raise their infants in sincere commitment to the psychedelic movement, giving them names not of common Anglo-Saxon or Judeo-Christian origin, but from astrology, Eastern metaphysics, and psychedelic mysticism.

Many names were taken from songs or symbols. For example, some of the children's names were Oran, Morning Star, Rama Krishna, Ongo Ishi, Star, and Ora Infinitya.

The dietary habits of the psychedelic communes also took a very naturalistic posture. Most commune babies were breastfed usually for as long as the mother was able and the child was willing. It was not uncommon to find a mother breastfeeding her child at two years of age. There was also a marked rejection of food supplements and many of the parents were quite proud of the fact that their child had never eaten any synthetic additives or artificial foodstuffs. It was felt that breastfeeding preserved the natural cycle of life as did eating food of a natural or dominantly vegetarian nature.

The number of individuals in the psychedelic commune ranged from six to seventy adults and the number of children ranged from one to ten. However, there were often various forms of communication and interaction between one psychedelic commune and another. It was felt that education could occur within the framework of the commune, or through a cooperative effort of various communes. The public school system was in general avoided for it was considered a major indoctrinator of the cultural values which the commune dwellers rejected.

Communal schooling for the young was based upon extensive folk art, music, singing and organic gardening which were, of course, general practices of communal life. There was an almost total absence of television in the psychedelic commune and most members stigmatized the mass-media. Although they could not articulate their theories, these young people had intuitively and emotionally interpreted many philosophies that are now so popular with the intelligentsia.

For example, Marshall McLuhan has described the contemporary world of electronic media as a global village. He feels that in an electronic age of mass communication almost everyone is in contact with dominant social values and, as a result, becomes gradually and subconsciously conditioned to them. The commune dwellers by rejecting the electronic media then were also rejecting this attempt at psychological conditioning. Dr. Stanislau Grof (6) found that repeated administration of LSD to his patients in Czechoslovakia eventually produced a situation in which they went through a psychological re-creation of their own death and rebirth. Very often he found that they were able to recall their own birth and that separation from their mothers following delivery had a destructive influence on them. Dr. Grof also found that his patients, after repeated LSD experiences, developed an orientation toward a natural way of life and toward making child birth and child rearing less traumatic, more loving and more natural. The commune dwellers appeared to be trying to minimize birth trauma and to provide an early life for their infants that was much more psychologically healthy than the ones they experienced with their own families.

The nature and organization of the psychedelic communes vary greatly, but they can roughly be grouped in the following six categories:

1. Crash-Pad Type

This type of commune generally had several core couples but had an open door policy to anyone that wanted to drop in and stay for varying periods of time. The crash-pad type commune was by far the most unstable and had the highest incidence of health problems for many of the individuals that participated (7) introduced destructive drug practices, disrupted the family organization, etc. The incidence of health problems was also greatest with this category. It became apparent that the crash-pad type of commune was for the most part short lived.

2. Nondrug
Family Commune Type

This type of commune seemed to be more centered around university campuses and very often involved professional students or young professional adults. Although marijuana and LSD were occasionally used, the drug experience did not have primary status in this type of commune. In addition, there was little sexual intermingling amongst the various commune couples as they viewed themselves to be brothers and sisters rather than "lovers." It was common in a commune consisting of ten to fifteen adults and one to three young children, to find several couples who were paired off or occasionally even married. Sexual experience within the commune was monogamous. Those individuals who did not have a sexual mate had their sexual experiences with individuals outside the commune. In the nondrug commune various types of consciousness altering techniques were used, such as medication, psychodrama, etc. It was apparent that this group was trying to achieve its psychological objectives using nondrug techniques.

3. Drug Family Commune Type

Although the family orientation of this type of commune was similar to the above nondrug commune it was readily apparent that the drug experience played a primary role. In this type of commune, marijuana was used almost continuously. Marijuana inhibited violence and its constant use seemed to inhibit interpersonal aggression and hostility, particularly in the more crowded communes. The young children in the drug family commune were exposed to drug experiences at an early age. The feeling was not that they should be deliberately given drugs but if they expressed interest or curiosity in having a drug experience then they were allowed to participate.

4. Nondrug
Group Marriage Commune

In this type of commune, sexual experience among various members of the commune was common practice. In one specific example, three males had intercourse with one female during her fertile period, so that the identity of the father would be unknown. Heterosexual intercourse and "wife swapping" was also frequently practiced. Drug experiences were usually limited to marijuana and LSD and were of a recreational nature.

Despite attempts toward enlightenment and sexual liberation, jealousies and rivalries relative to specific sexual issues frequently occurred between the various members and often produced group dissolution.

5. Drug
Group Marriage Commune

In this commune, drug experiences and sexual interaction among commune members played a major role. A very high premium seemed to be placed on sexual experience under the influence of LSD with multiple members of the commune and the subsequent psychotherapeutic effect of this experience. Very often several of the girls would have intercourse with one male, all under the influence of LSD, in an attempt to resolve some specific complex they felt he had relating to inferiority, etc.

6. Large Self-contained
Rural Commune

Occasionally several of the communes would combine to establish one large rural commune, often described as a school. There they would try to separate themselves completely from the outside world, develop their own educational system and establish their own basis for financial independence. All activities were carried on within the framework of the commune. Although principles were established regarding drugs and sex, the interpretation of these principles were left to the individual and no firm set of rules were practiced. Some of the rural communes included seventy to eighty young adults and as many as ten young children. Every large rural commune studied had a central Guru or father-figure who dictated in all disputes. If anything happened to this central figure, the commune almost always dissolved.

The number of young adults moving into the psychedelic commune is increasing. Very often the young adults have gone through a searching phase prior to entering the commune and when they establish themselves in the commune they are past their teens. The age range in our research was twenty to twenty-eight, the main age being around twenty-five. Most of the individuals in the psychedelic communes stated that they had found their answer to life, and it appeared that they had no intention of going "straight." As time passes it seems probable that an increasing number of older adults and older children will move into the psychedelic communes.

The authors do not wish to imply that attempts at communal living are a phenomenon of the 1960s. The Amish community in Pennsylvania, with their natural manner of living and nonviolent philosophy, are similar to the contemporary psychedelic commune. There are, of course, great differences between the two. The contemporary psychedelic commune places more value in sexual activities and certain types of drug experiences. In addition, the philosophy of psychedelic communes stems not from a Puritan-Christian tradition as seen in the Amish, but from Eastern religion. Although the old religious communes such as the Amish in Pennsylvania and the Mennonites in Colorado endured the test of the time and social stress, it is impossible to predict whether the psychedelic commune will survive.

However, the commune movement has developed some institutional characteristics. One is an outstanding underground monthly publication called WIN which focuses on techniques of alternative living and describes various communes throughout the United States.

In 1969, several large national magazines . . . published articles on communes presenting them as an alternative life style. It is the belief of the authors that unless the dominant culture in the United States comes to grips with the psychological stress and alienation experienced by its mechanized, dehumanized mass industrial society, more of its youth will seek communal life as a means of psychological survival and individual fulfillment.

References

1. McLuhan, M. *The Medium Is the Message* (New York: Bantam, 1967).
2. Shubart, P., Conrich, R. and Smith, D. E. "The Concept and Design of a Regionalized Medical Facility in the Haight-Ashbury District of San Francisco," *Journal of Psychedelic Drugs,* 1, no. 1 (1967): 113–115.
3. Smith, D. E., and Rose, A. J. "Health Problems in Hippie Subculture: Observations by the Haight-Ashbury Clinic," *Clinical Pediatrics,* 7, no. 6 (1968): 313–316.
4. Smith, D. E. "Changing Drug Patterns in Haight-Ashbury," *California Medicine,* 110 (1969): 151–157.
5. ———— "LSD and the Psychedelic Syndrome," *Clinical Toxicology,* 2, no. 1 (1969): 69–73.
6. Grof, S. "LSD, Mysticism and Religious Experience," *Journal of Psychedelic Drugs,* 3, no. 1 (1970).
7. Smith, D. E. "Health Problems in Urban and Rural Crash-pad Communes," *Clinical Pediatrics,* 9, no. 9 (1970): 534–537.

13

THE GROUP MARRIAGE
Larry L. and
Joan M. Constantine

The family is society's most ubiquitous group—and probably its oldest. Its origins indeed predate man and may well form part of our heritage from primate predecessors. From primordial beginnings, the family, and marriage, the relationship on which it is based, have changed and evolved in many ways but never so rapidly as in the past few generations. Though the pace of change is almost a world-wide phenomenon, the details vary.

The trends have been widely observed and discussed—with alarm, hope, or indifference. In general, the family has become increasingly unstable in various ways. The high and increasing divorce rate is common knowledge, though Department of Health, Education, and Welfare figures indicate it may be stabilizing in the United States. And desertion may well be more common than divorce. The very pace of events in the family history has been increasing. Leaving home, marriage, first child, last child, and the children's leaving in turn, are occurring on a compressed time scale.

Concomitantly, the family has undergone a progressive loss of function. Its purposes as an economic unit, socializing institution for children, even recreational facility have been seen by Nimkoff[1] and others as being partly and progressively surrendered to (or usurped by) society. Even in its (historically) recently stressed function in the personal fulfillment of its members, it is seen as seriously deficient. The gradual decay of the husband-wife relationship, the onset of boredom, the "seven year itch," the "thirty-sixth year crisis," and the disenchantment with marital age discussed by Pineo[2]—all are part of the picture of contemporary marriage. The almost pandemic extramarital affair and the rapid advent of mate-swapping are social phenomena that are pathognomonic of the failure of marriage and the family to fulfill many personal needs.

One of the most persistent and dramatic processes has been the gradual reduction in size of the family unit, not only in number of children but also in terms of extensions of the core family—the husband, wife, and children. While the progression from extended to nuclear family structure is not entirely unambiguous (some nuclear family orientation has character-

THIS is a previously unpublished article, printed by permission of the authors.

[1] M. F. Nimkoff, ed., *Comparative Family Systems* (Boston: Houghton Mifflin, 1965).

[2] Peter C. Pineo, "Disenchantment in the Later Years of Marriage," *Marriage and Family Living*, 23 (February 1961): 3–11.

ized the United States almost from the outset), it is crucial. Loss of function and functional diversity, failure in need satisfaction, instability—these are properties of a unit whose size has been reduced below critical levels.

Today's family is almost completely autonomous and nuclearized. Only the core of a man and wife and their children is left as a family unit. The autonomous nuclear family has advantages in a rapidly changing technological age. It is mobile and comparatively plastic. In keeping with the changed pace of family events, it reduces the ideological and stylistic conflicts of its predecessor, the multigeneration, or *extended,* family, which today would juxtapose generations whose culture and ideologies are separated by major discontinuities. But the nuclear family exacts a price of its members as well. The smaller group has a shorter, more uncertain lifetime. Its members are provided with ready opportunities for intimate interaction with one or at best a few others. Its children have limited models for adult roles and behavior and for sexual identification.

In diagnosing the statistical failure of modern marriage, we must go beyond divorce to other, less terminal, behavioral manifestations of degeneration. We must ask of the marriages and families that provide no happiness, or providing some measure, do not facilitate the personal growth of either children or adults.

It does not take an alarmed intuitive leap to recognize that the problem may not lie so much in marriage as practiced—in our culture's interpretation of the model—as in the model itself. If there are shortcomings in the model, no "return to normalcy" is possible.

If we look at marriage and the family (but not too closely), we find a single, constant idealized definition, a romantic love, one-man-one-woman, lifetime model which fits only some fraction of real marriages. The actual underlying model demands homage to the idealized form while being based on monogyny (one wife at a time) rather than monogamy (one lifetime mate). And, without real provision in either model, the majority of these monogynous marriages will at some time become involved with extramarital relations. This unitary design for marriage is what Cuber and Harroff[3] have termed "the monolithic code."

If we look at marriage more closely, as Cuber and Harroff have done in their study of the marriages of "successful" people, we find a variety of functional bases operative within the single structure. The typology they developed is broadly useful, for it recognizes that marriage must satisfy an impressive array of varying human needs. Thus the passive-congenial relationship, while lacking vitality and romance, may well best fit the casual companionship needs of its members. Even the conflict-habituated marriage of Virginia Wolff may satisfy important, even if neurotic, needs of both partners.

[3] Joan F. Cuber and Peggy Harroff, *The Significant Americans* (New York: Appleton-Century-Crofts, 1965).

THE INTUITIVE LEAP

Many concerned individuals want to build a stronger, more secure, more vital, more cohesive, more productive family, one that provides an enlarged framework for personal growth and an enriched environment for the nurture of their children. Some of these have been led to question the basic contemporary models of marriage and family structure. A few, among them popular utopian novelist Robert Rimmer[4] and science fiction writer Robert Heinlein, have proposed a new set of models based on multiperson marriages. A group marriage, through a larger "community of intimates" is offered as potentially providing exactly the size and diversity fundamentally lacking in autonomous, nuclear monogyny.

Of the many attracted by intellectual or endocrinological bent to the poetry and polemics of group marriage proponents, a small number have begun to put into practice a fundamentally new form of marriage. Their unusual relationships differ in concept and execution from most historically and anthropologically related forms of marriage. They are each trying to build a laterally expanded family, a marriage of equals tied together by deep bonds of love and caring, into a many-sided structure. We might properly call this *multilateral* marriage. As such, their present functioning and future potential depends on the nature and contributions of all bonds, including especially the bonds between members of the same sex.

Ten such families scattered across the United States are cooperating in an initial descriptive investigation of multilateral marriages today. Our experience in trying to locate functioning group marriages suggests that this is still an exceptional form of marriage. Pressed for an estimate, we would guess there may be fewer than a hundred, almost certainly less than a thousand group marriages in the United States. Nevertheless, interest in and speculation concerning such innovations in marriage and family relations have been considerable, as evidenced by *Psychology Today's* recent sex survey.[5] Most of this interest has surfaced in fictional accounts which, necessarily, idealized and simplify the nature of group marriage. Little of professional caliber has appeared beyond Herb Otto's collection on alternate models for the American family structure.[6] The formulations in both bodies of literature are, as might be expected, misleading. Practice is sufficiently divergent from theory that the potential participant basing his entrance on the experience of Rimmer's characters is in for genuine surprises if not serious difficulty.

It is important to differentiate what these groups are involved in from other, more widespread and better known social anomalies. Swinging, or organized mate-swapping, has an extensive participation, especially on the

---

[4] Robert H. Rimmer, *Proposition 31* (New York: New American Library, 1968).

[5] *Psychology Today*, 4, no. 2 (July 1970).

[6] Herbert A. Otto, *The Family in Search of a Future* (New York: Appleton-Century-Crofts, 1969).

West Coast. As a whole, swinging has been found to emphasize purely sexual, temporary liaisons, often carefully structured to avoid *personal* involvement. (Symonds[7] has, however, identified a minority subgroup, the utopian or ideological swingers, who emphasize interpersonal relations.) Clearly, too, the ubiquitous extramarital affair is a different phenomenon, being based on secrecy and isolation of the spouses rather than openness and mutual participation. Ironically, though mate-swapping and affairs are better known, they are in almost as sad a state as group marriage when it comes to formal study.

Our study emerged over a year's time from a desire to substitute understanding of the actual phenomenon for the surfeit of conjecture and argument. Locating active groups and devising a productive plan and philosophy for investigation have been the largest problems. An initial series of interviews with three families, when combined with our prior knowledge of attempted formations, suggested factors of prime interest and guided the study design.

The highest priority has been given to developing a primarily descriptive understanding of what group marriage in modern America is. The most basic questions are being investigated. Who is in it? Why? Does it work at all? Up to expectations? What are the special problems and difficulties? How can these be dealt with? The initial contacts suggested that a broad, comparatively unstructured approach to data gathering was needed. We chose to continue to rely on in-depth, face-to-face contact as our primary tool, supplemented with paper-and-pencil instruments where appropriate. The twenty odd historical, structural, and functional factors chosen for closer study have been divided between interview and reply schedule through several rounds of revision and trial using one group with whom close contact could be maintained.

Questions of methodology and instrumentation may be expected to continue to plague the project. One cannot meaningfully speak of a "sample" in this study, and most available instruments for family research are so heavily dependent on assumptions of "normality" that they are useless even for comparison purposes. We are working on adaptations of certain standard instruments, but the earliest stages are, necessarily, being conducted largely "by feel." In this preliminary "study for a study" type of operation dealing with so few respondents, we feel all sources are valuable and readily accept first-person narratives from participants.

If we have a research stance, it is decidedly that of humanistic psychology. We are convinced (and have objective independent evidence to support this conviction), that an open, informal, and personal relationship with the groups in the study has given us access to information and insights unavailable to others. While the same insights might have been

---

[7] Carolyn Symonds, "Pilot Study of the Peripheral Behavior of Sexual Mate Swappers," Unpublished Master's thesis, University of California, Riverside, 1968.

derived by psychoanalytic sociological methods like those of Hendin,[8] the combination of an open, though carefully structured relationship has worked as well without coversion or ulterior transactions. We have been aided in this by the respondents' genuine interest in their own and their groups' growth.

The questionnaires now being used are rather conventional in design with the possible exception of sections of the individual summary. There we are interested in the individuals' perceptions of their own motivations, their expectations and disappointments, and evaluation of problems. Because this data is requested individually, considerable insight into group structure and functioning can be derived. In addition, a final section asks the individual to select such targets as "preferred sex partner." From this, several potentially valuable sociograms, indications of the underlying structure of the group, can be developed. Some attention has been directed toward avoiding biasing "socially more desirable" replies.

It is now clear that the group marriage can be viewed as a very special form of intimate group and as an exceptional kind of marriage, one among three or more people. Both perspectives are valid, and a stereoscopic examination of group marriage as group and as marriage will structure our discussion. It is simplest, however, to dispense first with elementary social characteristics.

THE CONTEXT

Respondents in the current study are located in six states with "concentrations" in New England and California. They are not exclusively young; more than half are over thirty, with two distinct clusters, one in the midtwenties, another in the midthirties. The youngest participant is twenty-two; the oldest, sixty.

All but two groups have children, none more than three. If this is truly a general indication, the implications for population stabilization are substantial. The children range from infants through age thirteen. In every case, the children are an integral part of the expanded relationship. They are fully aware of their parents' involvement.

Unfortunately, most central tendencies are fictions in a sample of this size. The problem is exacerbated by the multidimensional diversity of the known participants. Among our respondents are group incomes ranging from below $10,000 per annum to in excess of $100,000, for example. Ten more unique marriages could hardly be found through deliberate search.

Occupationally, the respondents are so diverse that there are no duplications except in the category student in which there are four full time, and housewife, of which there are three. A physician, a high-school teacher, a commercial artist, and a rehabilitation aide have all chosen group marriage. Others are self-employed in small businesses, work as custodians, as postal letter carriers, teach ballet, or are unemployed. About one-third of the present participants entered as single individuals. If there is a pattern among the present respondents, however, it is for one married couple to act as a nucleus around which other couples or single individuals are drawn.

THE REASONS

It is interesting to ask why individuals would choose to enter group marriages. A multilevel interpretation of the psychology of participation is required. The public arguments offered are as important as the private ones, the surface reasons as interesting as underlying causes. How an individual perceives the origins of his involvement says much of the individual and the group marriage.

What we have now must be regarded only as tentative hypotheses. Though consistently supported in discussions and unstructured interviews, these will have to be verified by deeper analysis.

Public Pronouncements

Public justifications, that is, the readiest answers and reasons given on casual acquaintance, most often make reference to "community" and to "extended family." Participants seek a restoration of a lost sense of community, of family identification that is expanded. It is also evident that these are reasons with which the average person readily identifies. Benefits to children are also often cited. Similarly, the sexual dimension is often publically *deemphasized,* and this happens to be the element that the majority of people find the most threatening.

While these indications are not surprising, it *is* somewhat surprising that love is infrequently mentioned at this public level. The capacity for and benefits of multiple love relationships are important elements of the theoretical and fictional justifications of multilateral marriage.

Private Level

In deeper investigations, verbal and written, sex emerges as fairly central to participation in group marriages. It certainly does not appear to be a driving force for initial entry, but it is very frequently discussed as a retrospective benefit.

At this level, discussions of personal growth potential are dominant. The role of the group marriage as growth catalyst will be discussed in a later section.

Love still is relatively unimportant in these private responses. This may result from a special property of our sample. Our respondents include only one group in which the group marriage *began* with love relationships which later grew into sexual intimacy and finally cohabitation. All the others originated at more practical or intellectual levels, based on ideas of community, sexual freedom, economic efficiency, or admiration of the *concept* of group marriage. In many cases, these initially nonemotional relationships have *grown* into deep affection.

Deeper Reasons

One frequent and vital question is whether group marriage participation may not be motivated by deep-seated pathology in personality or in prior marriages. It is important in this to establish a broader notion of health than is usually available. In particular, conceptualizations of pathology based on *acts* which are simply labeled "sick" are clearly inadequate. If we begin by defining multiperson sex as pathological we will be unable to differentiate healthy and unhealthy reasons behind the act. As Ellis[9] and others have pointed out, extramarital and co-marital sex are not *intrinsically* unhealthy in their effects on individuals and marriages. This analysis must be extended to other elements of sexual and marital behavior.

Insofar as we can now evaluate, previously married participants who enter group marriage as a couple have at least normally healthy marriages. As a whole they are aware of the limitations they do have in their relationships and evidence constructive efforts to improve these aspects. Objective verification of the nature of their prior relationships presents major methodological difficulties, and available instruments are inadequate or inappropriate; new ones will have to be developed.

At this point, the only thing that is clear is that, in our opinion, very few of the prior dyadic marriages had *serious* marital problems. This applies only to our respondents, who by virtue of their continued existence must be regarded as successful. We do know of attempts to build group marriages that failed in which couples were previously experiencing substantial marital difficulties, and some were even motivated to try group marriage as a *solution* to their problems.

Lacking more penetrating study, it appears that people enter group marriage for the same reasons as people enter two-person marriage—love, security, sex, child-rearing, companionship, an almost endless list. The reasons are almost completely unique to the individuals and to the marriages. Our tiny sample includes passive-congenial relationships, marriages-of-convenience, even relationships based, apparently, on strong neurotic needs.

[9] Albert A. Ellis, "Healthy and Disturbed Reasons for Extramarital Relations," in Gerhardt Neubeck, ed., *Extramarital Relations* (Englewood Cliffs, N.J.: Prentice-Hall, 1969), pp. 153–161.

AS A GROUP

The majority of the group marriages involve four partners, a few include only three, and one has six. These sizes *may* reflect very fundamental processes. Triads appear to be especially easy to form. This is true of triads involving either two men or two women. They seem to be functionally stable but psychologically metastable; there is always a push to equalize the sex ratio. This makes four the first potentially stable point. But our respondents find numerous arguments for expansion, and most are actively trying. One group even deliberately experimented over a period of years with various sizes up to twelve. Now a fairly stable foursome, their conclusion is that six is maximal (and probably optimal). The limiting factor seems to be the capacity to build and maintain simultaneously a number of substantially equivalent, very deep, intimate relationships. While conclusions cannot be reached, a trend for four- and six-person groups is indicated by a number of independent factors.

As the size rises much beyond six, the group appears increasingly like a commune. Because the commune or small intentional community is the group that is most readily confused with a multilateral marriage, it provides a convenient contrast. It is difficult, however, to give a rigorous and noncircular set of definitions. We find that there are indeed two phenomena, differing in many dimensions, which are conveniently labeled as "group marriages" and "communities." Probably the definitive characteristic is the nature of commitment. The individual in a community either makes no commitment or commits himself to the community, its purpose, or its philosophy. Marriage is a fairly long-term commitment to other *individuals*. We have found it adequate to accept the individual's perception as an operational criterion. If he says he is married to all the others, we can assume he is. We also require a group to have confronted and creatively dealt with sexual sharing to be included. A "joint family" consisting of several monogamous couples, though an interesting alternate family structure, is simply not a group *marriage*.

Communes are short-lived, according to Rick Margolies,[10] averaging less than a year, and the population within is highly variable. Almost all respondents are seeking permanent or long-term associations. While they may not succeed, their intentions are the same as the typical couple at the altar. Because a group would have to last for some time to reach our attention, our respondents may well represent a biased sample. They have averaged twenty months together, and one is nearly four years old. None has broken up since the start of our study a year ago.[11]

[10] Rick Margolies, "Life in Urban Communes." Plenary address, 1969 meeting of the National Council on Family Relations.

[11] In the short period of ten days, while final manuscript revisions were being prepared, two of the groups in the study have disintegrated. One dissolved in the midst of an attempted transition from three to four participants, the other broke up

The interaction within a group marriage is typically intense and intimate, many times more so than one would encounter in any other group of comparable size. From our investigations, communities seldom reach this level of intimacy. It is often like an encounter group, the closest comparison, and one used by many of our respondents. It differs from the typical encounter group in being leaderless and exitless.

Coming from psychologically sophisticated segments of the population, most participants have first-hand experience in encounter groups and sensitivity training. This fact, coupled with the absence of trained leadership, may frequently contribute to dysfunctional intensity of interaction. This can be circumvented, as has been done, by bringing in an outside group therapist whose function is to facilitate *constructive* interaction. The extent to which strictly amateur application of the techniques embodied in Perls'[12] or Schutz's[13] formulations can facilitate growth and integration in group marriage has yet to be investigated.

The duration of the intense group process in multilateral marriage now appears to be of fundamental importance. Other intense, intimate groups of equals, which stress complete openness, have a well-defined termination. Even the marathon encounter, seemingly endless to focal participants, indeed ends. At this point, differential progress in contact and in personal growth cease to be a factor in the continued life of the individuals.

The group marriage has no such conclusion. We find that the increasingly differentiated growth rates in the group marriage leads to a characteristic "pressure to grow." This pressure to grow has its origins in the apparently nearly universal orientation of group marriage participants toward self-actualization and self-realization. It is the immediate consequence of the inevitability of some "slowest grower" and the importance of continued comparable progress by all for integration and maintenance of the group as a positive functional entity.

The function of intensity and duration in growth stimulating processes is not understood. In one of the best contributions to underlying theory of encounter, Arthur Burton[14] juxtaposed contradictory views on these variables without any attempt at reconciliation, which may indeed be impossible now. What we have found is that the intensity and subjectively experienced pressure to grow are very real, general phenomena in multilateral marriages.

---

apparently as the result of latent instabilities in a prior marriage. We have not had adequate time to analyze these dissolutions, but report them here in the interest of accuracy and currency. Intensive follow-ups in both cases are planned.

[12] Frederick Perls et al., Gestalt Therapy (New York: Delta, 1951).

[13] William C. Schutz, Joy: Expanding Human Awareness (New York: Grove Press, 1967).

[14] Arthur Burton, ed. Encounter: The Theory and Practice of Encounter Groups, (San Francisco: Jossey-Bass, 1969).

The relationship between growth toward self actualization and participation in multiperson marriages is too complex to explore in detail here. From the individual's standpoint, two broad issues have emerged: the participant's responsibility for openness, spontaneous disclosure, and continued growth in actualization, and the mechanisms within the group marriage that facilitate this process.

We now see that multilateral relations both permit and demand variety and flexibility in roles assumed by the participant. If we regard, as Jourard[15] does, self-disclosure and idiosyncratic feedback as the central ingredients in growth in self and self-realization, the intimate multiperson marriage must be optimal. First we find, as expected, mutual reinforcement in self-disclosure; in the group, this reinforcement is amplified. Second, genuine and deep disclosure is a prerequisite of worthwhile insight. Simultaneous intimate mutual relationships with several others enhances the probability that any particular insight will emerge. Finally, the unique contribution of each unique other person with whom a meaningful relationship can be built *and maintained* must be included. We do not have time-separated objective measures of self-actualization and its correlates, but our own unplanned observations of this factor and volunteered self-interpretations by participants are congruent with a model of group marriage as an exceptionally potent force for personal growth.

Some families do not appear to have completely mastered the effective channeling of this force without creating an unreasonable and dysfunctional pressure to grow. This pressure, in most such families, tends to fall more on one person than the others. The youngest or least secure is often the target and generally feels that the others frequently turn to him to catch up and outgrow his insecurity. The admonition, "Grow, damn it, grow!" is, needless to say, difficult to follow. In some cases during initial formation, individuals have been rejected for failing to respond to this command.

AS A MARRIAGE

Marriage takes on many forms. Of Murdock's 554 societies, only 135 had monogamy as the cultural norm.[16] At the same time, no society has ever been catalogued in which group marriage was the cultural norm, leading Nimkoff[17] to conclude that this form, while presenting special problems, possesses no special advantages. This leads us to conclude that Nimkoff and others never really looked at group marriage.

[15] Sydney M. Jourard, *The Transparent Self* (New York: Van Nostrand, Reinhold, 1964).

[16] George P. Murdock, "World Ethnographic Sample," *American Anthropologist*, 59 (1957): 686.

[17] Nimkoff, *op. cit.*

We shall resist the temptation of apologists who deemphasize the sexual element of multilateral marriage. The temptation originates with the opponents, who immediately pounce upon what they see primarily as legitimized promiscuity, evidencing further moral decline. The proponents then counter by playing down sex, emphasizing that it is but one dimension of any marriage.

We even find a similar Janus-like outlook among some of our respondents, for whom public, ready pronouncements place sex in a rank distinctly lower than evidenced by behavior and less guarded discussion.

Sex

No (other) formalized type of marriage provides for a variety of sexual partners for both sexes within the marriage. The provision of group marriage is important. It has often been argued that the cross-cultural preponderance of polygyny and rarity of polyandry evidences a higher male need for a variety of partners. In view of the historical importance of the family as economic and work unit and nearly universal male ascendency (even often in polyandrous cultures), this conclusion is unwarranted. It much more likely simply reflects male dominance. At this juncture, there is no a priori reason to assume a greater drive for multiple partners by either sex, and considerable behavioral basis for assuming they are biologically comparable.

What we find is that the majority of both the men and women in group marriages particularly enjoy the element of secure sexual variety afforded by their marriage. The criterion of responsibility and interpersonal involvement appears to be preeminent over sexual involvement. Thus, while some individuals engage in sexual activities outside the group marriage, these too tend to reflect interpersonal criteria and none would properly be described as promiscuous.

It is important not to confuse sexual variety, in the form of varied techniques and positions for intercourse, and varietism, in the form of different partners. The extent to which multiple partners are incorporated, by violation, into conventional marriage patterns is the best evidence that these represent distinct needs.

Reflected in reasons for entering group marriage, we find emphasized the dual aspect of sex in the group. At once, a depth of emotional commitment and involvement incongruent with most extramarital relations is possible, while a variety of partners are even more readily accessible. The group marriage seems to satisfy participants' needs for sexual varietism without the high emotional cost of clandestine affairs or impersonal swapping.

Early sexual involvement has been a pattern in all but one group, where one pair, after 18 months, have not had intercourse. The sexual involvement of many participants is not exclusively limited to their group marriage;

intimate relations do also occur with close friends and in a few instances, in casual encounters.

The mechanisms by which groups resolve the issues of sexual sharing and sleeping arrangements vary but have certain elements in common. Most multilateral families aspire to natural, spontaneous sexual relations. This has been difficult to achieve, and some have had to retreat occasionally to the dependability of formal rotation. Even after possessive jealousy recedes into the background, insecurity is manifest in the difficulty of deciding the sleeping arrangements. Unfortunately, immediate preference for one partner is too easily read as sexual rejection of another, and in our society that is tantamount to personal rejection. We would not describe the sexual sharing in any of the groups as truly spontaneous, though clear progress toward this is evident.

As a typical example, a group may spend a significant portion of its collective energy on this one decision, that is, who sleeps with whom. The decision-making time itself may be of short duration, but by observing other activities, it may be seen that this question arises early in the day, and there may be considerable tentative sounding and maneuvering prior to the actual confrontation. This may be the price of informality if not spontaneity. One can, hopefully, expect more efficiency with practice.

The fixed rotation scheme, say switching partners every week, so enthusiastically espoused by Rimmer,[18] does not work well in practice. It may, as he has suggested, assure (artificially) equal sexual demand for all partners; unfortunately, it not only utterly destroys spontaneity but avoids confrontation on an issue the facing of which is vital. Fixed rotation has generally been abandoned early, though it may serve as a useful transitional solution.

A novel compromise has evolved in one group which frequently begins by collecting unbiased, isolated, unprocessed preferences. Giving honest, purely personal first choices, without regard to the processing of the preferences of others, is a valuable general skill for group participation, and this framework is a good practice ground. If a conflict occurs in unprocessed choices of partners (which is not always), a group arbiter is selected who, while attempting to do best by the group as a whole, nevertheless makes a binding decision. Role of arbiter rotates, giving decision-making practice to all. Here is one way to turn a hassle into a learning experience.

Assignments of bedrooms vary. Groups with ample room give each individual his own bedroom, leaving a "your-place-or-mine" decision to each pair, at the same time solving the territoriality problem. Both primarily matricentric and patricentric sleeping have been tried. While assigning bedrooms permanently to the women may compensate somewhat for historical wrongdoing and residual male chauvinism, it has had no distinct advantages in practice.

[18] *op. cit.*

Group sex, with possible bisexual participation, is another area in which espoused or aspired directions diverge from practice. Multiperson and bisexual activities are generally either accepted as permissible or advanced as desirable despite the fact that very little has taken place. In only one group do three people consistently sleep together; in some others, group sex, though a live option, is rare. Consistent with reports from other sources, notably mate swappers and the sexual freedom movement, instances of three person participation with one man and two women account for the vast majority of those that do occur.

Multiple couple sex is quite rare, in contrast to its predominance among mate swappers. It has been found to be particularly conducive to triggering destructive jealousy. It also facilitates competition, especially male competition, which has sometimes been particularly destructive, in minimal cases manifesting temporary impotence.

Jealousy

Operationally, what most distinguishes multilateral marriage from a conventional dyadic one, is the potential for and necessity to deal with jealousy, possessiveness, and competition as an intrinsic part of group functioning. Two consistent and definite patterns emerged. First, the classic argument that jealousy is an inherent, irreversible quality of man's psychological makeup *seems* not to hold. While it would be difficult to prove now, there appear to be individuals who not only do not manifest behavior suggestive of jealousy but who also appear to have outgrown the feelings of jealousy that precipitate the behavior.

Actually this is somewhat inaccurate because what we traditionally lump under jealousy is really a variety of affective and behavioral phenomena. Close examination of some group marriages reveals at least the following structure. Jealousy itself appears to be more a behavioral manifestation of other emotional constructs than an affect that itself is felt, though this is not always true. Its origins may be in exclusivity, a desire for the exclusive love and affection of another. Or it may come from possessiveness and a desire to own or control the other person as an object. It might also be the result of fear of loss, the threat of which may or may not be genuine. A person showing jealousy may even be actually losing something at the time. Possessive jealousy seems to be the most common and also is frequently overcome.

What will happen in the long run, we do not know, but at present the vast majority of group marriage participants have largely outgrown or found effective ways of dealing with jealousy. On the other hand, no group reports being completely free of *some* residual problems. This is not surprising in view of the tremendous backlog of cultural conditioning which supports and even promotes jealousy and its variants.

Exposure of Scripts
and Contracts

As Eric Berne[19] would put it, in a marriage, look for a contract between children. The point is that *all* marriages include ulterior contracts which satisfy basic childlike needs and, though unwritten, are nevertheless binding on the parties. These contracts constitute tacit unconscious agreement to play certain roles and participate in predetermined complex patterns of behavior—scripts. For example, early in their marriage, Ursula might have found it easier to defer to Leo than express her own independent views, a role she most likely learned automatically, without plan or intent. Over time they find many ways effectively to ensure the continuance of these roles, though they are unaware of the contract itself. Contracts and scripts emerge almost automatically in marriage and once established, consistently determine behavior and persistently defy detection by the parties. It generally requires others to expose the contract, others intimately familiar with a couple in a clinical or personal sense.

The intense, intimate, continued interaction of a group marriage now seems to be an effective environment for discovery and productive working through of prior marital contracts. More strongly than that, it appears that, provided some premium is placed on reality and authentic disclosure, contracts and scripts will almost *inevitably* be revealed for what they are. This is not necessarily an unmitigated good. The contracts fulfilled a function in the dyadic marriage; if the motivating needs are still operative, then something else—in the group or perhaps a new contract—must assume the function. *New* contracts are not necessarily *better*. A further problem arises from one party's unilaterally canceling a contract, refusing to play his role in the script. This may happen because of that person's earlier perception or deeper feelings about the contract. It may leave the spouse in genuine despair.

In Transition

Four years may be too short a time for transition phenomena to settle down. At the present time, even in the best integrated expanded family, pair-bonds continue to take precedence or play special roles. Thus, while the definition of multilateral marriage is satisfied by the existence of comparable bonds between all pairs, these are not equivalent and some are significantly stronger. Our own respondents expect bonds between previously married pairs to continue to be differentiated.

In every aspect of group functioning, we find a recurrent theme—coping with complexity. All the mechanics of living are more complicated. Money,

[19] Eric Berne, *Transactional Analysis in Psychotherapy* (New York: Grove Press, 1961).

discipline, food, personality conflicts, all are multiplied in terms of problem potential. Fortunately, tradition, formal rules, and habit set in to reduce the continued level of complexity; unfortunately, this effect is only partial and the individual participant probably must be of that temperament that makes for the good member of a large family or a commune.

It can be surprising how important seemingly trivial aspects of life style can be. What may appear to be surface elements—brand of toothpaste, preferences in meat, which side of the bed to sleep on—emerge as being a persistent, ingrained, often intensely personal complex. These infinitely varied combinations of generally conflicting patterns have to be resolved in some way in every marriage. Needless to say, toothpaste can be more of a problem with six "newly weds" than with two. This appears to be more of a problem with groups exclusively formed of previously married couples. What seems to be operative is a tendency, once having made such adjustments in one marriage, to resist further accommodation, even if unconsciously.

The complexity which must be dealt with successfully is not only a product of particular individual personalities, but a fundamental property of the enlarged, intimate group. Between two people there are two interrelationships which must be built and maintained in a satisfactory manner. (An interrelationship is always directed; A can love B without B loving A, for example.) Among four there are twelve such interrelationships; among six there are thirty. While compatibility may be facilitated by initial selection, the basic mathematics of group structure cannot be countered.

THE FAMILY

The family based on a group marriage involves potentially new dimensions of interactions with children and of roles assumed by the parents. Some distinct patterns have emerged here.

Children

For the most part, all adults assume parental roles in rearing children in the group. These tend to be somewhat less sex-differentiated than in many conventional marriages. The husbands, as a rule, take very active roles in child care, in some cases rotating all such duties, from diaper changing on, with the wives. In terms of most mechanical aspects of child care, little distinction is made between biological parents and other members of the group marriage.

Most groups intend for the children to come to regard all the adults as parents, though all who are old enough are aware of their biological parents. In watching groups form, we find it takes very little time for children of any age to adjust and to accept new adults in parental roles, even if differentiated from those of their actual parents. Indeed, we have been impressed by the manner in which children have responded to an expanded family situation. The effects include behavioral manifestations such as increased self-confidence and, in one case, improved performance in school.

One child has been born into a group marriage. The fatherhood is in doubt, though believed to be the nonlegal co-husband rather than legal husband of the mother. Unrelated factors result in no other groups planning such "cross-couple" children. The effect of such children on group marriages is unknown as yet. In some cases young children have grown to employ relational forms of address like "Mommy" for other than actual parents.

A markedly differentiated pattern emerges in terms of discipline. While discipline may generally be administered by all adults, most groups report that the character of discipline is largely set by biological parents. In one group the patterns of child rearing for the two couples are very distinct, one being considerably more authoritarian and formalized. The resolution takes the form of general consistency among the four adults for each child, with the inconsistency between the two children. It is a source of friction.

Roles and Liberty

One of the central hopes of group marriage and other forms of expanded or extended families is greater flexibility in the assumption of specific roles. In a family with several breadwinners and several potential sources of child care, it should be easier for a man to become a "househusband" (or *hemman* as he is referred to in Denmark) or for a woman to pursue a full-time career.

We find *some* reduction in traditional sex roles. In general, participants are highly equalitarian in principle. In practice, the most noticeable manifestation is in terms of greater than average involvement by the men in child rearing and some household duties. On the other hand, much of the potential here has been unrealized as yet. Participants themselves feel their hopes for greater role freedom (and freedom in general) have been largely unfulfilled. One family intends in the future for one of two women to be principal wage-earner and the man involved will retire, but no such arrangements exist now.

It is intriguing to compare Talmon's analysis (in Nimkoff[20]) of the evolution of sex role differentiation among the Israeli *kibbutzim*. Equalitarian, undifferentiated ideals initially were followed with true revolutionary zeal. As expansion through recruitment gave way to internal population growth, roles became increasingly gender differentiated—and along traditional lines. Fundamental biological differences are seen by Talmon to be favoring this differentiation. If the women's liberation people can forgive

[20] *op. cit.*

us, we also see this as an intrinsic (not entirely conditioned) bias which, though it may be overcome, and perhaps more easily in a group than monogamous marriage, must be recognized as a reality to be compensated for, not merely dismissed as male chauvinism.

PROSPECT

What is the prognosis for the group marriages considered here and others like them? This is an involved issue, for it incorporates not only the intrinsic qualities of each groups' own relationships but also exogenous elements—the social milieu in which they are pioneering a new form of marriage. Very little of this environment is indifferent to their attempt; most, if their marriages were known, would be openly hostile.

A surprisingly large percentage of people have shown exceptionally strong negative reactions to even the abstract concept of multiperson marriage, appearing to be deeply threatened by it. In view of the inevitable increase in other potential "cultural shocks," this phenomenon is worthy of investigation in itself. Most such reactions give every appearance of either guilt over extramarital involvement or resentment over the greater freedom of others.

In itself, multilateral marriage is beginning to appear to be a viable alternative for some members of our society. We can absolutely assert short-to-intermediate-term success in the sense of continued existence. This is a stronger assertion than a similar one for dyadic marriage. For a conventional marriage to last four years only implies that the relationship is not so bad as to justify to its members the difficulty and disruption of an early divorce. In contrast, all exogenous forces (and perhaps more crucially, many culturally preconditioned internal personality forces) are working to disintegrate the multilateral marriage, making a four-year continuing commitment somewhat remarkable.

Moreover, we do see progress, if not what could be legitimately called success, in terms of meaningful self-insight and personal growth achieved through participation in group marriage. To the limited depth we have explored filiocentric factors, the conclusion is unmistakably in favor of the multilateral marriage as an improved child-rearing institution. In most families, we find committed, highly motivated individuals building a community of mutual trust and love, though this process is neither rapid, monotonic, nor universal.

But even if the observed variables were uniformly positive in terms of the internal processes of the multiperson marriage—and they are not—the laterally expanded family would have to be reconciled with contemporary society for it to be genuinely viable. In part, the currently active group marriages have remained viable through anonymity and their quiet minority position.

Open, direct, perhaps explosive confrontation with society seems all but inevitable. Rising interest in alternative family structures serves, in part, to release further xenophobic responses vectored on a moral scapegoat for current social dilemmas. Indeed, Nimkoff[21] has observed that pointing to family decline as a scapegoat for diverse social ills is a cross-cultural norm.

But we must not lose sight of the immense, psychological price paid by a society that espouses a single, monolithic conception of marital structure. While it remains unproven whether innate human needs are more congruent with nuclear or compound families, with monogamous or polygamous relations, it is certain that man's psychological polymorphism guarantees that anything short of cultural pluralism in marriage must deny, in sum, many intrinsic needs of many individuals.

Looking beneath superficial idealism in the *form* of modern monogamous marriage, and beyond ultimate emotional gains possible in the nonexistent perfect dyadic relationship, we see a forest of human needs and desires laid waste by our society's idolatry. The luckiest of conventionally married people will have one fully trusted confidant, one secure supportive relationship, one selective mirror of his or her self-reality, one intimate relationship with an autonomous equal. If he is in any other way a product of our age, he will long for a sense of community long lost, for an identification in more than a familial microcosm, for extended intimacy without guilt.

Our respondents continue to explore an uncertain answer to these needs. At present, not all are even in agreement among themselves about the likelihood of a continued relationship. Their mood fluctuates, although for most their ability to function cohesively increases fairly steadily. For groups having problems, there are no multilateral-marriage counselors to help them with the problems they and we see. It is essential to recognize that, as with conventional marriage, a break-up is not necessarily a total loss. Most participants themselves have stated that they regard their involvement as worthwhile regardless of final outcome. We concur in most instances. They will not necessarily have failed—only chosen not to choose each other permanently. Irreversible positive effects of their difficult commitment are already evident.

MORE

In view of the psychological stakes, the emotional cost of wrong models and the growth and happiness possible in right ones, much more intensive study is needed. Our immediate plans call for continued work with our present respondents and expansion of the sample as fast as new groups can be located.

We have begun investigating the personality makeup of participants in group marriage, and eventually will be relating this to population norms,

21 *Ibid.*

to group function, and to success and failure in multilateral relations. The Edwards Personal Preference Schedule, which measures some fifteen normal personality needs, has been chosen as the primary instrument for this purpose. The EPPS is being used not only to measure personality but also to study the interpersonal relationships involved. A framework which focuses on an individual's needs, his perceptions of others' needs and his perceptions of their perception of his (metaperception) has been used by Drewery[22] with dyadic relationships and is being adapted by us to multilateral ones. Besides the broad descriptive process underway, we are also focusing in on personal growth and sexual relationships as specific dimensions of multilateral marriage.

The long term will be even more indicative, and we plan regular follow-up for some distance into the future. It is hoped eventually that a separate study by qualified child psychologists will be undertaken to ascertain the real impact on children of multiple parents.

Perhaps the fruit of the tree will be the most telling.

References

Constantine, Larry L.   "Personal Growth in Multiperson Marriages," *Radical Therapist*, 2, no. 1 (April–May 1971).

Constantine, Larry L., and Joan M.   "Multilateral Marriage: Alternate Family Structure in Practice," in Robert H. Kimmer, *You and I for Tomorrow* (New York: Dell, 1971), pp. 157–173.

———. "The Pragmatics of Group Marriage—Year One," *The Modern Utopian*, 4, no. 3 (Summer 1970).

———. "Where is Marriage Going?" *The Futurist*, 4, no. 2 (April 1970): 44–46.

---

[22] James Drewery, "An Interpersonal Perception Technique," *British Journal of Medical Psychology*, 42 (1969): 171–181.

Adams, B. N., 3n.
Albee, G., 93
Almquist, E. M., 12
Angrist, S. S., 12
Arensberg, C. M., 2, 5
Ariès, P., 8, 15n., 21, 44, 45n., 57
Axelrod, M., 6n.

Bailyn, B., 44, 57, 58
Bales, R. F., 7n.
Bauer, R. A., 120, 122, 128n.
Beckel, C., 50n., 55n.
Beissel, C., 46
Bem, D., 11
Bem, S., 11
Ben-Gurion, D., 93
Berne, E., 217
Bestor, A. E., 46n.
Blau, Z. S., 104n.
Boehler, P., 55n.
Bowlby, J., 93, 98
Bronfenbrenner, U., 117, 119–142
Brun-Gulbrandsen, S., 11n.
Burgess, E. W., 15
Burton, A., 212

Calhoun, A. W., 45
Cole, M., 96
Cole, S., 96
Conrich, R., 203
Constantine, J. M., 172, 204–222
Constantine, L. L., 172, 204–222
Cooper, D., 21–22
Cornford, F. M., 25n.
Coser, L., 46n.
Cuber, J. F., 205

Dahlström, E., 11n., 13n.
Dayan, M., 93
Dederich, C., 176
Demos, J., 2, 3, 7n.
Doll, E. E., 46n.
Donahue, W., 112n.
Drake, J. T., 112n.
Drewery, J., 222

Ellis, A., 210
Engels, F., 120, 125n., 136
Erbe, H., 47n., 48n., 52n., 53n.
Eshkol, L., 93

Fonzi, G., 171, 180–195
Frazier, E. F., 45n.
Freedman, E. A., 104n.
Friedan B., 13

Geiger, K., 120n., 125n., 139n.
Gluckman, M., 105n.
Golan, S., 96
Goldberg P., 11
Goldberg, S., 12n.
Gollin, G. L., 23, 24, 44-58
Goode, W. J., 9–10
Goodman, P., 97
Goodsell, W., 45
Greer, S., 6n., 20
Greven, P. J., 2, 4n.
Grønseth, B., 158n.
Grof, S., 200, 203

Haavio-Mannila, E., 118, 154–169
Haller, M., 50n.
Hamilton, K. G., 54n., 56n.
Harroff, P., 205
Havighurst, R. J., 104n., 109n.
Heinlein, R., 206
Heiskanen, V. S., 159n.
Hendin, H., 208
Herzog, E., 85n.
Hindus, M., 119
Holter, H., 157, 161
Howard, G. E., 45
Huxley, A., 71n., 138

Inkeles, A., 120, 122, 124, 126, 128n.
Ironside, C. E., 45

Janowitz, M., 20
Jansson, B., 158n.
Jordan, J. W., 53n.
Jourard, S., 213

Kanter, R. M., 171, 173–179
Kephart, W. M., 23, 24, 59–77
Kharchev, A., 137, 138, 139
Khrushchev, N., 128, 129, 130, 131, 134n., 138, 139
Kimball, S. T., 2, 5
Kluckhohn, F. R., 102n.
Knani, D., 115n.
Kohen-Raz, R., 98
Kolbanovsky, V. N., 136, 139
Kononenko, E., 137n., 140n.

Laing, R. D., 21
Laslett, P., 2
Lenin, V. I., 120, 126, 127
Levshin, A., 137
Lewis, M., 12n.
Lipinski, B., 11
Litwak, E., 108n.
Lyman, M., 176

McLuhan, M., 196, 200
Makarenko, A., 125, 126n., 127
Margolies, R., 211
Mariagin, G., 137n.
Marsh, R., 155n.
Marx, K., 120, 125n.
Mehnert, K., 138
Michel, L. C., 109n.
Miner, H., 2, 5
Morgan, E. S., 6n., 44, 45, 57
Mosley, P. E., 120
Murdock, G. P., 81, 82, 83, 85, 86, 88,
    89, 90, 91, 92, 167, 213
Myrdal, J., 118, 143–153

Nimkoff, M. F., 204, 213, 219, 221
Noordhock, J., 158n.
Noyes, G. W., 72n.
Noyes, H. H., 72n.
Noyes, J. H., 24, 59, 60, 61, 64, 65, 66,
    70, 71, 73–76, 174

Orwell, G., 138
Osgood, C. E. 154, 168
Otto, H., 206

Parsons, T., 7, 8, 9, 20
Peleaz, C., 178
Perls, F. S., 178, 212
Pierre, A., 120
Pineo, P. C., 204
Plato, 14, 23, 24, 25–43
Plitt, J., 49n.
Poloma, M. M., 12, 13n.
Protopopova, A., 137n.

Rabin, A., 98, 99
Rabkin, K., 79, 93–100
Rabkin, L., 79, 93–100
Rapaport, D., 99
Rapp, G., 174, 176
Redfield, R., 88, 89n.
Reichman, F., 46n.
Rimmer, R., 172, 206, 215

Rose, A. J., 203
Rosow, I., 17, 18n., 114n.
Roszak, T., 181
Rothman, D. J., 58

Sarell, M., 102n.
Sawyer, J., 154, 155
Schlesinger, R., 119, 121n., 123n., 127n.
Schutz, W., 178, 212
Seidensticker, O., 46n.
Sennett, R., 8, 9, 20–21, 22
Shanas, E., 4n., 16
Shubart, P., 203
Siegel, A., 100
Sjoberg, G., 2
Skinner, B. F., 173, 191
Slater, P. E., 21
Smelser, N. J., 6, 7
Smith, D. E., 172, 196–203
Solov'ev, N., 137, 138, 139
Sorokin, P. A., 3n.
Spangenberg, M., 48, 49n., 52n., 53
Spiro, M., 14, 79, 81–92, 99, 103n.
Stalin, J., 125n.
Sternfield, J. L., 172, 196–203
Stockwell, E. G., 15n.
Streib, G. F., 16n., 17n., 19n., 104n.
Strumilin, S., 135, 136, 138
Suelzle, M., 11n.
Sussman, M., 5
Sverdlov, G. M., 126
Sweetser, D. A., 2n.
Symonds, C., 207

Talmon, Y., 19, 46n., 80, 101–115, 219
Terman, L., 11
Tibbits, C., 104n.
Townsend, P., 16n., 107n., 110n.
Tyler, L., 11

Uttendoerfer, O., 49n., 50n.

Walkley, R. P., 18n.
Wigley, E. A., 2
Willmott, P., 4n.
Wirth, L., 20
Worden, H. M., 62n.

Young, M., 4n.

Zborowski, M., 85n.
Zetkin, C., 126
Zinzendorf, N. L., 48, 49, 52, 53, 54